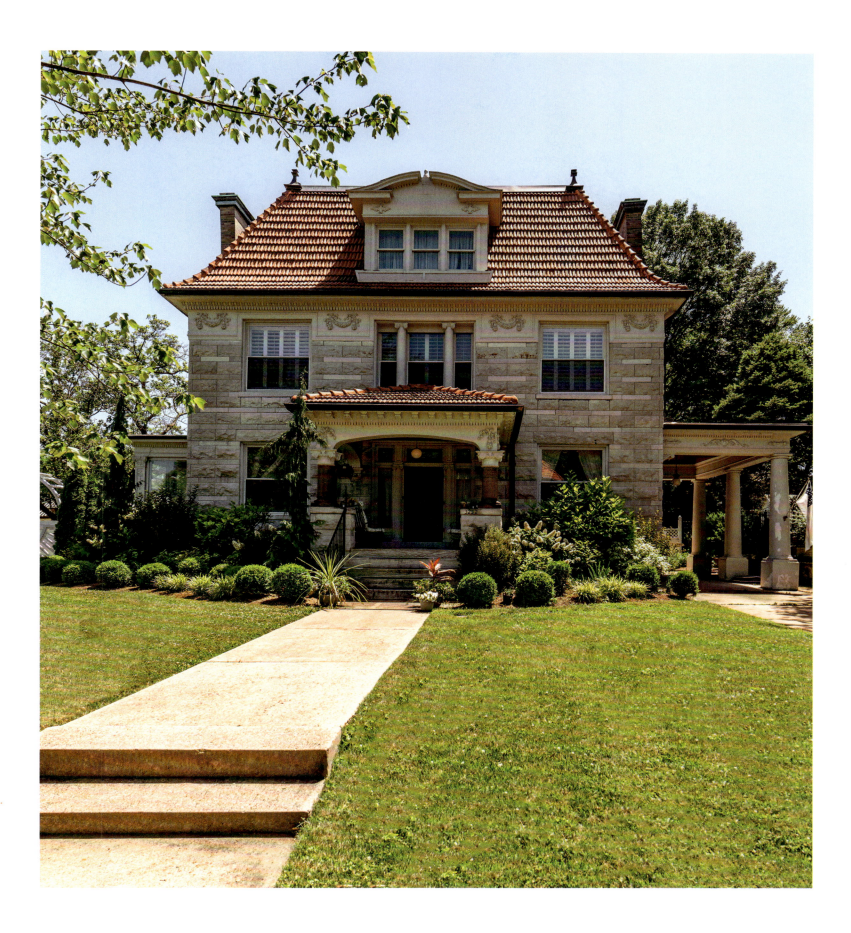

PREVIOUS
3222 Hawthorne Boulevard.

NEXT
52 Westmoreland Place.

Photos by Reed R. Radcliffe, 2022.

A. A. FISCHER'S ST. LOUIS STREETSCAPES

NANCY MOORE HAMILTON

Missouri Historical Society Press

Distributed by University of Chicago Press

ISBN 979-8-9855716-2-2

27 26 25 24 23 • 1 2 3 4 5

© 2023 by Missouri Historical Society Press

All rights reserved. No part of this book may be reproduced in any form without written permission of the copyright owners. All images in this book have been reproduced with the knowledge and prior consent of the artists concerned and no responsibility is accepted by producer, publisher, or printer for any infringement of copyright or otherwise, arising from the contents of this publication. Every effort has been made to ensure that credits accurately comply with information supplied.

Library of Congress Control Number: 2022952279

Distributed by University of Chicago Press

Designed by Mary Haskin Designs, LLC

Printed and bound in the United States by Holland Litho Printing Service

FRONT COVER
Russell Boulevard and Westminster Place streetscapes.

BACK COVER
Vernon Avenue streetscape.

NEXT
Vernon Avenue streetscape (left to right) with 5237, 5233, and 5231 Vernon.

Photos by Reed R. Radcliffe, 2022.

CONTENTS

xi	INTRODUCTION
xxvii	GLOSSARY
1	CHAPTER ONE: THE FISCHER FAMILY
15	CHAPTER TWO: A CHANCE MEETING
27	CHAPTER THREE: BUILDING ST. LOUIS, 1890–1911
111	CHAPTER FOUR: FROM BROKEN FRIEZES TO BROKEN DREAMS
121	CHAPTER FIVE: DIRECTORY OF A. A. FISCHER BUILDS
461	NOTES
465	ACKNOWLEDGMENTS

INTRODUCTION

This book has two stories to tell. They are related, as you will see, but each has its own chronology. The more important story is that of Alexander August Fischer, who built several hundred houses in St. Louis between the 1890s and the 1920s. The other story is the account of my experiences researching Fischer's life and work.

Since I began researching A. A. Fischer in the mid-1990s, technology has advanced considerably, and research methods have evolved right alongside it. Much of my research began with microfilm and pencil and paper, and for years some of my manuscript was stored on Zip disks. But the final phase of my research has been conducted using computers and other modern tools.

Many people have asked me, "Why St. Louis? You live in Michigan. Why Fischer?" So I must begin by attempting to answer those questions. Most of my life has been spent in medium-size cities: Peoria, Illinois; Champaign, Illinois; and Kalamazoo, Michigan. Early on I discovered Chicago and was immediately captivated by the fact that it was not simply bigger than, but very different from, the smaller cities I was accustomed to. Had my life taken some other turns when I was young, I might now be writing about a Chicago builder rather than a St. Louis one. But I am happy that I found St. Louis.

I first arrived there in the spring of 1958, the ink scarcely dry on my University of Illinois diploma. I had earned a bachelor's degree in geography and had been persuaded by a campus recruiter to apply for a job with the Aeronautical Chart and Information Center, a government installation that was mostly civilian but made maps for the United States Air Force. For $18.50 a week I had a private room, breakfast, and supper every day at the Evangeline Residence, an old hotel at 18th and Pine streets that the Salvation Army had turned into a home for working women. I made some good friends there and still keep in touch with them more than 60 years later. In August 1958, while paying a visit to my alma mater, I met Ray Hamilton, who was completing his master's degree in bacteriology. He began working at the Upjohn Company in Kalamazoo in January 1959. In June of that year, I married Ray and moved there.

My year in St. Louis, short as it was, changed my thinking forever. I experienced the pleasures of walking in a city where there was always something interesting to see, and the nearest grocery store was just around the corner. I appreciated the fact that public transportation was so good that I had no need for a car. The architecture of ordinary houses was particularly fascinating. I could ride the bus or streetcar for miles and see no end to the phalanxes of houses: mostly brick (occasionally stone), two or three stories high, very close together, all of them embodying styles of architecture from the past. They were alien and intimidating yet somehow inviting. I have never tired of savoring the size, the structure, the brickwork, the amazing variety of these houses. How can so many houses look so much the same at first glance yet be so different upon closer inspection?

The lighting in St. Louis adds to the mystique. Much of the brick is dark, and most streets are narrow. The city's age has given the trees time to mature, to cast shadows over the houses and their diminutive front yards. The sun seems to come from odd angles and can be cruel: When you drive west on Lindell Boulevard late on a summer afternoon, you can hardly tell whether the traffic lights are red or green because of the sun in your eyes. Photography is difficult because of the contrasting bright light and shadows—usually it works best to take pictures on cloudy winter days, when only branches obstruct the architectural details one is trying to record for posterity.

I should confess that it is tempting for me to idealize St. Louis and push aside in my mind the very real challenges the city has faced since my initial sojourn in the 1950s. It is well known that St. Louis has endured decades of high crime and racial segregation, but the consequences of how these realities have shaped everyday life for all St. Louisans are not as widely comprehended.

For me it was a revelation to hear just how many streets and parts of entire neighborhoods are widely deemed unsafe by locals.

—

Who built all these houses? I wondered about this many times while I lived in St. Louis and continued to ponder it during my occasional visits in the decades that followed. Over the years I had plenty of other things to think about, but my interest in cities, architecture, and historic preservation gradually increased. In the early 1960s, I was so excited about Jane Jacobs's *The Death and Life of Great American Cities* that I persuaded the program chair at the Kalamazoo YWCA to let me review the book at one of its meetings.

Although I attended many tours of historic homes in Kalamazoo and surrounding towns, I generally found the exteriors more interesting than the interiors. My filing cabinets bulged with snapshots, and my shelves were crowded with books such as *A Field Guide to American Houses* by Virginia and Lee McAlester and *Houses by Mail* by Katherine Cole Stevenson and H. Ward Jandl. Whenever I was able to visit St. Louis, I would go to a bookstore and find the "Local Interest" section. This was how I discovered, bought, and eagerly read *St. Louis: Landmarks & Historic Districts* by Carolyn Hewes Toft, the executive director of the Landmarks Association of St. Louis. As I read and re-read the book, I kept returning to two sentences on page 80 where the author described the Skinker DeBaliviere/Catlin Tract/Parkview District.

> "Although prestigious architectural firms were active in the District, especially in Parkview and the Catlin Tract, the majority of the buildings were designed by contractors with the prolific Alexander A. Fischer, responsible for some 75 structures. His trademark, the "broken" or interrupted frieze at the roof line, is stamped on entire streetscapes."

In vain I searched the book for pictures of the broken frieze, thinking, "Where are those streetscapes? I've got to see them." Although

PREVIOUS
Cabanne Avenue streetscape with 5247 Cabanne in the foreground followed by 5243, 5241, and 5239.
Photo by Reed R. Radcliffe, 2022.

RIGHT
Cabanne Avenue streetscape with 5201 Cabanne in the foreground followed by 5205, 5209, and 5211.

CENTER
Cates Avenue streetscape with 5165 Cates in the foreground followed by 5169, 5171, and 5175.

BOTTOM
Vernon Avenue streetscape with 5247 Vernon in the foreground followed by 5249, 5253, 5255 (razed), 5259, and 5263.

Photos by Reed R. Radcliffe, 2022.

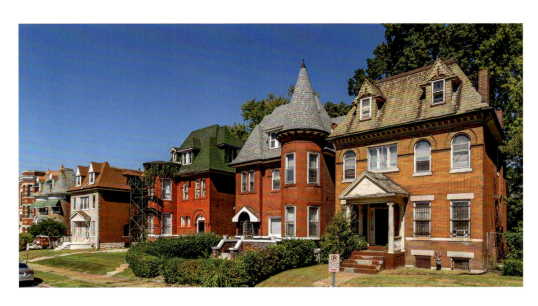

OPPOSITE TOP
Home at 3222 Hawthorne Boulevard in the Compton Heights neighborhood with A. A. Fischer's signature broken frieze. It was built in 1905.

OPPOSITE BOTTOM
Detail of broken frieze at 3222 Hawthorne.

Photos by Reed R. Radcliffe, 2022.

ABOVE
Broken frieze at 3222 Hawthorne.
Photo by Reed R. Radcliffe, 2022.

individual, monumental houses usually receive more attention from writers and photographers, I have never found them as exciting as streetscapes. It is the sense of place—the variety within the repetition of shapes, the way streets are framed by the lines of houses—that somehow moves me. I'd never seen a broken frieze, but I knew immediately that they were important to me. Fischer's signature broken frieze, with wreaths and/or swags that descend into the spaces between the upper-story windows rather than extending straight across the façade below the cornice, would in time become very familiar.

Although Fischer unabashedly described himself as an architect, his lack of formal architectural training required him to hire architects to design the homes and apartment buildings that his workers would then erect. Fischer sought top-notch talent when hiring architects, demonstrating his respect for this occupation that was rapidly professionalizing.

Fischer acted more as a contractor, or builder, than he did any other professional role. Eventually he also participated in real estate—the buying and improving of property, the selling of homes—as well as financial speculation. He brought much to each of these roles, including an abundance of creativity paired with a frugality that ultimately allowed him to build multiple homes from a single set of plans, all while making the houses look different from one another by mirroring the layouts and varying decorative elements, such as the types of friezes and the brick colors used. On other occasions, Fischer and his firm were hired to erect or modify structures on behalf of independent architects or architects associated with competing firms.

———

Like many other women of my generation, I happily spent several decades raising a family and supporting my husband in his career. Unlike many other women of my generation, when my husband retired, the focus of our lives shifted to accommodate my interests. In the fall of 1993, I attended the annual meeting of the National Trust for Historic Preservation. St. Louis was hosting. During the meeting, which lasted a week, I went on as many local tours as possible.

The first day's bus tour was "St. Louis on Wheels," a broad overview of the city's historic districts. Carolyn Toft, the author of the book I had enjoyed so much, was the leader. As participants climbed onto the bus, which was parked at the south end of Union Station, Carolyn handed each of us a map. When the bus was full, she picked up the microphone and began to speak. She told us that, after traversing the whole route in her car, she knew the tour would take exactly three hours. She planned to talk extensively, and there would be no stops to get off. Any traveler who needed it could use the onboard bathroom.

What followed was one of the most interesting afternoons of my life. Carolyn was knowledgeable, articulate, and funny. She had done a superb job of planning the route so that we could see and learn as much as possible. She knew how to direct the bus driver to stop where we could actually see what she wanted us to see. (I learned later, in taking bus tours led by less-expert leaders, that this is a rare talent.) In the National Trust bookshop, I bought another of Carolyn's books, *Compton Heights*, which she had written with Jane Molloy Porter. The book helped me find my first broken frieze: It adorned the house at 3222 Hawthorne Boulevard, which A. A. Fischer had built in 1905.

An idea was germinating in my mind. Perhaps there was some way I could do research on St. Louis architecture and help the Landmarks Association in the process. It took me another year and a half to act. Foolishly, perhaps, I went out on a limb and wrote to Carolyn. I asked her if Landmarks ever accepted help from temporary volunteer researchers. I think I expected her to say no, but instead she replied that it depended on qualifications. She then asked the obvious question: Would I commute? *Absolutely.* Plans for a weeklong trip turned into a monthlong trip. I wrote back to Carolyn, told her about my bachelor's degree in geography, my associate degree in data processing, and various other experiences I felt had prepared me for research of this kind. She replied that my qualifications sounded fine. Now, what topic should I work on?

I sent a list of ideas and was willing to take on whichever one she chose, but privately I hoped Carolyn would pick A. A. Fischer. Her next letter explained that other people had already spoken for all but one of the topics I had suggested. She concluded, "I guess it will have to be A. A. Fischer." Our correspondence culminated in a brief phone conversation, during which I let her know that I would visit St. Louis for a few days the following week. I would meet Carolyn (who, after all, could not be expected to remember me from the bus tour), discuss the research, and find a place where I could stay for a month. My husband, Ray, accompanied me on this trip and helped me with research from the very beginning.

The Landmarks Association office was then located on the seventh floor of the St. Louis Design Center at 917 Locust Street in downtown St. Louis. At the time of our first visit, in August 1995, the only people working there besides Carolyn were Cindi Longwisch and John Saunders. Cindi was the acknowledged local authority on William Butts Ittner, the architect who had designed about 50 buildings for the St. Louis Public Schools. She was helping Landmarks consultant Mimi Stiritz with the book *St. Louis: Historic Churches & Synagogues* and had taken many photographs for it. John was the friendly, capable office worker and jack-of-all-trades. The office itself was a charming mixture of antiquity and efficiency, with creaky wooden floors, lots of rolled-up maps (and a big table for unrolling them), an overflowing bookcase, a large literature rack, and numerous filing cabinets.

Cindi gave me photocopies of everything in the Fischer file. There were only a few sheets, but they were very helpful. There was a typewritten list of Fischer houses in the Skinker DeBaliviere neighborhood. Also included was an article from the June 1905 issue of the *Builder*, illustrated with a head-and-shoulders photo of Fischer; a picture of the home he built for himself at 5256 Vernon Avenue; and a panorama of several Fischer houses along the north side of Vernon Avenue east of Union Boulevard. The article stated that Fischer's houses, if placed side by side, would stretch from the Mississippi River to Forest Park, a distance of over 4 miles.

Cindi said that Carolyn wasn't in the office but suggested it was a good time to visit city hall and the public library to show me how to find building records. The first step, she explained, could be done at the Landmarks office. On the wall was a large map of St. Louis that showed the official city block number for every block in the city. She instructed me to sit down by the map, find the city block number for Fischer's home, and write it down.

This was an educational day. Among other things, I learned that I was going to have to equip myself with some better tools to do effective research. My bifocals weren't useful at all. I needed reading glasses because so many of the things I'd be reading were on vertical surfaces. Cindi and I walked from the Landmarks office to St. Louis City Hall at Tucker Boulevard and Market Street. She lamented how difficult it was to drive around the city, noting that parking was expensive and hard to find, and walking was faster if the destination wasn't too far. We were both wearing comfortable shoes, so we walked.

Cindi explained that the building permit information in city hall had been copied to microfilm as a Works Progress Administration project during the Depression. Workers typed data from the actual building permits onto 3-inch-by-5-inch cards, and then the cards were lined up and photographed for storage on microfilm. Many errors crept in because the workers were trying to read handwritten records, and they often misinterpreted them. They used old typewriters with letters and numbers that were not uniformly inked, so it's often hard, for example, to tell an *E* from a *K* and a *1* from a *0*. Worst of all,

OPPOSITE
In July 1905, the *Builder* published a feature on A. A. Fischer that explained his strategic approach to business and the values his homes embody.

The Builder
Fischer's Houses would make a Line from Forest Park to the Mississippi River

An entire block of Houses on Vernon Avenue and Union Boulevard, planned, built and formerly owned by A. A. Fischer.

Phenomenal Building Record of 517 High Class Dwellings Built in West End in Recent Years by one man

A. A. FISCHER

Were A. A. Fischer's houses placed in a line on 40-foot lots they would make an imposing architectural column extending from the Mississippi River to Forest Park.

Over five hundred high-class houses standing to the credit of one man's enterprise and representing an individuality of taste and skill would seem to represent the limit of one busy man's ability; yet they are the products of Mr. Fischer's work in the past few years only.

Having studied the wants of home owners, subserved the showy for the comfortable and substantial and yet a charm to all, Mr. Fischer has devised a style of dwellings that is in demand as fast as he can get the ground, devise the plans, let the contracts and assemble the materials. His methods are rapid but thorough. They are the speed that comes of good generalship and experience and not that of slighted details and unworkmanlike construction.

Mr. Fischer believes in labor and time saving devices. Whenever he starts a job—it is usually two or more houses at a time—a temporary telephone is installed. This often saves a day's time in reaching the mills or yards or labor headquarters. He is thus always in touch with his foreman.

The Fischer houses are noteworthy because of the particular attention paid to the plumbing, ventilation, light and sanitary features. These matters are often neglected in houses built for sale, though the neglect proves very costly in the years to come. Abundant closet room is another feature which receives careful attention, as being a concession that women folks appreciate in the houses where they necessarily spend most of their lives.

The Builder shows herewith a halftone of Mr. Fischer's own home at 5256 Vernon avenue. It is a typical Fischer house, showing the fine artistic lines, the splendid light from cellar to attic, the wise distribution of room space and the substantial and dignified general effect of the structure. The interior is in keeping with the exterior.

The offices of the firm at Nos. 604-06 Chestnut street on the ground floor are probably the most strikingly pleasing on Chestnut street. They are fitted up on a green and mahogany tone with gold trimmings that charms the eye and lulls the sense. The different departments are divided by low mahogany partitions, which permit a sweep of the eye and preserve the harmony of the scheme. All the little touches of comfort in benches, settees, palm settings, telephone conveniences and facilities for examining plans or for work have been introduced.

Patrons and employes can transact business there expeditiously. The Fischer offices are emblematic of the Fischer houses.

A force of draughtsmen and superintendents form the staff under whose jurisdiction the Fischer houses are created.

Mr. Fischer was born 38 years ago in Washington, Mo., but acquired his early education in the St. Louis Schools. His first thoughts towards real estate and building matters were directed by his experience gained as bookkeeper for the old Tower Grove Building & Loan Association. Mr. Fischer soon saw that the ownership of a home was a natural craving of mankind. To satisfy this craving and to make the homes of St. Louis more beautiful and comfortable became his life work. He is an enthusiast on the subject. There is no excuse, he maintains, for an unsightly and ill-arranged home.

Mr. Fischer worked along these lines, branching out into the real estate business first with H. M. Mepham for six years and then for himself, later organizing the company that bears his name. The business is now incorporated and the company is equipped to buy and sell ground, furnish plans, build houses and supply the funds for the purpose.

And the proof of success lies, as stated at the beginning of this article, in the fact that the houses Mr. Fischer has so far built would make a line from the Mississippi River to Forest Park.

RESIDENCE OF A. A. FISCHER, 5256 VERNON AVENUE.

occasionally the microfilming was so carelessly done that some cards overlapped with others. "The record you absolutely have to have is always the one that's covered up," Cindi joked. Some microfilm rolls are clear and sharp, while others are very faint, with little contrast between the writing and the background. Still, Cindi said, it was better than many other cities' records: She'd heard of one that retained its building permits for just 10 years before throwing them out.

St. Louis is unique in the attention it gives these records. One particularly valuable resource is the Address and Property Search database made available through the City of St. Louis's official government website. It includes official addresses, alternative addresses, city block numbers, a detailed record of the most recent building permits filed for each address, and photographs of properties from various angles, in addition to maps and other details. Over the course of my research, it has been fascinating to watch and benefit from the increasing sophistication of recordkeeping and the greater accessibility to records made possible by the city, the St. Louis Public Library, the Landmarks Association, and the Missouri Historical Society.

St. Louis City Hall was built in the French Renaissance Revival style. It was designed in 1891 but not completed until 1904, owing to the parsimony of the city fathers. The exterior's first floor is pink granite, and its upper stories are yellow sandstone. Inside we found lots of gleaming marble on the main level, but the basement—our first stop—was much more austere, with an asphalt-like substance covering the floors. Cindi led us into the microfilm room in the basement's northeast corner; the microfilm itself was kept inside a walk-in vault. We went into a dimly lighted room that contained several microfilm readers.

Each box of microfilm was marked on the outside and contained two rolls of microfilm, but the rolls themselves were not marked— you couldn't tell which roll was which until it was put on the machine. "Invariably, I put the wrong roll on first," Cindi said. "Sometimes I try to outwit the system by trying the bottom roll instead of the top one, but that doesn't

ABOVE
St. Louis City Hall.

Photo by Reed R. Radcliffe, 2022.

OPPOSITE
Building permit for A. A. Fischer's home at 5256 Vernon Avenue in the Academy neighborhood.

Building Division of the City of St. Louis.

PERMIT No.	LOCATION	DATE	BLOCK No.
D-5126	5256 Vernon Avenue	11-21-01	5145

USE	2 Story Brick Dwelling	COST	$4,000.00

OWNER	A.A. Fischer

ARCHITECT	Owner and Builder

FORM NO. 277-M

work either." Neither of us were surprised when the roll on the machine turned out to be the wrong one. But when the second roll didn't have the right city block on it either, Cindi realized I'd made a mistake in writing down the city block number for Fischer's home when we were in the Landmarks office and instructed me to look it up on the map beside the microfilm reader again. Embarrassed, I did so. The correct box was retrieved from the vault, and eventually the right roll of microfilm was placed onto the machine.

Again, I found that bifocals were unsuitable for the job because the microfilm screen was vertical, and the print was small. Cindi had brought standard Landmarks forms for recording the building permit information, but there were only a few square inches of desk space next to the machine. I silently told myself to bring a clipboard and a magnifying glass next time, along with reading glasses. But we did find the building permit data for A. A. Fischer's home.

We returned the microfilm and took the elevator back to the first floor. Next, Cindi would show me how to do abstract searches. The new objective was to find the current owners of Fischer's home, see who sold it to them, and trace the transactions backward in time to determine when the house was built. The office had a counter separating the employees from the public; this barrier contained horizontal slots for dozens of large, heavy map books, perhaps measuring 30 inches by 18 inches. Each page was devoted to just one city block, and each book was labeled with the beginning and ending city block numbers for the maps it contained. House numbers and property lines were marked in India ink. For each property, the current owner's name was written in pencil, along with the date of the most recent transaction and a hyphenated number. The number to the left of the hyphen referred to the book in which the transaction could be found, and the number to the right of the hyphen referred to the page number in that book. The more recent books were ones you could pick up and hold, but the older books were on microfiche, not microfilm as the building permits were.

We were to use the hyphenated number on each transaction record to find the book and page for the previous transaction. Most transactions indicated a dollar amount. If the amount was several thousand dollars in one transaction and only $1,000 in the previous transaction, it usually indicated that a house was built on the lot after the earlier transaction and before the later one. If the date of the building permit was between the dates of the two transactions, so much the better. In cases where no building permit could be found or there was uncertainty as to which building permit applied to the house in question, the abstract search assumed a greater importance in determining the age of the house.

Cindi had brought along a Landmarks form for abstract searches, and she taught me some tricks to speed up the process of recording the data. For example, instead of writing "grantor" and "grantee" every time, she wrote the grantor's name, drew a horizontal arrow, and then wrote the grantee's name. She explained that *hw* in the records meant "his wife," and *hh* meant "her husband." In the case of Fischer's own home, we were lucky to fit the entire history of the building onto one sheet of paper—properties can change hands numerous times over a century. Cindi also advised me to always write all four digits of a year whenever recording information so there'd never be a question about which century the information was from.

We left city hall and walked north to the St. Louis Public Library's central branch, cutting through the series of parks that run from east to west for several blocks between Market and Chestnut streets. We went to the library's microfilm room in the southwest corner of the basement. It housed the *St. Louis Daily Record*, where building permits are published the day after being issued. We needed to look at the *Daily Record* from November 22, 1901—the day after the date of the permit for Fischer's home, November 21, 1901. Fortunately, there was only one roll of *Daily Record* microfilm in each box. The machines were a little different from those at city hall, but before long we found the record for Fischer's home.

Cindi showed me how she wrote the *Daily Record* data on the same form that she had used for the building permit, only this time in red ink to make it clear that the data came from a different source. She put a red checkmark to indicate that the data were the same in both sources. The data agreed this time, but it wasn't always so. In the case of a contradiction, I'd have to record all the information and determine which parts were correct some other way.

We walked back to the Landmarks office. John told us Carolyn had waited for me that morning until she had to leave, but she asked me to come back late in the afternoon. I said that I could. After saying goodbye to Cindi and John and then eating lunch downtown, I looked for Fischer houses in two neighborhoods, Academy and Skinker DeBaliviere. Both had examples of streetscapes stamped with the broken friezes that Carolyn had referred to in her book.

In the first neighborhood, Academy, I found 5256 Vernon Avenue—Fischer's home. Even though interesting architecture was everywhere, I only took three pictures: Fischer's home, the house next door, and a house across the street. In the second neighborhood, Skinker DeBaliviere, I walked up and down the 6100 block of Westminster and took numerous photos. Recordkeeping was awkward because I still didn't have a clipboard.

Late in the afternoon I returned to the Landmarks office and finally met Carolyn. As I walked in she was clattering away on an ancient upright typewriter. Visible from her office window were the twin towers of the Shrine of St. Joseph several blocks to the north at Biddle and N. 11th streets. To my chagrin I found out that she thought we'd had an appointment at 11 a.m., which is why she had waited for me. I had been unaware of such an appointment, as was Cindi, who at that time was showing me around city hall and the library. I'd wanted so much to make a good first impression, but I'd already managed to mess up.

When I arrived, Carolyn told me she had been thinking about my research topic. The team really needed a survey of Union Sarah West, the area bounded by Kingshighway, Page, Delmar, and Union boulevards. It also contained a significant number of Fischer houses, including his house on Vernon. It would be my job to document all the buildings. She asked if I'd been to the neighborhood. I said yes and mentioned my brief visit to Union Sarah West earlier in the afternoon.

Satisfied, Carolyn walked over to the map racks, rummaged around, and handed me two large rolled-up maps. One of the maps was of the Skinker DeBaliviere neighborhood, which had been surveyed. It showed the architect or builder and year of construction for every house. The other was for my surveying assignment, Union Sarah West. My duty would be to find and fill in the same information. Carolyn emphasized that I had to be accurate. She told me that if there were any indication something was off, someone else would have to redo the entire project.

This was an unexpected turn of events: Carolyn was changing my assignment, and she didn't seem to have much confidence in my ability to do an accurate survey. Had Cindi told her that I'd misread the city block number on the map? Of course, from Carolyn's point of view, I had missed an appointment and kept her waiting. I asked to think about it and call her the next day, which she agreed to. She said regardless of my assignment, I'd spend much of my time at city hall and the library. She also brought up the matter of my room and board, recommending the Mansion House Apartments on 4th Street between Olive and Locust streets. It wasn't inexpensive, but it was centrally located.

After a little more conversation, Carolyn returned to her typing. I toured the Mansion House and decided to rent a unit there for a month in the fall of 1995. With my husband's encouragement, I contacted Carolyn to say I would take on the Union Sarah West project. I made a point to emphasize my intention to do a thorough, accurate job.

In January 1998, I submitted to the Landmarks Association of St. Louis a report on the Union Sarah West neighborhood. My objectives were: to find the architect and/or builder and year of construction for each of the more than 800 structures in the neighborhood, to discover something of the district's history, to call attention to some buildings of particular interest, and to consider the possibility that the entire district might be a candidate for the National Register of Historic Places. Relevant sections of the report are woven throughout this book. Compiling the Union Sarah West report proved to be excellent practice for my deep dive into the career of A. A. Fischer.

—

ABOVE
A report written by Nancy Hamilton, 1998.

As it worked out, researching Fischer and his career became my foremost interest and hobby for the next two-plus decades. In my quest to learn all that I could about Fischer, I was fortunate to establish a relationship with two of his grandchildren, siblings Lorraine Fischer Cruise and Norman Fischer, both of whom are now deceased. When I met the siblings in February 2000, Lorraine was 79 years old, and Norman was 77. Kenneth, their eldest sibling, was already deceased.

Kenneth, Lorraine, and Norman were the children of A. A. Fischer's only child, Roland Fischer, and his wife, Irene. Lorraine and Norman were young teens when their grandfather died, and they both held fond and detailed memories of him. My correspondence with the Fischer grandchildren eventually developed into a genuine friendship, and they even invited me to attend an upcoming Fischer family reunion. Not only would I have the opportunity to meet his grandchildren and great-grandchildren but I was also asked if I would like to give a presentation on their patriarch. In June 2009, it was my honor to travel to St. Louis and do just that.

In 2006, I published an article about A. A. Fischer in the newsletter of the Missouri Valley chapter of the Society of Architectural Historians. The article, "From Broken Friezes to Broken Dreams: The Fleeting Prosperity of A. A. Fischer, St. Louis Builder," drew heavily on the interviews and conversations I had with Fischer's descendants, making use of details remembered by family members rather than historians. The article begins: "A. A. Fischer could yodel. He fished for turtles and made good turtle soup. During the 1904 World's Fair, he had a gondola on Post-Dispatch Lake. His grandchildren remembered him as a kind, gentle man who was always tinkering and inventing things."

Over time my fascination with A. A. Fischer had expanded from his career and buildings to include personal information about the man

OPPOSITE
Roland and Irene Fischer's family at the Lake of the Ozarks in Missouri, 1940.

STANDING, FROM LEFT:
Norman A. Fischer,
Roland Fischer,
Kenneth R. Fischer.

SEATED, FROM LEFT:
Unknown woman,
Lorraine Fischer Cruise,
Irene Knopp Fischer.

Courtesy of Diane Barrett.

himself. I became engrossed in the details of his social network, from his family relations to his business associates, as well as the individuals to whom he sold houses.

Included in the back cover of this book is a map of St. Louis with close-up views of the various neighborhoods in which Fischer built; each of his structures is marked. The purpose of these maps is to demonstrate how significantly Fischer shaped the city's architectural identity and to show how he built houses and apartment buildings in clusters, thus magnifying the impact his structures have. Should you wish to scout out and visit Fischer structures on your own, the maps are designed for practical use; all street names and addresses are contemporary.

Shortly before the onset of the pandemic in 2020, I began seriously preparing this manuscript for publication. My biggest concern was fact-checking. The life and career of A. A. Fischer are built upon thousands and thousands of facts. Because many years had elapsed since beginning my research, I felt it prudent to check my own work as thoroughly as possible. Given the challenges COVID-19 posed to traveling and in-person research, I enlisted support in the form of a dedicated St. Louis–based researcher named Lori Berdak Miller. Lori gamely retraced my steps and consulted the primary source materials needed to fact-check my manuscript. Lori is also responsible for a great number of the house photos featured throughout this book. It has been a special experience to share my passion for A. A. Fischer with a fellow researcher, and I delight in the opportunity to share it here with you, too.

RIGHT
Grandchildren of A. A. and Frances Fischer, 1987.

FROM LEFT:
Kenneth R. Fischer,
Lorraine Fischer Cruise,
and Norman A. Fischer.

Courtesy of Bill Fischer.

NEXT
Westminster Place streetscape with 6182 Westminster in the foreground followed by 6186 and 6188.

Photo by Reed R. Radcliffe, 2022.

INTRODUCTION | xxiii

LEFT
Home at 3655 Flora Place.
Photo by Reed R. Radcliffe, 2022.

GLOSSARY

BROKEN FRIEZE
A decorative course that descends into the spaces between the upper-story windows rather than extending straight across the façade below the roofline.

CARTOUCHE
A decorative element consisting of scrollwork that is often placed above doorways or windows, or on ceilings, as a means of framing the space.

COLONNADE
A row of columns used to support a roof or upper story.

COURSES
The continuous horizontal layers of building materials (such as brick or stone) that are used to erect a building.

DENTILS
A repeating series of decorative blocks below the soffit.

FRIEZE
A decorative course. A. A. Fischer's friezes usually featured wreaths and/or swags below the roofline that are uninterrupted by windows or doorways.

PILASTER
An architectural feature very similar to a column but with square or rectangular edges.

PORTE-COCHÈRE
A covered porch through which a carriage may pass and/or park while passengers enter and exit.

QUOINS
Stones or bricks used at the corner of a building that are in some way visually distinctive from the type(s) of stone or brick used on the rest of the façade.

SOFFIT
The underside of roof eaves.

TRIPARTITE
Consisting of three distinct parts: a building's base (foundation, front steps); its center floors; and the upper portion of the building, which may include visually distinctive floors or visually distinctive elements, such as a frieze or broken frieze.

CHAPTER ONE

THE FISCHER FAMILY

The oft-quoted John Donne so famously wrote, "No man is an island." That is, no individual can be viewed entirely in isolation: People constantly interact with their immediate and extended families, as with the family one marries into. Even long-deceased ancestors play their part. This seems particularly true of German families, including the Fischers. The pattern certainly runs throughout the life of Alexander August "A. A." Fischer, so this biography begins not with his birth in 1866, but instead with his ancestors.

GERMAN ORIGINS AND IMMIGRATION

When A. A. Fischer's ancestors immigrated to Missouri from the northwestern part of present-day Germany, they left behind a region that was not yet a unified nation, but rather a hodgepodge of duchies, kingdoms, city-states, and other small entities. Some of his ancestors left before the failed 1848 revolution, and others came later. One avowed reason for going to America was "keine König da," meaning, "no king there."[1] The German populace had suffered greatly as a result of Napoleon's wars, forced conscription, economic inequality, and overpopulation.

Fischer's ancestors settled in Washington, Missouri, a hilly, picturesque town on the south bank of the Missouri River, about 50 miles west of St. Louis. (The reader must now break the habit of assuming that any reference to "Washington" means Washington, DC.) Washington is in Franklin County, but it is not the county seat; that honor goes to the town of Union.

THE PATRIARCH: FRIEDRICH LUDWIG AUGUST FISCHER

First among Alex's ancestors to emigrate from Germany was his father, Friedrich Ludwig August Fischer, commonly known as August Fischer. Records conflict regarding the year of August Fischer's birth, but they are consistent in date and location: He was born on May 5 in either 1839 or 1840 in the town of Schlangen in the principality of Lippe, a very small area in northwest Germany. August Fischer was christened in Schlangen's Evangelical church on June 8, 1840.[2, 3]

Two of August Fischer's names—"Friedrich" and "Ludwig"—were probably given to him by his godparents at the time of his christening. Every US record concerning August lists him simply as "August Fischer." August had two younger siblings, also born in Schlangen: a brother, Hermann Heinrich Ferdinand Fischer (known as "Herman"), born August 1842[4], and a sister, Henriette Marie Johanne Karoline Fischer (known as "Marie"), born February 1849.[5] The parents of these children (A. A. Fischer's grandparents) were August Gottlieb Fischer and Louise Helene Auguste Gallenkamp, who were married in Schlangen's Evangelical church in 1839.[6]

In 1854, 14-year-old August Fischer Jr., claiming to be 15, left Detmold, Germany, for the United States. He was one of 13 "cabin passengers" aboard the ship *Louisiana*, which sailed first from Bremen in the north of Germany, to London, England, and on to New York Harbor.[7] According to the ship's passenger list, August described himself as a merchant. Once in New York, August prepared for the last leg of his journey to Washington, Missouri—his final destination. Like so many other immigrants, August followed in the footsteps of friends and family from his homeland who had already established themselves in America, among them two of his mother's sisters.

Four years later, in 1849, August's maternal uncle Charles F. W. Gallenkamp immigrated to the United States, arriving in New Orleans. While Charles likely traveled directly to Washington, where his sister and brother-in-law had settled, his whereabouts are unconfirmed until September 1852, when he married fellow German immigrant Johanne Mary Stumpe in Franklin County, Missouri. So by the time August Fischer bade farewell to his mother and siblings in 1854, he already had two sets of aunts, uncles, and cousins waiting for him in Washington.

Four years after August emigrated from Germany, on June 14, 1858, the ship *Rosalia* arrived in New Orleans from Bremen.[8] Every passenger on the ship was of German origin, including August's mother, Louise Fischer, age 42, and sister, Marie Fischer, age 9. How exactly Louise and Marie traveled from New Orleans to Washington—a distance of approximately 700 miles—is unknown. They may have taken a steamboat north up the Mississippi River to St. Louis, and then gone west by stagecoach to Washington.

Other records indicate that August's brother, Herman Fischer, did not immigrate to the United States until after the Civil War.[9]

ABOVE
Inset of the German principality of Lippe.

Courtesy of the David Rumsey Map Collection, David Rumsey Map Center, Stanford Libraries at Stanford University.

PREVIOUS
Westminster Place streetscape with 6150 Westminster in the foreground followed by 6154, 6158, 6160, and 6164.

Photo by Reed R. Radcliffe, 2022.

RIGHT
Map of Germany, 1854.

Courtesy of the David Rumsey Map Collection, David Rumsey Map Center, Stanford Libraries at Stanford University.

ABOVE
The Calvin Opera House in Washington, Missouri, built in 1909.

Photo by Reed R. Radcliffe, 2022.

LIFE IN WASHINGTON, MISSOURI

Young and full of vigor, August Fischer immersed himself quickly and completely in his new community of Washington. Within a few years of his arrival, his various orbits—family, work, and church—heavily overlapped, and he was settling into a new life as an American. A particularly revealing event occurred on April 17, 1859, when August served as one of three godfathers to a baby baptized at St. Peter's Evangelical Church.[10] The baby was his first cousin, born to his aunt Johanna Gallenkamp Arcularius John and her second husband, Rudolf John (who, like her late first husband, was the church's minister).

The closeness of the Gallenkamp brood was not limited to their relationships. It also extended to their living arrangements. The 1860 Census reveals that August's mother and sister were living with William Gallenkamp and his family. (William was Louise and Johanna's brother.) Living separately was 22-year-old August, who boarded in the home of a man named Edward Schuller and worked as a clerk in his store.

Part of August's community immersion was his participation in cultural-enrichment groups. Germans had brought the Turnverein (literally, "gymnastic society") with them to Washington, with the goal of cultivating members who were well rounded in both mind and body. The group hosted debates on moral and political problems; conducted physical and intellectual exercises; and held balls, parades, and picnics.[11] As a member of the Turnverein, the able-bodied August Fischer enlisted for a three-year term in the Missouri infantry in September 1861, not long after the Civil War began.[12]

NEXT
6217 Waterman Avenue.

Photo by Reed R. Radcliffe, 2022.

AUGUST FISCHER IN THE CIVIL WAR

August and other Washington members of the Turnverein became part of the Union's Company G, 17th Missouri Infantry. Union Major General Samuel R. Curtis had been successful at Pea Ridge, and now he wanted to attack Little Rock, the capital of Arkansas.[13] Because the terrain of northwest Arkansas was so rugged, General Curtis took his 17,000 men east to West Plains, Missouri, and then south into Arkansas. Food for the infantry's horses was running low, but on May 19 an abundance of it was found on the flat land near the town of Searcy Landing, Arkansas. August Fischer's Company F, along with companies G and H, were commanded to go on a foraging expedition. His written report states:

> Arrived at the first large farm on the road, we proceeded to load some of the wagons with fodder and sent them back to camp, proceeding on with the remaining train. . . .
>
> We heard heavy firing about half a mile in the rear, and I instantly marched Company F in that direction. The 2 mounted men who had been left with me had galloped some distance and presently returned, shouting, "They are coming," upon which they fled.
>
> We discovered that the woods around us were swarming with the enemy, who attacked us from all sides. My men continued to defend themselves until at last I saw none standing except Sergeant Schaub and myself, upon which I called him to surrender, which I also did. My sword and revolver were taken from me, and after having been a prisoner some five minutes I was shot in the shoulder by one of the enemy. Upon the approach of our troops that were hurrying to our rescue from camp the rebels fled, leaving us few survivors at liberty. I have seen the enemy barbarously hacking and shooting our brave wounded soldiers after all resistance on their part was impossible.
>
> I have the honor to be, colonel, very respectfully, your obedient servant, AUGUST FISCER [sic], Second Lieutenant, Company F, Seventeenth Missouri Vols.[14]

Although August survived, being shot changed his life. No surgeon was ever able to remove the ball from his shoulder because it was too close to his spine. He finished the remaining two years and four months of his three-year term in the Union Army but was hospitalized several times.

The 17th Missouri Volunteers fought in numerous battles and were part of the Vicksburg campaign. Following the Chattanooga campaign in the fall of 1863, August was promoted to captain. During the Atlanta campaign in June 1864 he led Company E through the Battle of Kennesaw Mountain. The 17th Missouri Regiment was mustered out of service on September 26, 1864, at which time August returned to Washington.

OPPOSITE
Portrait of August Fischer by Gustav A. Cramer, ca. 1870s.

Courtesy of Diane Barrett.

BELOW
Undated photo of A. A. Fischer's mother, Maria Heining Fischer.

Courtesy of Diane Barrett.

THE FAMILY OF AUGUST AND MARIA HEINING FISCHER

After coming home to Washington, August Fischer married Maria Heining at St. Peter's on March 27, 1865.[15] The daughter of Henry Heining and Catherine (or Katarina) Esselbruegge Heining, Maria Heining Fischer (referred to as "Maria Fischer" in this book) was born in Washington on September 3, 1843. According to the 1860 Census, Maria's parents were born in Prussia[16] and married in Franklin County on June 12, 1841.[17] The 1850 and 1860 censuses record Henry Heining's occupation as brickmaker, but by 1870 he was working in a retail store.

On May 14, 1866, August and Maria welcomed their first child and the subject of this book, Alexander Heinrich Carl August Fischer.

August and Maria Fischer had six children, only three of whom—Alexander, Hugo, and Clara—lived to adulthood.[18] Hugo was born on March 1, 1868,[19] and Clara was born on November 14, 1870, both in Washington. According to the 1870 Census, August Fischer was working as a "retail merchant."[20] The family stayed in Washington until 1874, then lived in St. Louis from 1874 to 1877. From 1875 to 1876, August was described in a city directory as a clerk for the Pittsburgh Brewery at 2506 Carondelet Avenue, and in 1877 he was described as a brewer for the same company. During their St. Louis years, the Fischer family lived at 532 Sidney Street, 2506 Carondelet, and 2524 Carondelet.

August Fischer's friend William G. Ruge had also been a part of the 17th Missouri Infantry during the Civil War. He knew about August's chronic health issues that stemmed from his war wound and encouraged him to think about moving to a warmer climate. In 1878 they went to Arkansas and found a place for the Fischer family to live. After August and his family moved to Sub Rosa, Arkansas, Ruge bought some land nearby.

Although the town of Sub Rosa no longer exists, in the late 1800s it was a thriving little community. *Goodspeed's History of Franklin County, Arkansas* from 1888 says, "Sub Rosa, Vista, and Alston are vigorous small business points, especially Sub Rosa, which has five business houses, seven residences, two secret societies, three religious societies, one physician and a notary public."[21] August, Maria, Alexander, Hugo, and Clara lived in Sub Rosa until 1889, when 23-year-old Alex moved to St. Louis and began a career of his own.[22] Not long after, in February 1890, Alex married Frances M. E. Peterson in his former home of Washington.

NEXT
McPherson Place streetscape with 6186 McPherson in the foreground followed by 6182, 6178, 6174, 6170, and 6168.

Photo by Reed R. Radcliffe, 2022.

CHAPTER ONE | 9

LEFT
Washington's C&W Gallenkamp Building, where it's believed A. A. Fischer was born.

Courtesy of the Washington Historical Society.

OPPOSITE
5237 Vernon Avenue.

Photo by Reed R. Radcliffe, 2022.

Back in Sub Rosa, on April 5, 1890, Alex's sister, 19-year-old Clara, died of consumption. She was buried in the large Lowes Creek Cemetery. Even though it's in a remote area south of Ozark and east of Fort Smith, it has been well maintained. Clara's beautiful gravestone, inscribed with a poem, sits beneath a large tree.

After Clara's death, only Hugo was available to help his parents—that is, until he was badly hurt in a tornado in Fort Smith on January 11, 1898. A brief news item in the *Arkansas Democrat* announced that as a result of his injury, "Mr. Hugo Fischer of Sub Rosa, Ark., had his right arm amputated above the elbow."[23]

More sadness soon followed for the Fischers. August Fischer died in Sub Rosa on July 23, 1899, and he was buried in Washington. Five different stories were published about him in local newspapers, including this one, printed in *Die Washingtoner Post*:

> 1899-07-28   August Fischer formerly of Washington died in Arkansas and was buried in Odd Fellows Cemetery [in Washington] Wednesday, July 26, 1899.
>
> Age 60. Leaves a widow and two grown sons. James C. Kiskaddon [an attorney] praised his record as a captain during the civil war. Card of thanks was signed by Alex Fischer, son, and Herman Fischer, brother. August Peterson [and] Herman Fischer of St. Louis attended the funeral.

It is unknown how long August's widow Maria remained in Sub Rosa, but by 1910 she had returned to Washington, where she lived in a rented home by herself.[24] By the time Maria died in Washington on May 7, 1919, her eldest son, Alex "A. A." Fischer, had built more than 300 structures in St. Louis.

12 | A. A. FISCHER'S ST. LOUIS STREETSCAPES

CHAPTER TWO

A CHANCE MEETING

Alex Fischer was 12 years old when his father's friend from the Civil War persuaded his family to move to the warmer climate of Sub Rosa, Arkansas, where he spent his adolescence before returning to Missouri in 1889. It seems by this point 23-year-old Alex had had enough of small-town living, for he did not return to his birthplace of Washington, but rather went to the nearby big city of St. Louis. It would not be long before his path crossed with a young entrepreneur named Walter Jefferson Lewis.

PREVIOUS
Westminster Place streetscape with 6163 Westminster in the foreground followed by 6159 and 6155.

Photo by Reed R. Radcliffe, 2022.

PREVIOUS ILLUSTRATION
Undated pencil sketch by Alex A. Fischer, later known as A. A. Fischer.

Courtesy of Diane Barrett.

WORK WITH WALTER JEFFERSON LEWIS

Walter Jefferson Lewis had already led an eventful life by the time he settled in St. Louis in 1889. Born in Morgan County, Ohio, on March 13, 1858, Walter was the son of Walter and Nancy Carter Lewis.[25] By 12 years of age he was working on his father's farm while continuing to attend school. Lewis was educated in the Federal School in Morgan County, Ohio, until he was 20 years old. From 1878 to 1879 he attended Atwood Institute in Albany, Ohio.[26]

Then came a decade of change. According to *The Book of St. Louisans* from 1912, Lewis spent a year in sawmill and lumber camps in Florida and Alabama, followed by a year in surveying and bridge construction with the International–Great Northern Railroad in Mexico.[27] In 1882 he acquired an interest in a sheep ranch in Austin, Texas, and by 1883 he was in the hotel business in Abilene. In 1884 he purchased a ranch 15 miles south of Abilene and remained there for five years.[28] Lewis's account of this time span suggests that he had some financial capital at his disposal.

In 1889, when he was 31, Lewis picked up stakes again and moved to St. Louis. That same year he organized a real estate business he called the Tower Grove and Southwestern Building Association, located at 2604 S. Jefferson Avenue.[29] Lewis had probably been in the real estate business only a short time when Alex Fischer arrived in St. Louis. Lewis needed a bookkeeper and Fischer needed a job, so Lewis hired him—a pivotal event in both of their lives. It is also a pivotal point in the research because it poses an intriguing question that might never be answered.

TWO WEDDINGS

The question involves two weddings. On February 20, 1890, Alex Fischer married Frances Peterson in Washington.[30] Exactly three months later, on May 20, 1890, Walter Lewis married Alex's first cousin, Emma Simon, also in Washington.[31] Did Fischer introduce Lewis to Simon? Or did she already know Lewis and play some role in getting him to hire Fischer? We can consider two possible scenarios.

In the first, Fischer moves from Sub Rosa to St. Louis in 1889. He looks for work and is hired as Lewis's bookkeeper. Now that he's living in St. Louis, it's easy for him to take the train to Washington to visit relatives and friends. He courts Frances Peterson, they arrange to be married, and Fischer invites Lewis to the wedding. Fischer's cousin Emma Simon is also at the wedding; she and Lewis meet, and they are married three months later.

The second scenario stems from the fact that Emma Simon's sister Melinda had married William C. Kruse in 1887[32], and the Kruses were living in St. Louis. In this situation, the Kruses somehow meet Lewis. They introduce him to Simon. Then they mention to Lewis that Fischer is looking for a job, or they tell Fischer that Lewis is looking for a bookkeeper.

There are some chronological ambiguities that must be addressed. First, consider an item in *Die Washingtoner Post*, a weekly newspaper that was originally published in German. On August 30, 1889, it reported (with the all-too-common misspelling of *Fisher*), "Alexander

Fisher of Arkansas, son of our former citizen August Fisher, came to Washington Thursday to visit friends."[33] Was the newspaper editor correct in saying that Fischer was living in Arkansas, or did he just make that assumption? Did Fischer already have his bookkeeping job in St. Louis? If he did, why was he able to get away from work on a Thursday?

Fischer himself is not helpful in clarifying things. The data he provided for his entry in *The Book of St. Louisans* states, "From age of 12 years to age of 23 years, lived on father's farm in Franklin Co., Ark.; came to St. Louis, 1889, and took position with the Tower Grove and Southwestern Building and Loan Association as bookkeeper. . . ."[34] That part is straightforward enough, but Fischer never specifies when he began his employment. But the data he submitted for *The Book of St. Louisans* say he and Frances Peterson were married on February 20, 1889, whereas all other records—including Missouri marriage records—say they were married on February 20, 1890.[35] So just how reliable was his memory? After all, men forgetting their wedding anniversaries is a well-worn punch line.

This was an era when a young man postponed marriage until he had a job and could support his wife. It is certain, then, that Alex Fischer was already working in St. Louis—most likely for a few months—when he and Frances were married. This puts him beginning work sometime in 1889, either before or after his August 30, 1889, visit to Washington. The *St. Louis City Directory*, which was published early in the year, mentions Fischer in 1890 but not 1889.

Then there are two news items that reported on the wedding itself.

> Married—Thursday, Feb. 20, '90, by Rev. Holke, at the residence of the bride's mother, Mr. Alex Fisher to Miss Frances Peterson. The accomplished and pretty bride is well known in our city and very popular; the groom is engaged in the real estate business in St. Louis. We join with the many well-wishers in wishing the newly married couple a long, happy and contented married life.[36]
>
> – *Franklin County Observer*, February 21, 1890

> Alexander A. Fisher and Miss Frances Peterson were married Thursday, Feb. 20, 1890. Rev. Holke officiated, they moved to St. Louis the next day.[37]
>
> – *Die Washingtoner Post*, February 28, 1890

It is highly unlikely that the newspapers would have reported the Fischer-Peterson wedding in 1890 if it had taken place in 1889. While it seems all but certain that Fischer simply incorrectly recorded his marriage year as 1889 instead of 1890, closer examination yields some unexpected insight. In the second scenario, Simon's sister and brother-in-law, Melinda and William Kruse, introduce Alex Fischer to Walter Lewis.

ABOVE
Portrait of Frances Peterson Fischer by E. A. Atwater, ca. 1900.
Courtesy of Diane Barrett.

NEXT
Washington Place streetscape with 5137 Washington in the foreground followed by 5133 and 5129.
Photo by Reed R. Radcliffe, 2022.

OPPOSITE TOP TWO
Portraits of a young Roland Fischer by E. A. Atwater, ca. 1900.
Courtesy of Diane Barrett.

OPPOSITE BOTTOM
Portrait of the A. A. Fischer family in Centralia, Illinois, ca. 1900s.
FROM LEFT:
A. A. Fischer, Roland Fischer, Frances Fischer.
Courtesy of Richard Fischer.

St. Louis was already a large city in 1889, so how would the Kruses have known Walter Jefferson Lewis, a relative newcomer to the city? St. Louis directories provide an important clue. It's documented that Lewis's office was at 2604 S. Jefferson. According to *Gould's St. Louis Directory* for 1889[38], William C. Kruse was the proprietor of a barber shop at 2601-A S. Jefferson, which was located right across the street from Lewis's office. Furthermore, William and Melinda Kruse lived at 2608 S. Jefferson, which was *next door* to Lewis's office. William Kruse would have had to walk past Lewis's office on his way to and from work. This information tips the scales in favor of the second scenario—in which Fischer's first cousin and her husband make the introduction that facilitates his employment with Walter Lewis.

A third, speculative piece of evidence in favor of an 1890 marriage is the fact that Roland August Fischer was born at the end of November 1890[39], exactly nine months from the date of Alex and Frances's wedding. In the era before modern birth control, babies were often born within the first year of marriage.

The circumstances of Alex Fischer's introduction to and relationship with Walter Jefferson Lewis are essential to this story for one simple reason: Lewis was in the real estate business. If Fischer would have been hired as a bookkeeper for a shoe manufacturer or brewery instead, would he have built any houses in St. Louis at all, let alone several hundred? Fischer became a far more prolific builder than Lewis ever was, but it was Lewis who gave Fischer his start.

While on paper it looks like Fischer's job as a bookkeeper was a modest (even menial) position, it is critical to understanding how he became a builder whose contributions to the St. Louis streetscape can be viewed to this day. Fischer was inducted into the industry in an apprentice-like fashion that was far more common in a time when most people didn't have a formal education. There is no doubt that, as a bookkeeper for Lewis, Fischer learned about the expenses involved in construction and real estate. Fischer was a young man who had grown up in a first-generation American farm family. He lacked a formal education in real estate, construction, and architecture, but over time he would learn to profit from all three.

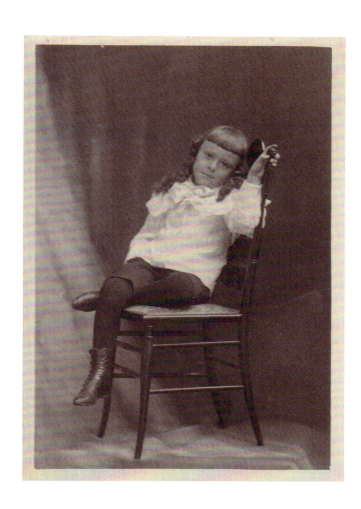

CHAPTER TWO | 21

THE WALTER JEFFERSON LEWIS CONNECTION

Walter and Emma Lewis were married three months to the day after Alex and Frances Fischer. As reported in *Die Washingtoner Post* on May 23, 1890: "Miss Emilie Simons and J. W. Lewis of St. Louis married Tuesday May 20, 1890. Rev. Holke performed the ceremony."

Although this news item contains at least three mistakes—the bride's first name was Emma, not Emilie; her last name was Simon, not Simons; and the groom's name was W. J. Lewis, not J. W. Lewis—the account is reliable. The state's marriage records corroborate the details of Walter and Emma Lewis's wedding.[40]

Within a year of founding his new business venture, Walter Lewis seems to have had enough work that he could employ at least two bookkeepers. In addition to Alex Fischer, who worked there for 18 months, there was William Haase, who stated in his own entry in *The Book of St. Louisans* that from 1890 to 1894 he was "bookkeeper for W. J. Lewis, secretary of Tower Grove and Southwestern Building Association."[41] The major portion of Tower Grove's business involved lending money to other builders, who paid them back with interest. Lewis did build a few houses, but a study of them will have to wait for another day. (A cursory examination shows they did not resemble the homes Fischer built.)

Walter and Emma, like many St. Louisans of that era, rented their home and moved frequently. In 1890 the couple lived at 2231 Sidney Street; in 1891 their address was 2821 Missouri Avenue; and by 1892 the Lewis family was living at 2344 Gravois Avenue. Each of these homes was within a few blocks of Lewis's office at 2604 S. Jefferson.

As Lewis's real estate business grew, so did his family. The Lewises' first daughter, Rhea, was born June 10, 1893—the year the family moved to 2331 Sidney. Rhea's younger sister, Grace, was born March 22, 1895, and on October 1, 1898, the family was made complete with the birth of Clifton Carter Lewis. In 1898 or 1899 the Lewises left their south St. Louis neighborhood of straight streets, brick houses, and flats for a very different environment: a residential enclave called Clifton Heights.

According to Charles C. Savage in his book *Architecture of the Private Streets of St. Louis,* Clifton Heights originated as a Methodist settlement.[42] Surveyed and platted by Julius Pitzman—who also surveyed and platted private streets, such as Vandeventer Place and Benton Place—the streets curve around Clifton Park, which contains a small lake.[43] Clifton Heights doesn't feel like a city neighborhood at all. The houses sit farther apart. They're made from wood-frame construction and look like the middle-class homes common to many midwestern towns.

Savage's book mentions the names of some of those who built Clifton Heights, including "M. J. Lewis" (who is likely W. J. Lewis). Savage states, "A 1901 roll of the members of the Fry Memorial [Methodist] Church [nearby] shows that almost the entire membership lived in Clifton Heights."[44] The neighborhood's Simpson Avenue was named after Matthew Simpson, a Methodist bishop who lived in Pennsylvania. Census and city directory records show various Lewis family members living at 6255, 6131, and 6138 Simpson.

In his entry for the 1912 edition of *The Book of St. Louisans,* Walter Lewis stated that he was the secretary of the Tower Grove and Southwestern Building Association; the former vice president of the Jefferson Gravois Trust Company; the secretary and treasurer of the State League Building and Loan Association of Missouri in 1911; the owner of Pineolia, a 4,000-acre resort at Citronelle, Alabama; and the president of Clifton Realty Company. He was also a member of the Civic League of St. Louis, a Republican, and a Protestant. His stated recreation was "bee raising and the production of fancy comb and pure extraction honey." His office was listed at 2608 S. Jefferson, and his residence was 6255 Simpson.

On April 12, 1914, Walter J. Lewis died in Mobile, Alabama, at the age of 56, following a short illness.[45] At that time he was likely living at or near his Alabama resort. The *St. Louis Republic* reported on April 13, 1914, that Walter died after an operation for appendicitis. His widow, Emma, outlived him by more than a decade, dying in St. Louis on December 4, 1927. Both Walter and Emma are buried in her birthplace of Washington, Missouri, in the old section of St. Peter's Cemetery.

OPPOSITE
6224 Washington Avenue.
Photo by Reed R. Radcliffe, 2022.

ABOVE
Union Boulevard streetscape (left to right) with 1344, 1342, 1338, and 1336 Union.

Photo by Reed R. Radcliffe, 2022.

CHAPTER THREE

BUILDING ST. LOUIS
1890–1911

As St. Louisans were pulling down tattered 1890 calendars and replacing them with crisp new ones for 1891, Alexander August Fischer was working as a bookkeeper for the Tower Grove and Southwestern Building Association, Walter J. Lewis's real estate company. But that would soon change.

ST. LOUIS IN THE 1890s

Now that Fischer knew more about the real estate business and had a wife and infant son to support, he was ready to pivot to the career he really wanted: house builder. It came at a good time. St. Louis was flourishing and growing rapidly. Most Americans assumed the prosperity would continue, unaware that a recession would take hold just a few years later. Just as Fischer and his ancestors had done, disillusioned men and women from farms, small towns, and other countries were coming to St. Louis to seek their fortunes. Many residents of St. Louis's oldest neighborhoods along the riverfront now found their homes cramped and lacking in amenities. For them, moving farther west in the city and the land just beyond was a way to attain something better and improve their lives.

Each decade the federal census confirmed that the nation's population center was moving westward. St. Louisans had long considered their city to be at the center of things, and there had even been talk of relocating the United States capital to St. Louis from Washington, DC. St. Louis was booming.

In early 1891 the Lewis and Fischer families were living at 2821 Missouri and 2702 Missouri—both within easy walking distance of the men's office at 2604 S. Jefferson. The two young families may have gotten along splendidly, but because Lewis's business was primarily about financing houses rather than building them, Fischer was still on the lookout for a different job.

PREVIOUS
By 2012 the home at 2244 S. Jefferson had been brought back to its former glory. It's one of many historic-home restorations taking place across the St. Louis area.

Photo by Reed R. Radcliffe, 2022.

OPPOSITE
With details similar to those found at 2244 S. Jefferson, this Fischer home at 3665 Shenandoah Avenue was built three years later in 1897.

Photo by Reed R. Radcliffe, 2022.

A NEW PARTNERSHIP

At some point in 1891, Alexander Fischer left the employ of Walter J. Lewis and went to work for Harry W. Mepham, a house builder. By 1892, Mepham was working in real estate out of an office at 1901 S. Jefferson, and Fischer was working as a bookkeeper with no business address given. According to their entries in *Gould's St. Louis City Directory* for 1892, the men were sharing a residence at 2010 S. Jefferson.

The *St. Louis Daily Record* began publishing in late 1890, just in time to record all of Fischer's building permits and probably most of Mepham's, too. The first time Fischer's name appears on a building permit is July 10, 1894. The house is 2244 S. Jefferson.

The permit lists A. A. Fischer as the owner and Franz Schroeder as the builder. The house is a two-story dwelling measuring 22 feet by 50 feet. This red brick home was in disrepair in 2000: It had a boarded-up window, a makeshift porch roof, and some damaged brick on the façade. Happily, by 2012 it had been brought back to life, looking beautiful at age 118, as it continues to today.

The house is two stories high and two bays wide. The entrance is in the left bay. Brick arches, with patterns of dentils inside, are above all four openings. Pairs of small round brick columns flank the recessed entry, which has two doors. Just below the flat roof is a band of perhaps a dozen darker brick courses that are occasionally punctuated by a decorative square three courses high. In 1897, Fischer would build a home that looked remarkably similar to this one, a bit over a mile west at 3665 Shenandoah Avenue.

Following the construction of 2244 S. Jefferson, Fischer embarked on his next project—or rather, *projects*—two homes at 3667 and 3669 Russell Boulevard. On October 25, 1894, the *Daily Record* published the building permits of these two structures, describing them as brick dwellings 22 feet wide by 50 feet deep. They were each two stories high and separated by just 3 feet. The permits offer tangible proof of Fischer's partnership with Mepham, as both of their names appear on the paperwork.

Building permits from the late 19th century could be frustrating to decipher. Misspellings were common, and businesses were incorrectly named. It's possible that hired carpenters were sent to city hall on behalf of Fischer and Mepham, and they gave their own names for the buildings rather than the names of their bosses. Thankfully, today's recordkeeping is much more streamlined.

ABOVE
July 10, 1894, is the first time A. A. Fischer's name appeared on a building permit; it was for this house at 2244 S. Jefferson Avenue. When this photo was taken, the house was in a state of partial disrepair.

Photo by Nancy Moore Hamilton, 2000.

RUSSELL BOULEVARD: 1894 AND 1902

On October 25, 1894, two side-by-side structures—3667 and 3669 Russell—appeared in the *Daily Record*, listing A. A. Fischer as the owner and H. W. Mepham as the builder. Despite being some of Fischer's earliest work, elements of these two homes would reappear time and again. Both 3667 and 3669 Russell feature recessed entryways supported by colonnades, decorative brick, and either stacked bay windows or rounded arched windows.

The third house on Russell Boulevard attributed to Fischer is 2326, which bears a strong resemblance to the house he would later build for himself and his family on Vernon Avenue. Erected in 1895, 2326 Russell is built of limestone and features a grand centered porch flanked by decorative colonnades. A broken frieze bedecks the home's top windows.

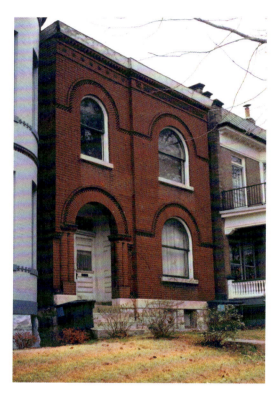

LEFT
These homes at 3667 (right) and 3669 Russell Boulevard were built in 1894. Records list A. A. Fischer as the owner and H. W. Mepham as the builder of both.

Photos by Nancy Moore Hamilton, 2001.

BELOW
These side-by-side Fischer homes at 3667 (right) and 3669 Russell are the jewels of their block in St. Louis's Shaw neighborhood.

Photo by Reed R. Radcliffe, 2022.

CHAPTER THREE | 31

BELOW
Fischer streetscape of eight homes from west to east on Vernon Avenue in the Academy neighborhood.

Photo by Reed R. Radcliffe, 2022.

OPPOSITE
The same Vernon Avenue streetscape was used to illustrate the July 1905 article in the *Builder* in which A. A. Fischer was profiled.

Missouri Historical Society Collections.

CHAPTER THREE | 33

LEFT TO RIGHT

5263 Vernon Avenue.
5259 Vernon Avenue.
5255 Vernon Avenue, razed.
5253 Vernon Avenue.
5249 Vernon Avenue.
5247 Vernon Avenue.
5243 Vernon Avenue, razed.
5237 Vernon Avenue.
5233 Vernon Avenue.
5231 Vernon Avenue.
5227 Vernon Avenue, razed.

Photos by Reed R. Radcliffe, 2022.

1896: THE FIRST FISCHER STREETSCAPE

Fischer built a total of 24 structures on Vernon Avenue between 1896 and 1907. As of spring 2022, the status of Fischer's Vernon builds ranges from restored to condemned to razed. Of the 23 structures on Vernon, 10 have been razed, 11 are occupied (1 of which has been restored), 2 are under renovation, and 1 has been condemned. In addition to a streetscape of three houses on Vernon (5248, 5252, and 5256) and a pair of duplexes side by side (5616-5618 and 5620-5622), Fischer is responsible for a stretch of 11 homes on the street (west to east from 5263 to 5227). It's the first Fischer streetscape to grace St. Louis.

The two earliest permitted Fischer structures on Vernon Avenue are located at 5249 and 5253.

When ground was broken on these properties in late summer of 1896, they were the first 2 of 10 houses that were part of what appears to be a very intentional building plan for the block, which was carried out over the next three years. In addition to these houses on the north side of the street, in 1902 Fischer was responsible for the erection of two additional Vernon Avenue homes on the south side of the street (5252 and 5248).

Before the broken frieze became Fischer's trademark, he was already making a name for himself as a man who built houses in groups and prided himself on running his business with great efficiency.

CHAPTER THREE | 35

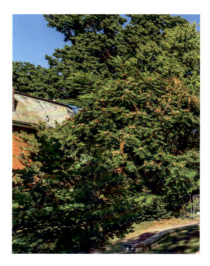

LEFT TO RIGHT, TOP TO BOTTOM
5263 Vernon Avenue.
5259 Vernon Avenue.
5255 Vernon Avenue, razed.
5253 Vernon Avenue.
5249 Vernon Avenue.
5247 Vernon Avenue.
5243 Vernon Avenue, razed.
5237 Vernon Avenue.
5233 Vernon Avenue.
5231 Vernon Avenue.
5227 Vernon Avenue, razed.

Photos by Reed R. Radcliffe, 2022.

RIGHT

Fischer must have been particularly proud of this streetscape of eight homes on Vernon Avenue at Union Boulevard: He used a photograph of it to decorate his company's letterhead in 1901.

Courtesy of Richard Fischer.

ABOVE, TOP
By 2012 the home at 2631 Allen Avenue was missing its rear retaining wall.

ABOVE, BOTTOM
After many years of decline, the Fischer home at 2631 Allen Avenue was razed in early 2018.

City of St. Louis Address and Property Search.

LEFT
By 2022 the home at 2629 Allen had been condemned, and its neighbor to the west, 2631 Allen, had also been lost.

Photo by Reed R. Radcliffe, 2022.

FAR LEFT
Fischer home at 2631 Allen Avenue. It has since been razed.

LEFT
This Fischer home at 2629 Allen Avenue was one of two side by side in St. Louis's Fox Park neighborhood.

Photos by Nancy Moore Hamilton, 2001.

ALLEN AVENUE

Sandwiched between the cross streets of Ohio and California avenues in the Fox Park neighborhood is the 2600 block of Allen Avenue, where Fischer built two houses side by side. Both of the Allen homes—numbered 2629 and 2631—appeared in the *Daily Record* on December 10, 1895.

These two houses were built on the north side of the street and seem to mimic each other architecturally while also sharing components with the very first Fischer house at 2244 S. Jefferson. The exteriors of all three structures have brick façades and porches. However, the two homes on the north side of Allen are more architecturally intricate and have features that would later become defining characteristics of Fischer homes. While the home on Jefferson has brick detailing and arched windows that accentuate the façade, the homes on the north side of Allen are distinguished by stacked bay windows on their left sides that look almost tower-like. With the exception of the shape of the bays—the ones on 2629 are rectangular whereas the windows on 2631 are round—the two Allen houses are mirror images of each other.

It is worth noting that 2629 and 2631 are not the only homes on Allen built in such a style: Several houses west, the same core architectural features appear once again. The house at 2637 Allen has the same brick façade, recessed porch, and tripartite organization as the two Fischer homes built on Allen Avenue. While it cannot definitively be linked to Fischer because the building permit is no longer on file, it wouldn't be surprising to learn that Fischer was associated with it in some way.

Building on Allen may have been particularly appealing to Fischer because of the area's strong German presence. The German newspapers *Anzeiger des Westens*, *Westliche Post*, and *Amerika* all ran stories in the 1890s and early 1900s regarding activity on the street. According to McCue and Peters in *A Guide to the Architecture of St. Louis*, earlier generations had "speculated, took their profits, and moved on," whereas the Germans who came to St. Louis were looking for a permanent residence. As a result, they "built carefully, of brick and stone, to last and look good."[46] Fischer's homes, made with both structural surety and architectural flair, would have fit this bill.

At least one more Fischer home was built on the south side of Allen Avenue in the years that followed. The confirmed Fischer house is 2144 Allen, built in 1902. Constructed of red brick and featuring a canopied porch, its façade closely resembles the two homes on the north side of Allen, minus the stacked bay windows. The two larger, rectangular windows on the top floor of 2144 break up a frieze—its white brick creates a striking contrast with the red brick on the rest of the home.

OPPOSITE LEFT
Undated photograph of A. A. Fischer (foreground) in his office.

OPPOSITE RIGHT
Undated photograph of A. A. Fischer (far right) and associates in his office. The name of the business— A. A. Fischer Architectural & Building Company—is partially visible in the window in the background.

Photos courtesy of Richard Fischer.

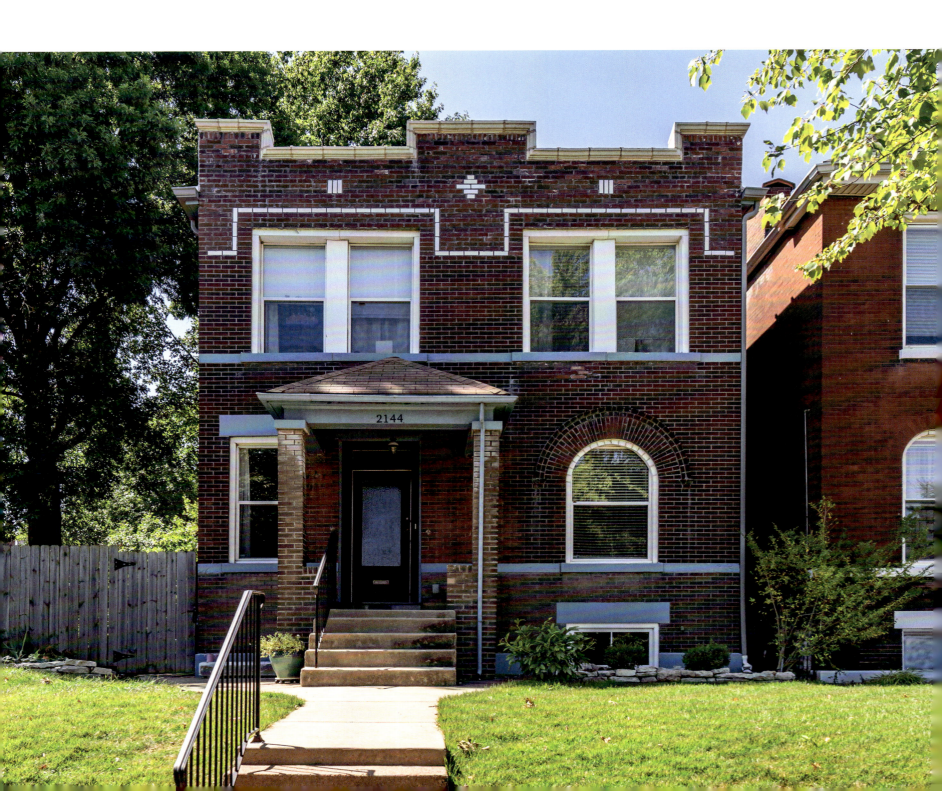

1898

The final two years of the 19th century were pivotal in A. A. Fischer's career. Although he's credited with only 15 buildings during this period, he was busy working behind the scenes, preparing to set out on his own and build on a far larger scale than he ever had before. When *The St. Louis City Directory* was published at the beginning of 1898, Fischer and Mepham were still sharing offices at 1821 S. Jefferson, but by August, Fischer had moved his office to 813 Chestnut Street, and soon thereafter Mepham moved his office to 3642 Cleveland Avenue. These separate offices are representative of the pair's business relationship: For the next few years Mepham had a home office and concentrated on building in the Shaw neighborhood, while Fischer had his office downtown and built all over the city, with a particular concentration in Mount Cabanne–Raymond Place and Skinker DeBaliviere. In Mount Cabanne–Raymond Place—bounded by Kingshighway, Union, Page, and Delmar boulevards—Fischer built 96 houses from 1896 to 1908, and in Skinker DeBaliviere—bounded by Skinker, Delmar, DeBaliviere Avenue, and Forest Park Parkway—he built 68 houses and 16 apartment buildings from 1907 to 1911.

The year 1898 is also significant because it marks the first time Fischer lists himself in the city directory as a contractor rather than a bookkeeper or in real estate. The A. A. Fischer Architectural & Building Company was officially incorporated the following year.[47] The 1906 edition of *The Book of St. Louisans* has a short biography on Fischer that states after his five-year partnership with Mepham, he "embarked in real estate and speculative building on [his] own account, from which evolved the A. A. Fischer Architectural and Building Company."

OPPOSITE
The house at 2144 Allen Avenue, built in 1902, is the third and final home attributed to Fischer on this block.

Photo by Reed R. Radcliffe, 2022.

CHAPTER THREE | 41

ABOVE
At the time this photograph was taken, the Fischer homes at 5312 and 5314 Maple Avenue were 124 years old.

Photo by Reed R. Radcliffe, 2022.

5312 AND 5314 MAPLE AVENUE

Over the course of Fischer's career, he built at least 15 homes on Maple Avenue that spanned the Academy, Visitation Park, and West End neighborhoods. His first three structures were 5240 Maple, for which a building permit was issued in March 1897, followed by 5312 and 5314 Maple, both of which appeared in the *Daily Record* in October 1898. Of these houses, 5240 has been razed, but 5312 and 5314 have both fared quite well. They closely resemble each other and were likely built from the same plans, but they're made with a different color of brick. Both have ground-floor arched windows and the elaborate frieze (not yet broken) below their rooflines. According to city records, between 2000 and 2015, both 5312 and 5314 benefited from significant reinvestment on behalf of their homeowners.

PREVIOUS
When these exquisite Fischer homes were erected in 1899, the name of their street was Berlin Avenue. In 1915 it was renamed Pershing Place for General John J. Pershing, who was from Missouri.

FROM LEFT:
4620 Pershing Place,
4624 Pershing Place.

Photos by Reed R. Radcliffe, 2022.

RIGHT
Work began on this Fischer home at 5137 Washington Place in 1899.

Photo by Reed R. Radcliffe, 2022.

1899

Shortly before the dawn of the 20th century, Fischer left his mark on the Central West End neighborhood with a pair of striking two-and-a-half-story structures with stone façades and unbroken friezes. At the time of their erection, their street was known as Berlin Avenue—today recognized as Pershing Avenue and Pershing Place. These grand homes, numbered 4620 Pershing Place and 4624 Pershing Place, are neighbors that have withstood the test of time and represent two fine examples of Fischer's architecture restored to their original glory.

Less than a mile northwest of the Pershing Place homes is a streetscape of three homes on the south side of Washington Place, also in the Central West End neighborhood. The three homes from west to east are 5137, 5133, and 5129 Washington Place. All three are in fine condition, with 5137 and 5133 earning the highest rating possible: restored.

BELOW

Archival documents suggest that Fischer was constructing this home at 5133 Washington Place while also working on its neighbor to the west, 5137 Washington.

Photo by Reed R. Radcliffe, 2022.

BELOW
Within a year of breaking ground on 5137 and 5133 Washington Place, Fischer went slightly farther east to build 5129 Washington.

Photo by Reed R. Radcliffe, 2022.

BELOW, TOP LEFT
Fischer's own home at 5256 Vernon Avenue in 2017, after many years of decline.

City of St. Louis Address and Property Search.

BELOW, TOP CENTER
By the spring of 2019, it looked as though 5256 Vernon Avenue would not be saved.

City of St. Louis Address and Property Search.

OPPOSITE LEFT
Fischer's Vernon Avenue home, as it was pictured in the July 1905 issue of the *Builder*.

Missouri Historical Society Collections.

OPPOSITE RIGHT
5256 Vernon Avenue during its historic renovation project in 2022.

Photo by Reed R. Radcliffe, 2022.

2017

2019

2021

June 2022

July 2022

August 2022

1901

The second year of the new century was most significant for A. A. Fischer. Of the 13 homes he constructed in 1901, none was more personally meaningful than the one he designed and erected for his own family at 5256 Vernon Avenue in the Academy neighborhood. His trademark, the broken frieze—wreaths and/or swags that descend into the spaces between the upper-story windows rather than extending straight across the façade below the cornice—is completely realized in this structure that embodied his architectural style and his growing economic status. Innovated in 1901, the broken frieze would grace the majority of Fischer's homes from 1902 to 1908.

Above, you can see how 5256 Vernon looked when it was new. The elegant, ornate house sits on the south side of the street and faces north on a 60-foot lot. This unusually large lot allows a driveway to run along the west side of the house from street to stable. The east wall, which is very close to the house next door, is constructed from unornamented brick, but the other three walls abound with decorative flourishes. Even the front porch, with steps on its west side, is oriented toward the driveway. The façade and west wall are limestone, alternating wide, rough-faced courses with smooth and narrow ones. The broken frieze on the façade has both wreaths and swags, but when it wraps around to the west wall, it becomes a frieze of continuous swags except when it encounters a window.

In late 2021, Fischer's home at 5256 Vernon was a shell of its former self, with only the front (northernmost) wall remaining standing. Its entire insides were hollowed out, and a chain-link fence ran around the perimeter of the property.

According to the City of St. Louis's online Address and Property Search portal, in 2021 the building's owners invested more than $450,000 in construction costs toward the restoration of this property. As of 2022 the home had been restored and is seemingly ready for the next 120 years.

OPPOSITE
The property was bought in 2019 for $5,000, and its new owners embarked on an ambitious historic renovation project.

Top right photo by Lori Berdak Miller, 2021.

Bottom row photos by Reed R. Radcliffe, 2022.

5266 AND 5268 MAPLE AVENUE (1901)

One block north of Fischer's Vernon Avenue home and streetscape is a cluster of four houses on Maple for which Fischer obtained permits in 1901: 5268, 5266, 5258, and 5252 (from west to east). They've all seen hard times, but as of 2022 they are pictures of resilience and rejuvenation: 5268 and 5258 Maple are both under renovation, and together they have enjoyed more than half a million dollars in published construction costs since 2019. Meanwhile, 5266 Maple is fully restored, having benefited from comparable investments in 2020 and 2021.

PREVIOUS
Side by side, the Fischer houses at 5266 Maple Avenue (left) and 5268 Maple make a striking impression.
Photo by Reed R. Radcliffe, 2022.

OPPOSITE
A. A. Fischer advertised his build at 5266 Maple Avenue as a "bargain" in the July 1901 issue of the *St. Louis Republic*.
Missouri Historical Society Collections.

OPPOSITE
Fischer's houses at 5266 Maple Avenue and 5268 Maple (foreground) have been restored to their original glory.
Photo by Reed R. Radcliffe, 2022.

LEFT
The home at 5268 Maple Avenue (right) undergoing extensive renovations, as its next-door neighbor at 5266 Maple (left) waits its turn in January 2020.
City of St. Louis Address and Property Search.

5266 Maple Ave.—A Bargain.

In Raymond place, just east of Union boulevard. A very attractive rough-stone front residence, containing 8 rooms and bathroom. The first floor contains Reception Hall, Parlor, Dining-Room and Kitchen; the second floor contains four rooms and bath. The Reception Hall and Staircase is finished in Oak, the Parlor is finished in Gloss White, the Dining-Room, Kitchen and second floor finished in Cypress, natural-wood finish. Polished Oak floors. The stair front in Reception Hall is neat and attractive and has Oak Columns with carved caps, an arched beam and carvings, which makes it very attractive. The bathroom contains White Enameled Bathtub, Marble Washstand and Tank closet, and has an ornamental tile floor; hot-water connections for Bathroom, Kitchen and Laundry. The entire cellar is cemented, has brick piers supporting the girders. Also contains sink, a water closet and a good large Hot-Air Furnace. Has a very large front porch, with two large square columns, with carved caps and ornamental trimmings.

This is the neatest, prettiest and lowest-priced house in Raymond place. Examine it and convince yourself. A special low price will be made to a quick buyer. A. A. FISCHER, 915 Chestnut st.

1902

Fischer is responsible for the erection of a confirmed 24 structures in 1902. Geographically, his turf was continuing to expand, particularly in two clusters north of Forest Park, one on the west end in the Skinker DeBaliviere neighborhood and the other on the east end in the Academy neighborhood.

Standing side by side, 5575 and 5579 Chamberlain Avenue are considerably farther northwest than the earliest Fischer structures, reflecting the trend that by the turn of the century, St. Louisans who could afford it were moving to homes farther away from the river.

PREVIOUS
This pair of Fischer homes at 5579 and 5575 Chamberlain Avenue have similar aesthetics and were likely built from the same plans, but there are variations in their façades. 5579 Chamberlain was built from stone, while 5575 Chamberlain was built using yellow brick. Their porches are also different.

Photo by Reed R. Radcliffe, 2022.

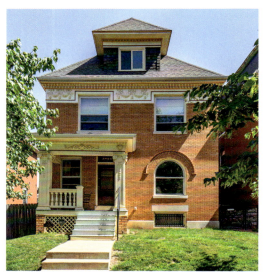

3825 Cleveland Avenue.

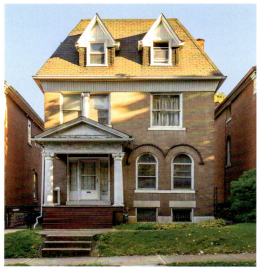

3823 Cleveland Avenue.

BELOW
The homes in Fischer's Cleveland Avenue streetscape are located on the north side of the street.

Photos by Reed R. Radcliffe, 2022.

3821 Cleveland Avenue.

3817 Cleveland Avenue.

3815 Cleveland Avenue.

RESUMING AN OLD PARTNERSHIP

It is unclear whether Fischer and Mepham collaborated on building projects between 1898 and 1901, but we know with certainty that the men resumed a partnership in December 1902 when they incorporated Cleveland Realty & Building Company. At this time Harry Mepham held 10 shares; his wife, Ella, held 1 share; and A. A. Fischer held 9 shares. The value of the total capital stock was $2,000.[48]

In December 1902, Fischer was issued building permits in the Shaw neighborhood for a stretch of five houses on Cleveland Avenue—3815, 3817, 3821, 3823, 3825—all of which remain standing. In fact, three of the homes (3815, 3821, and 3825) are considered restored.

One interesting aspect of this block is that the three houses immediately west of Fischer's streetscape—3839, 3835, 3851—were all built in 1895 and are all attributed to Mepham. Research shows that the men were working together in 1895, so it's possible Fischer had a role in their construction as well.

CHAPTER THREE | 59

ABOVE
The same view of Fischer's Union Boulevard streetscape as the ad in the May 1902 *St. Louis Republic*.

Photo by Reed R. Radcliffe, 2022.

OPPOSITE
In May 1902, A. A. Fischer advertised "6 New Residences" on Union Boulevard in the *St. Louis Republic*. Three of the four homes pictured—1391, 1395, and 1399 Union—are still standing. The home at 1397 Union Boulevard has been lost.

Missouri Historical Society Collections.

SPECIAL RESIDENCE BARGAINS.

6 NEW RESIDENCES BUILT BY THE
A. A. Fischer Architectural & Building Co.,
S. W. Cor. Union Boulevard and Ridge Ave., 2 blocks north of Page Ave.
2 of which were sold last week.

These houses vary in size and arrangement. A general description follows:

The fronts of the buildings are of rough Carthage stone and light-colored brick. Several have red tile roofs, some green slate and some dark slate roofs. The porches vary in style of architecture, making all attractive and neat in appearance.

The first floor contains a square reception hall, with a pretty oak paneled stair front, a parlor finished in gloss white, a dining-room finished in hardwood, and a good, light kitchen, with china closet. The second floor has four bright rooms and a neat bathroom, with tile floor, white enameled tub, tank, closet, washstand of Italian marble and a medicine case, with mirror. The third floor has two nicely finished rooms, and the basement has a cemented floor, hot and cold water connections; good hot-air furnace and brick piers supporting the building. The houses are wired for electric light, have separate pipes for fuel and illuminating gas, and other modern conveniences. The entire yards are sodded, and each house has seven shade trees.

PRICES FROM $5,850 TO $6,500.
They Are Well Built, and Attractive in Architectural Style and Beauty, Which Has Made Us a Reputation.
WE HAVE BUILT 53 AND SOLD THEM AS SOON AS COMPLETED.
Our prices are always low; that is why we sell quickly. Examine them. Open daily.

A. A. FISCHER ARCHITECTURAL & BLDG. CO., 915 Chestnut St.

Agents are invited to show their clients these houses.

ABOVE
Ridge Avenue streetscape from left to right: 5312, 5314, 5320 (razed), and 5322.

Photo by Reed R. Radcliffe, 2022.

NEXT
Cates Avenue streetscape with 5163 Cates in the foreground followed by 5165, 5169, 5171, and 5175.

Photo by Reed R. Radcliffe, 2022.

1903

In 1903, A. A. Fischer Architectural & Building Company was responsible for the erection of 10 houses in a row on the north side of Cates Avenue in the Academy neighborhood. West to east, the addresses are 5179-81, 5177, 5175, 5171, 5169, 5165, 5163, 5159, 5157, 5153-55. This streetscape survives in its entirety, albeit in varying states of repair.

ABOVE
An intact streetscape of 10 Fischer homes on Cates Avenue, from west to east.

LEFT TO RIGHT
5179-5181 Cates Avenue
5177 Cates Avenue
5175 Cates Avenue
5171 Cates Avenue
5169 Cates Avenue
5165 Cates Avenue
5163 Cates Avenue
5159 Cates Avenue
5157 Cates Avenue
5153-5155A Cates Avenue

Photos by Reed R. Radcliffe, 2022.

ABOVE
Home at 3655 Flora Place in the Shaw neighborhood.

Photo by Reed R. Radcliffe, 2022.

In December 1903, Fischer was issued a building permit (#D-9616) for erection of a two-story brick residence at 3655 Flora Place in the Shaw neighborhood. The owner of the building was C. A. Sevenson. It cost a whopping $17,000, and the result was spectacular. Fischer built two other homes on Flora, and all three are in restored condition. The other two homes, 3832 and 3924, were built in 1904 and 1908, respectively.

TOP
With generous space on either side of its western and eastern exterior walls, 3832 Flora Place fits in among its stately neighbors.

Photo by Reed R. Radcliffe, 2022.

BOTTOM
Although mature vegetation partially obscures 3924 Flora Place from drivers, pedestrians are rewarded with a view of this majestic 1908 Fischer home.

Photo by Reed R. Radcliffe, 2022.

CHAPTER THREE | 69

In November 1904, Fischer was issued building permits for a mini-streetscape of three homes on Clarendon Avenue. The houses at 915, 917, and 919 Clarendon were all occupied in 2021. These specimens of Fischer's work are particularly interesting as their location on an alley allows for easy side and rear views of the homes.

Sadly, many of Fischer's streetscapes are fractions of what they once were. His work on Lafayette Avenue in the Gate District neighborhood is one such case, with only four of the five houses that once comprised a streetscape still standing and occupied. The fifth, 3244 Lafayette, was razed for construction of the Interstate 44 off-ramp.

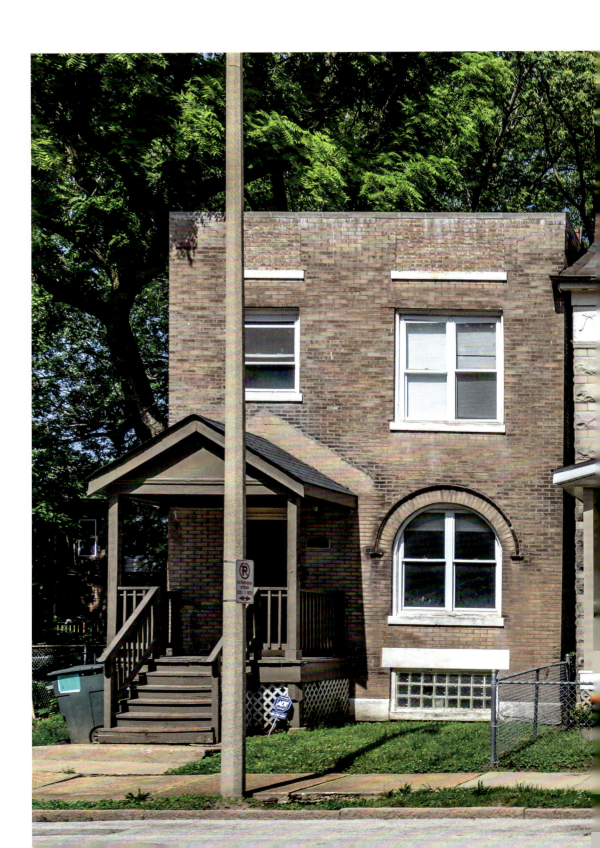

BELOW
Fischer's 1904 streetscape on Clarendon Avenue in the Academy neighborhood—915, 917, and 919 Clarendon—shows an array of his preferred architectural features.

Photo by Reed R. Radcliffe, 2022.

RIGHT
The Clarendon Avenue streetscape's alley location allows for views from the rear.

Photo by Reed R. Radcliffe, 2022.

ABOVE
Originally a streetscape of five Fischer structures, four remain on Lafayette Avenue as of 2022. The easternmost home, 3244 Lafayette, was razed and is now a vacant lot. Streetscape pictured from left to right: 3228, 3232, 3236, 3240 Lafayette.

Photo by Reed R. Radcliffe, 2022.

NEXT
Kensington Avenue streetscape with 5235-5237 Kensington in the foreground followed by 5231, 5229 (razed), 5227, 5225 (razed), and 5223.

Photo by Reed R. Radcliffe, 2022.

BELOW NEWSPAPER AD
On October 16, 1904, A. A. Fischer advertised three of his Kensington Avenue streetscape homes in the *St. Louis Republic*.
Missouri Historical Society Collections.

BELOW STREETSCAPE PHOTOS
Fischer's Kensington Avenue streetscape was originally composed of 14 houses, several of them duplexes. By 2022, four of the structures had been razed.

Photos by Reed R. Radcliffe, 2022.

LEFT TO RIGHT, TOP TO BOTTOM
5235-5237 Kensington Avenue.
5231 Kensington Avenue.
5229 Kensington Avenue, razed.
5227 Kensington Avenue.
5225 Kensington Avenue, razed.
5223 Kensington Avenue.
5221 Kensington Avenue.
5219 Kensington Avenue, razed.
5215-5217 Kensington Avenue.
5211 Kensington Avenue.
5209 Kensington Avenue.
5207 Kensington Avenue.
5205 Kensington Avenue, razed.
5201 Kensington Avenue, razed.

1904–1905

Not far from Fischer's Clarendon Avenue streetscape, there's another streetscape of 14 homes on the north side of Kensington Avenue. He built them in 1904.

1905

When interviewed for the *Builder* in 1905, Fischer said he "saw that the ownership of a home was a natural craving of mankind."[49] Perhaps it was his perception of home ownership that motivated him to build homes at vastly different scales in widely varied neighborhoods throughout St. Louis and University City. In the same *Builder* story Fischer claims to have built 517 structures. In fact, the story begins with a striking claim and powerful visual: "Were A. A. Fischer's houses placed in a line on 40-foot lots they would make an imposing architectural column extending from the Mississippi River to Forest Park." But even painstaking research has failed to uncover anywhere near that many that can definitively be linked to A. A. Fischer—let alone during the first 10 years of his building career.

HALLIDAY AVENUE

In the spring of 1904, Fischer filed building permits for three houses on Halliday Avenue: From west to east was a pair of houses at 3925-3531 and 3525-3527, and one block farther east was 3441 Halliday.

OPPOSITE
Home at 3441 Halliday Avenue.
Photo by Reed R. Radcliffe, 2022.

ABOVE LEFT
The duplex at 3525-3527 Halliday Avenue is an excellent representation of Fischer's work.

ABOVE RIGHT
Duplex at 3529-3531 Halliday Avenue.

Photos by Reed R. Radcliffe, 2022.

On the 4800 block of Dr. Martin Luther King Drive, A. A. Fischer built five mixed-use structures. Four of these structures were built in 1905: From west to east they are 4861, 4859, 4853-4855-4857, and 4851. In 1911, Fischer built a fifth structure, 4849, at the east end of his existing streetscape. At the time of the houses' erection, the street was known as Easton Avenue. It's easy to imagine a lively thoroughfare where Fischer's five structures—storefronts on the bottom and apartments upstairs—would be witness to the daily comings and goings of hundreds, if not thousands, of St. Louisans.

A notable aspect of the fifth structure, 4849 Dr. Martin Luther King, is that the owner and builder is listed as Herman Laube, and the architect is listed as Roland Fischer—A. A. Fischer's son, who was no more an architect than his father. Laube was the manager of Builders' Manufacturing & Supply Company, an entity he owned along with A. A. Fischer, Fischer's son, wife, and two others. In April 1906, Fischer would file a charter for Builders' Manufacturing & Supply Company and two other business ventures.

Fischer's Martin Luther King structures make up his only commercial streetscape. Although these buildings have seen better days, all but one (4853-4855-4857) remain standing as of 2022.

BELOW
This partially extant Fischer streetscape is the only streetscape of a commercial nature attributed to the builder.
Photo by Reed R. Radcliffe, 2022.

CHAPTER THREE | 81

An especially grand Fischer home is located at 5225 Lindell Boulevard. Built in 1904, it's directly across the street from Forest Park in the Central West End neighborhood. Although it seems Fischer reveled in the chance to showcase his work in the city's more affluent neighborhoods, he didn't pass up building on working- and middle-class blocks, either.

LEFT
This extravagant Fischer home at 5225 Lindell Boulevard, just across the street from Forest Park, was built in 1904.

Photo by Reed R. Radcliffe, 2022.

In 1905, Fischer was responsible for a pair of houses on Maple Avenue in the West End neighborhood, 5614-16 and 5618-20, both of which remain occupied. These two houses sit side by side, so it's all the easier to identify them as being the same fundamental design and almost certainly from a single set of plans. The only obvious difference between the two two-family houses is the color of their brick.

From the front, each house appears to have a full third story with a flared, hipped roof and a centered dormer. The house to the east of 5614-16 Maple has been demolished, and its side view reveals that the impressive roof is actually just a few feet deep. The house itself has only two stories—a common characteristic among Fischer builds. Fischer houses must be inspected one by one because some of these roofs do signal a genuine third story. Houses in St. Louis were built close together, so it was common for builders to lavish most of their attention on the view from the street.

ABOVE

This pair of fraternal twin Fischer duplexes at 5614-5616 Maple Avenue (left) and 5618-5620 Maple were both erected in 1905.

Photo by Reed R. Radcliffe, 2022.

RIGHT
The duplex at 5614-5616 Maple Avenue was built directly to the east of another Fischer duplex at 5618-5620 Maple. The roofing material and brick color are their most noticeable differences.

BOTTOM RIGHT
Duplex at 5618-5620 Maple Avenue.

Photos by Reed R. Radcliffe, 2022.

The years 1905 and 1906 were good to Fischer in many ways. His business was thriving, he was forming new partnerships, and he was expanding his range of services. The July 1905 *Builder* story explains that Fischer's "business is now incorporated and the company is equipped to buy and sell ground, furnish plans, build houses and supply the funds for the purpose." It goes on to say, "A force of draughtsman and superintendents form the staff under whom jurisdiction of the Fischer houses are created." What Fischer could not do himself for lack of specialized training, he farmed out to other competent men and women.

These years also presented Fischer with multiple opportunities to leave his mark on the city's private streets. In 1905 he built the extraordinary residence at 3222 Hawthorne Boulevard in Compton Heights, the only structure in this affluent neighborhood for which he is definitively responsible.

The home at 3222 Hawthorne has a number of fascinating features, among them the detail that the hipped, flared roof doesn't cover the whole house. Rather, it's there to hint that something grander exists than actually does (as seen at 5614-16 and 5618-20 Maple Avenue). The roof has a triple dormer with a broken pediment, and below the roofline is Fischer's iconic broken frieze; the façade alternates wide courses of rough stone with narrow courses of smooth stone. The west and east sides of the house are stone too, and the frieze wraps around to both sides. This home features the same porch roof style as Fischer's own home at 5256 Vernon: Stone piers support squat granite porch columns with Ionic-style capitals. The final element worth noting on this home is the wooden *porte cochère* on its west side.

Fischer is credited with two additional builds on private streets in 1906: 36 Portland Place and 52 Westmoreland Place, both in the Central West End neighborhood.

―――

April 1906 was a significant month for A. A. Fischer and his expanding business empire. On a single day—April 20—three charters were issued for three Fischer businesses: the A. A. Fischer Realty Company, the Builders' Manufacturing & Supply Company, and the Vernon Realty and Construction Company.[50]

RIGHT
The home at 3222 Hawthorne Boulevard remains in pristine condition.

NEXT
This three-story home in the Central West End is among the most spectacular examples of Fischer's workmanship.

Photos by Reed R. Radcliffe, 2022.

BELOW
House number slips were used to show how the house and lot were oriented in relation to nearby streets. This one, for 52 Westmoreland Place (address changed from 5284), earned a stamp of approval from the St. Louis Street Commissioner's Office on July 20, 1905.

Courtesy of the St. Louis Public Library.

RIGHT
The home at 52 Westmoreland Place in the Central West End is a gleaming example of Fischer's work and range as a builder.

Photo by Reed R. Radcliffe, 2022.

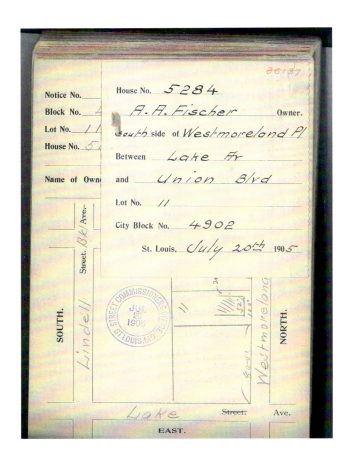

90 | A. A. FISCHER'S ST. LOUIS STREETSCAPES

ABOVE
West Cabanne streetscape (left to right) with 5968, 6002, and 6006 West Cabanne.
Photo by Reed R. Radcliffe, 2022.

1908: WASHINGTON BOULEVARD STREETSCAPE

There was no buyer of Fischer homes more passionate than Rachel Baer Elgas. She purchased five of them, and she's the only person who bought more than one Fischer house on Washington Boulevard. Numbered 6148, 6152, 6154, 6158, and 6160 from east to west, the houses stand side by side in the middle of a block that extends along the south side of Washington between Rosedale and Skinker. The A. A. Fischer Realty Company obtained building permits for all five houses in July and August 1908. Although each house has its own combination of architectural features that distinguishes it from the other four, all of them have dimensions that harmonize with the nearby homes.

6148 Washington Boulevard
24 × 33. Red brick. Shaped parapet. A colonnade divides a double window in the left bay of the second floor. The right bay of the second floor contains a single window. The broken frieze has one wreath at each corner and a double swag between the double window and the single window. The first floor has a single window in the left bay and a porch in the right bay. The porch has a gable roof supported by full-height rectangular wooden columns. The east wall of the house has bay windows on the first and second floors.

6152 Washington Boulevard
24 × 33. Brown brick with quoins on each side. Hipped, flared roof. The centered dormer has its own gable roof. The two dormer windows, which may be artificial, are flanked and separated by Corinthian pilasters. The first floor has a single window in the left bay and a porch in the right bay. The porch has a gable roof supported by stone columns. The stones are white and of many different shapes and sizes. The mortar is brown. A stone wall below the left windows extends eastward from the porch to the east corner of the façade. The east wall of the house contains bay windows on the first and second floors.

BELOW

Rachel Baer Elgas purchased five side-by-side Fischer homes on Washington Boulevard. On the south side of the street, from east to west, the houses are numbered 6148, 6152, 6154, 6158, and 6160 Washington.

All photos by Reed R. Radcliffe, 2022.

6154 Washington Boulevard

24 × 33. Light brown brick. Flat roof a few feet higher than what is probably the second story's actual ceiling. The second floor has two double windows, one in each bay. Both are divided by Corinthian-capital columns. The columns are white, and the capitals are brown. The first floor has a single window in the left bay and a porch in the right bay. The porch roof is nearly flat but sloped enough for drainage. It is supported by full-height white columns with brown Corinthian capitals. A shallow brick porch with a low wooden fence extends from the main porch across the left side of the façade to the east corner of the house. The east wall of the house has bay windows on the first and second floors.

6158 Washington Boulevard

24 × 33. Dark red brick with quoins on each side. Flat roof a few feet higher than what is probably the second story's actual ceiling. False gable extends only slightly higher than the false roof. This house lacks double windows on the façade. The second floor has two single windows, one in each bay, and the first floor has one window in the left bay. The porch roof is nearly flat but sloped enough for drainage. It is supported by full-height columns with Tuscan capitals. The east wall of the house has bay windows on the first and second floors.

6160 Washington Boulevard

30 × 32. Brown brick. Flat roof a few feet higher than what is probably the second story's actual ceiling. Four single windows are on the second floor of the façade. They are almost evenly spaced, but there is a little more room between the windows closest to the center. The broken frieze has a wreath at each corner, a swag between the two center windows, and a smaller ornamentation in the space between the first and second windows, as well as in the space between the third and fourth windows. The porch is centered and has a single window on each side, but the door is not centered with the porch. It is right of center, leaving room at left for the mailbox to be protected by the porch roof. The porch roof is nearly flat but sloped enough for drainage. It is supported by narrow half-height brown granite columns.

Although the building permits' dates suggest that all five houses were built around the same time, Elgas bought them one at a time over a stretch of two years.

Purchased	Relative Date of Building Permit
May 5, 1909	Middle (Aug. 1, 1908)
Oct. 14, 1909	Last (Aug. 15, 1908)
Apr. 22, 1910	Middle (Aug. 1, 1908)
Jan. 27, 1911	First (July 13, 1908)
May 25, 1911	Last (Aug. 15, 1908)

It is easy to assume that finances explain why she had to buy the houses one at a time—first saving money before buying another—but it also makes sense that she would have preferred to own five adjacent houses to avoid traipsing around to look after them. But why weren't other people buying some of them in the meantime?

During each of the four intervals between house purchases, other houses nearby were being sold for comparable (if slightly higher) prices. There are several possible explanations: Perhaps Rachel Elgas and A. A. Fischer agreed in 1908 that she would buy these particular houses, but that isn't very likely unless she first made a down payment. No record of any such payment has been located in the *Daily Record*.

It is more likely that Fischer did not build these five houses all at once, even though he had the permits. After all, he was a busy man. Between 1907 and 1911 his crews were building multiple houses in Skinker DeBaliviere, and he had to keep them on track.

Elgas's purchases were fairly evenly spaced:
- Five months and nine days between the first and second houses
- Six months and eight days between the second and third
- Nine months and five days between the third and fourth
- Four months lacking two days between the fourth and fifth

On the other hand, these intervals are not exact. This could mean that Fischer's crews were sometimes busier than others and/or that Elgas's income from her husband's optical practice was a variable factor.

The home at 6144 Washington (immediately to the east of Elgas's five houses) was on the same permit as her houses at 6148 and 6152 Washington. Joseph P. McGrath bought it on May 27, 1909, less than a month after Elgas bought 6148. Meanwhile, 6164 Washington (immediately to the west of Elgas's five houses) was on the same permit as her house at 6160 Washington. Harvey E. Jones bought it on August 17, 1909, when Elgas had only purchased one house.

The house McGrath bought bears a strong resemblance to Elgas's house at 6158 Washington. They are identical except that 6144's brick is light brown and 6158's is dark red. Their dimensions, 24 feet by 33 feet, are also the same. Elgas's house at 6160 Washington and Jones's house at 6164 Washington both measure 30 feet by 32 feet. Because these homes are adjacent, it seems some effort was made to disguise the fact that they were basically the same design; these houses can be thought of as cousins rather than twins.

When the 1910 Census was enumerated in April, Rachel and Edward Elgas were living at 6158 Washington Boulevard.

ABOVE
6144 Washington Boulevard.

Photo by Reed R. Radcliffe, 2022.

BELOW
Rachel Baer Elgas and her husband, Richard, lived at the home on the left, 6158 Washington Boulevard. The home in the foreground is 6160 Washington.

Photo by Reed R. Radcliffe, 2022.

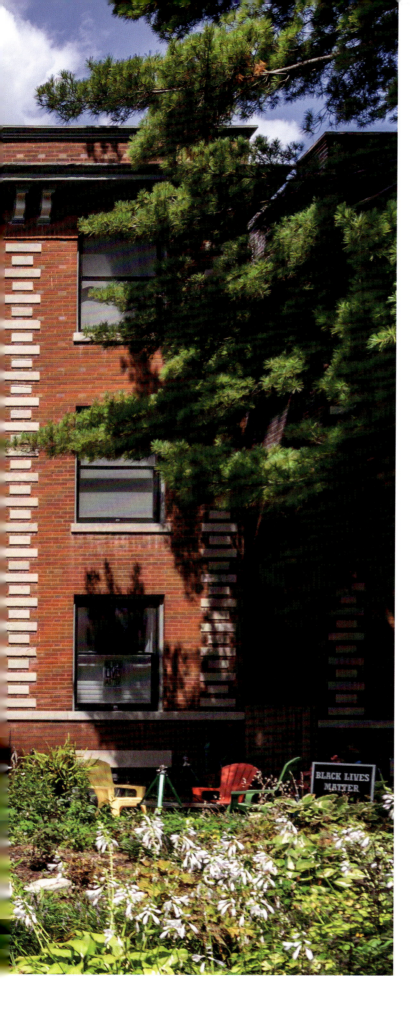

1909

In addition to building single- and two-family homes throughout St. Louis, Fischer was also responsible for the erection of numerous apartment buildings. Most of them remain standing, and many have been converted into condos.

MORE WEST END APARTMENTS.

The A. A. Fischer Architectural and Building Company will at once begin the erection of thirteen apartment houses in the West End. Three of these will be on the north side of Kingsbury boulevard east of Rosedale avenue. They will occupy lots of fifty feet each, will be three stories high, built of brick, and will contain accommodations for six families each in apartments of four, five and six rooms.

The other ten houses will be in Washington Heights. One will have 300 feet front and will contain thirty-six apartments of five and six rooms each. It will be composed of six adjoining buildings of fifty feet frontage and will cost approximately $150,000.

The Fischer Company is completing an apartment house at Nos. 6040-42 Kingsbury boulevard. It is a three-story brick building and contains apartments of four and five rooms each. It will be ready for occupancy about the time construction is begun on the others.

The Fischer Company has built sixty houses during the last twelve months. With few exceptions it has sold the houses as soon as finished. Many have been sold long before completion.

LEFT
The apartment at 6045-6047 Kingsbury Avenue is the westernmost of the three apartment buildings located on the north side of Kingsbury, east of Rosedale.

Photo by Reed R. Radcliffe, 2022.

ABOVE
The story "More West End Apartments" detailed some of Fischer's work in the West End and Washington Heights neighborhoods in August 1909.

Courtesy of the St. Louis Public Library.

BELOW
6040-6042 Kingsbury Avenue sits across the street from two other Fischer apartment buildings: 6041-6043 and 6045-6047 Kingsbury.

Photo by Reed R. Radcliffe, 2022.

OPPOSITE TOP
The apartment at 6041-6043 Kingsbury Avenue is one of the three apartment buildings located on the north side of Kingsbury, east of Rosedale.

Photo by Reed R. Radcliffe, 2022.

OPPOSITE BOTTOM
The apartment at 5931-5933 Kingsbury Avenue is the easternmost of the three apartment buildings located on the north side of Kingsbury, east of Rosedale.

Photo by Reed R. Radcliffe, 2022.

CALVIN OPERA HOUSE

In 1909, Fischer returned to his birthplace of Washington, Missouri, to collaborate with Lawrence H. Caugh and Edmund C. Little (both of whom helped design the Missouri Building for the 1904 World's Fair)[51] in the design and erection of the Calvin Opera House at 311 Elm Street. Caugh assisted Little in designing the building—with a flat roof, straight parapet, and centered pediment—which was then constructed by the A. A. Fischer Architectural & Building Company. A 1909 photo shows that the arched, broken pediments in the left and right bays were originally above double doors, and the center bay contained a large triple window.[52] By 2000, as shown here, the entrance had been moved to the center bay and was shaded by a marquee.

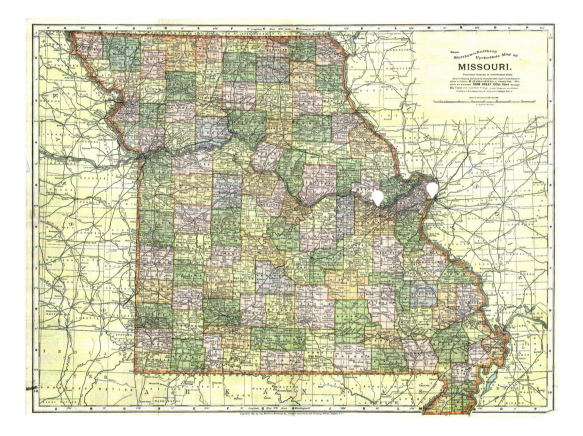

ABOVE
The Matthews-Northrup Up-to-Date Map of Missouri, 1895, showing the location of Washington, Missouri (left teardrop), in relation to St. Louis, Missouri.

Map courtesy of the David Rumsey Map Collection, David Rumsey Map Center, Stanford Libraries at Stanford University.

NEXT
Westminster Place streetscape with 6155 Westminster in the foreground followed by 6159, 6163, 6165, 6169, 6173, 6175, and 6179.

Photo by Reed R. Radcliffe, 2022.

OPPOSITE
The Calvin Opera House was built in Washington, Missouri, in 1909. It was a collaboration among Fischer and Lawrence H. Caugh and Edmund C. Little, who also helped design the Missouri Building for the 1904 World's Fair.

Photo by Reed R. Radcliffe, 2022.

ABOVE
Streetscape with 6173 Westminster Place in the foreground followed by 6169, 6165 (under renovation), 6163, and 6159.

Photo by Reed R. Radcliffe, 2022.

WESTMINSTER PLACE STREETSCAPE

On the one-block section of Westminster Place—between Skinker Boulevard on the west and Rosedale Avenue on the east—Fischer built 15 houses on the north side, 12 of which formed a streetscape, and 20 houses on the south side of the street, which formed another one. There is no greater place to experience the buildings of A. A. Fischer than to walk from the corner of Westminster and Skinker east, toward the center of the block. Fischer homes line both sides of the street. There were 35 originally, and 34 of them remain. Many have friezes, some do not, but all of them exhibit Fischer's vision for what a St. Louis city street should look and feel like.

The 1905 *Builder* story reveals some insight into why Fischer built in clusters. It states, "Mr. Fischer believes in labor and time saving devices. Whenever he starts a job—it is usually two or more houses at a time—a temporary telephone is initiated. This often saves a day's time in reaching the mills or yard or labor headquarters. He is thus always in touch with his foreman." Not a moment was wasted. An analysis of the map in the back of this book shows that while Fischer frequently built houses along the same block, he also built houses back-to-back with great regularity.

1910: APARTMENT BUILDINGS

By 1910, Fischer was listed in the census as the head of household at 5256 Vernon Avenue, along with his wife, son, and two live-in servants. Fischer's hard work was paying off—just years earlier he had been a farm boy, then a bookkeeper, then a builder. Now Fischer could boast that he owned and operated a successful architectural and real estate business, in addition to having built a home for his family.

Fischer's success is evident in the 1908, 1909, and 1910 advertisements and flyers that proudly proclaim the A. A. Fischer Architectural & Building Company's work on large-scale apartment buildings.

1911: MOMENTUM LOST

After a busy year in 1910 erecting 23 structures—11 of them apartment buildings—Fischer's momentum slowed to almost a complete halt. He is credited with just three structures in 1911: 6209 Pershing Avenue, 5740 Waterman Boulevard, and 4849 Easton Avenue. The final address is present-day 4849 Dr. Martin Luther King Drive, the fifth of five Fischer structures on that street, and even more notably the very last structure attributed to him until a full decade later. In 1912, Fischer would repair fire damage to a home at 5215 Cabanne Avenue, but otherwise, the record on him goes silent in 1912.

Despite his inactivity, Fischer worked hard to maintain his image, submitting an entry to the 1912 *Book of St. Louisans* that identifies him as the president of two businesses: the A. A. Fischer Architectural & Building Company and the A. A. Fischer Realty Company and Builders' Manufacturing & Supply Company.[53] Fischer and his son, Roland, maintained their offices at 724 Chestnut Street through some point in 1915. The 1916 city directory indicates that the father and son moved to a fifth-floor room at 105 N. 7th Street, surely a downgrade from their former accommodations. The city directory also reveals that both men (and presumably Frances Fischer) were living in Kirkwood, a western suburb of St. Louis. A. A. Fischer, builder and provider, had lost his own exquisite home on Vernon Avenue, as well as the success he had once known in business.

OPPOSITE
This commercial structure at 4849 Dr. Martin Luther King Drive (originally 4849 Easton Avenue) is the fifth of five Fischer structures on this block.
Photo by Reed R. Radcliffe, 2022.

FAR LEFT
Home at 5740 Waterman Boulevard in the Skinker DeBaliviere neighborhood.

NEAR LEFT
Fischer built this home at 6209 Pershing Avenue in 1911. It is one of only three structures attributed to him that year.

NEXT
Cabanne Avenue streetscape with 5211 Cabanne in the foreground followed by 5209, 5205 and 5201.

Photos by Reed R. Radcliffe, 2022.

CHAPTER THREE | 109

CHAPTER FOUR

FROM BROKEN FRIEZES TO BROKEN DREAMS

In retrospect, Fischer was too optimistic about Skinker DeBaliviere. Profit margins were narrow. He frequently took out two deeds of trust on each property: the first to acquire the land, and the second to buy the building materials and pay his workers. A typical deed of trust for the latter was $5,000 at 6 percent for three years. Some houses were sold within a few months, but as time went on, it was not unusual for a house or apartment building to remain unsold when it came time to repay the loan. For a while Fischer bought time by taking out second deeds of trust on the same properties to pay the first ones.

FINANCIAL COLLAPSE

But then construction came to a screeching halt. Ultimately, many houses and apartment buildings were put up for auction by the holders of the deeds of trust and sold for much less than their actual value. Other houses were sold directly for $100 or less, according to his granddaughter. Often the buyers were Fischer's workmen, whom he would have been unable to pay in any other way.

By the end of 1916, Fischer had lost most of his properties—including his home at 5256 Vernon—and live-in help quickly became a thing of the past. Alex and Frances lived in Kirkwood for a few years before moving to a brick building near a suburban streetcar stop in Pine Lawn. The building they lived in also housed a grocery store, a barbershop, and at least one other apartment, which was occupied by Frances's brother.[54]

A few years earlier, in 1912, Alex and Frances's son, Roland, had eloped with a young woman he met at business school. Roland and Irene Knopp were married at the Clayton courthouse in June 1912. They welcomed their first child, Kenneth Roland Fischer, into the world just over two years later. We know from Roland Fischer's World War I draft registration card that by 1918 he and his family were living in Kirkwood, as were his parents. It is worth noting that during this time Roland provided his occupation as self-employed "architect and builder," but no homes had been attributed to either Roland or Alex since 1911.[55]

How exactly Alex and Roland kept afloat financially during these years is unclear, as is the nature of their day-to-day lives. But it is known that life changed almost overnight for the Fischers—first with Alex's professional rise and second with his unexpected professional decline. To survive such fluctuations would require great personal resilience, a trait neither man lacked.

THE COMEBACK

Alex and Roland attempted a comeback in 1921 and 1922, their eyes now focused on nearby University City. By this time Roland had become a father again, his wife giving birth to a daughter named Lorraine.

On Cabanne Avenue between North Drive and Eastgate Avenue, Fischer built a stretch of nine one-story brick bungalows, capped on either end by a two-story, four-family brick bungalow, making for a streetscape of 11. While five of these homes have been razed, six were extant and occupied as of spring 2022.

Fischer's bungalow at 6272 Cabanne is worth mentioning for the elaborate scrolled brackets tucked beneath its eaves. Although Fischer's style had evolved with the times, he had not lost his penchant for decorative touches. The ornamental brackets are under the roofline and between the windows—just as the broken frieze had been on his earlier houses.

Sadly, all 13 of Fischer's structures on nearby North Drive have been razed. Roland's collaboration with his father on homes on Cabanne Avenue and North Drive in University City in 1922 apparently marked the last time the two worked together. Afterward, he worked for other real estate companies and later became a brick vendor.[56]

LEFT
Elaborate scrolled brackets beneath the eaves of a home at 6272 Cabanne Avenue in University City.

Photo by Reed R. Radcliffe, 2022.

ABOVE
Two Fischer homes in an extant streetscape on Cabanne Avenue in University City.

FROM LEFT:
6300 and 6304 Cabanne.

Photo by Reed R. Radcliffe, 2022.

NEXT
Two Fischer homes in an extant streetscape on Cabanne Avenue in University City.

FROM LEFT:
6270 and 6272 Cabanne.

Photo by Reed R. Radcliffe, 2022.

CHAPTER FOUR | 113

In 1923, Fischer returned to the West End neighborhood to build a three-story apartment building at 5434 Page Boulevard. The structure was razed in early 2019, but it reveals some significant history-friendly, preservation-minded efforts undertaken by the City of St. Louis concerning the demolition of structures in extreme disrepair. When major changes are planned for a house or apartment building within city limits, photographs are taken to document the structure in its "before" state and again in its "after" state. All photographs can be accessed online through the city's Address and Property Search portal. In the case of 5434 Page Boulevard, the before photographs show the structure as condemned, and the after photographs show the vacant lot following demolition. (There are also more uplifting transformations evidenced on the portal, such as the major reinvestment in and ultimate restoration of 5312 and 5314 Maple Avenue, discussed in Chapter 3.) By taking on this responsibility, the City of St. Louis has supplemented the documentation that's been done by the Landmarks Association of St. Louis for decades. Many of the archival images in this book originated from Landmarks.

In 1925, Fischer built a Spanish Revival house designed by William W. Sabin for Adolph Boldt at 7327 Westmoreland Drive in University City. The home is undeniably handsome—and today, restored and occupied. Surely he was proud to have worked on it. But given Fischer's own creativity, it's possible he had conflicted feelings about erecting the designs of others.

After Westmoreland, Fischer went four years having little to no work. His name doesn't appear on any building permits or newspaper advertisements. He many have worked for others during this time. In May 1929, Fischer is credited with building a porch on a pre-existing home on Dorset Avenue in University City. It's the very last time his name appears in the *Daily Record*.

LEFT
Condemned Fischer apartment building at 5430–5434 Page Boulevard, April 2016.

City of St. Louis Address and Property Search.

ABOVE
This Spanish Revival home at 7327 Westmoreland Drive in University City was designed by architect William W. Sabin and built by A. A. Fischer in 1925.

Photo by Reed R. Radcliffe, 2022.

Prosperity never returned to Alex and Frances Fischer. The last home they shared was a narrow, one-story house on Kempland Place in University City. Alex died of bronchial pneumonia at the age of 70 on September 16, 1936, and he was buried in Washington.⁵⁷ Frances outlived Alex by 21 years. She never again had a home of her own, living among the homes of her sister, her son, and her three grandchildren. (Roland and his wife had gone on to have their third and final child, Norman, in 1925.) Frances also outlived her son by almost a decade. At the time of Roland's death in 1948 at the age of 57, he was living in Granite City, Illinois, and was president of the R. A. Fischer Brick Corporation—yet another testament to the junior Fischer's resilience.⁵⁸ Given the ages of Roland's children at the time of his own father's death, the elder two, Kenneth and Lorraine, had particularly vivid memories of their grandfather. They've provided many important details for this book.

OPPOSITE
Undated photograph of Roland Fischer and a man identified only as Mr. Kemp showcasing a variety of of brick.

OPPOSITE
Letterhead of R. A. Fischer Brick Company.

Courtesy of Diane Barrett.

ABOVE
Undated portrait of Frances Fischer.

Courtesy of Richard Fischer.

LEFT
Undated photograph of Frances and A. A. Fischer.

Courtesy of Diane Barrett.

LEGACY

Make no mistake: The story of Alexander August Fischer is not a sad one. It is a quintessentially American account of one man's dream, hard work, and extraordinary success that was ultimately beset by overoptimism. Regardless of how his building career ended, evidence of his extraordinary talent can be seen and appreciated today on streets throughout the city and beyond. Indeed, the memory of the man who built these hundreds of foundational structures deserves to be lauded. The homes of A. A. Fischer—be they single-family, two-family, or apartment buildings—have provided safety and shelter to generations of St. Louisans, who in turn have given their own gifts to the city. This book seeks to preserve the legacy of what is no longer extant while celebrating the structures and streetscapes that remain.

CHAPTER FIVE

DIRECTORY OF A. A. FISCHER BUILDS

Each of A. A. Fischer's 333 confirmed structures (with exception of the Calvin Theatre in Washington, MO) is listed in this chapter, as are associated data from historical records, contemporary research, and photographs of the structures. The photographs are a mix of modern and archival depictions based upon the availability of resources and whether the structures remain extant. All verifiable data has been included for each structure. If information was not available, the data field has been omitted.

Over his nearly four-decade-long career Fischer established innumerable partnerships and participated in several real estate ventures beyond those that bore his name. Among them was the Cleveland Realty & Building Company, which he incorporated with Harry Mepham in 1902. For this reason, the count of Fischer structures also includes builds by the Cleveland Realty & Building Company. In 1906, A. A. Fischer incorporated three additional businesses: A. A. Fischer Realty Company, Builders' Manufacturing & Supply Company, and Vernon Realty and Construction Company. Fischer was the majority stockholder for each of these businesses, and his wife and son joined him as minority stockholders. Other minority stockholders included his known business associates Levi F. Gardner, Lawrence H. Caugh, and Herman Laube.

PREVIOUS
520 Skinker Boulevard.

Photo by Reed R. Radcliffe, 2022.

ABOVE
3924 Flora Place.

Photo by Reed R. Radcliffe, 2022.

The *St. Louis Daily Record* began publishing in 1890, and it continues today. Its content includes news from City of St. Louis courts, as well as the legal and business communities. During the years A. A. Fischer was building—1894 through 1929—the *Daily Record* printed summaries of building permits filed the previous day (or days) at city hall. For each structure or set of structures, these summaries included assigned numbers, which usually match—or very nearly match—the building permit numbers. At times, the building permit numbers are preceded by a letter that isn't reflected in the *Daily Record* summaries; accordingly, data from the *Daily Record* is transcribed exactly as it appeared (unless otherwise noted).

The official journal of the Master Builders Association of St. Louis, the *St. Louis Builder*—as well as its later iterations, the *Builder* and the *Realty Record and Builder*—was printed monthly from 1899 to 1911. Billed as "an illustrated journal of architecture," it published a variety of real estate news, as well as building permit transcriptions. Its name changed throughout its 12-year run, and the name that appears in the following directory depends upon the year the information was provided and the publication's official name at that time. Entries in the *Builder* list the name of a property's owner, architect, and builder/contractor, as well as a brief description of the structure, such as dimensions, number of stories, and intended use.

Several Fischer homes in the Skinker DeBaliviere/Catlin Tract/Parkview neighborhoods were identified as such by the Landmarks Association's Carolyn Hewes Toft and Jane Molloy Porter, who produced an architectural survey map of the neighborhoods in 1983 (then revised in 1986) for the Heritage and Urban Design Commission. The map is annotated to include the architects and the "builder/contractors" to which each structure is attributed—it's a powerful illustration of Fischer's tendency to build in clusters. Some Fischer homes have been so significantly modified that iconic Fischer features have been completely obscured or eliminated. In the directory that follows, the field "Landmarks" refers to this particular map and the research behind it.

A final note: This directory is the most complete record available for each of A. A. Fischer's confirmed structures, but the data are almost certainly imperfect. In many instances, handwriting had to be decoded and conflicting information had to be reconciled using best judgments.

CATEGORIES

BUILDING PERMIT NO.

BUILDING PERMIT DATE

DAILY RECORD NO.

APPEARED IN THE *DAILY RECORD*

THE REALTY RECORD AND BUILDER NO.

APPEARED IN *THE REALTY RECORD AND BUILDER*

HOUSE NUMBER CERTIFICATE

LANDMARKS

ARCHITECT

OWNER

BUILDER

DESCRIPTION

BROKEN FRIEZE

PART OF A STREETSCAPE

NEIGHBORHOOD

SIDE OF THE STREET

STATUS IN 2021

NOTES

STATUS

RESTORED

OCCUPIED

CONDEMNED

UNDER RENOVATION

RAZED

OPPOSITE
Map of St. Louis, 1903.

Courtesy of the David Rumsey Map Collection, David Rumsey Map Center, Stanford Libraries at Stanford University.

DIRECTORY OF BUILDS TABLE OF CONTENTS

Allen Avenue
2144 Allen
Page 128

2629 Allen
Page 129

2631 Allen
Page 130

Aubert Avenue
906-904 Aubert
Page 131

908 Aubert
Page 132

910 Aubert
Page 133

Botanical Avenue
3855-57 Botanical
Page 134

Cabanne Avenue
5095 Cabanne
Page 135

5201 Cabanne
Page 136

5205 Cabanne
Page 137

5209 Cabanne
Page 138

5211 Cabanne
Page 139

5215 Cabanne
Page 140

5219 Cabanne
Page 141

5223 Cabanne
Page 142

Cabanne Avenue continued
5226 Cabanne
Page 143

5228 Cabanne
Page 144

5230 Cabanne
Page 145

5233 Cabanne
Page 146

5234 Cabanne
Page 147

5236 Cabanne
Page 148

5237 Cabanne
Page 149

5238 Cabanne
Page 150

5239 Cabanne
Page 151

5241 Cabanne
Page 152

5242 Cabanne
Page 153

5243 Cabanne
Page 154

5244 Cabanne
Page 155

5247 Cabanne
Page 156

5249 Cabanne
Page 157

5251 Cabanne
Page 158

5253 Cabanne
Page 159

5514 Cabanne
Page 160

Cabanne Avenue continued
5520 Cabanne
Page 161

6254 Cabanne
Page 162

6256 Cabanne
Page 163

6258 Cabanne
Page 164

6262 Cabanne
Page 165

6264 Cabanne
Page 166

6268 Cabanne
Page 167

6270 Cabanne
Page 168

6272 Cabanne
Page 169

6300 Cabanne
Page 170

6304 Cabanne
Page 171

6305 Cabanne
Page 172

6306 Cabanne
Page 173

6407 Cabanne
Page 174

West Cabanne Place
5968 West Cabanne
Page 175

6002 West Cabanne
Page 176

6006 West Cabanne
Page 177

Cates Avenue
5007 Cates
Page 178

5009 Cates
Page 179

5034-5036 Cates
Page 180

5038 Cates
Page 181

5107 Cates
Page 182

5109 Cates
Page 183

5153-5155A Cates
Page 184

5157 Cates
Page 185

5159 Cates
Page 186

5163 Cates
Page 187

5165 Cates
Page 188

5169 Cates
Page 189

5171 Cates
Page 190

5175 Cates
Page 191

5177 Cates
Page 192

5179-5181 Cates
Page 193

5965-5967 Cates
Page 194

5971-5973 Cates
Page 195

6003 Cates
Page 196

Cates Avenue continued
6007 Cates
Page 197

6029 Cates
Page 198

Chamberlain Avenue
5575 Chamberlain
Page 199

5579 Chamberlain
Page 200

Clarendon Avenue
915 Clarendon
Page 201

917 Clarendon
Page 202

919 Clarendon
Page 203

Clemens Avenue
5725-5727 Clemens
Page 204

Cleveland Avenue
3815 Cleveland
Page 205

3817 Cleveland
Page 206

3821 Cleveland
Page 207

3823 Cleveland
Page 208

3825 Cleveland
Page 209

Copelin Avenue
3253 Copelin
Page 210

Dorset Avenue
7320 Dorset
Page 211

Enright Avenue
5032-5034 Enright
Page 212

Flora Place
3655 Flora
Page 213

3832 Flora
Page 214

3924 Flora
Page 215

Halliday Avenue
3441 Halliday
Page 216

3525-3527 Halliday
Page 217

3529-3531 Halliday
Page 218

Hartford Street
3631 Hartford
Page 219

Hawthorne Boulevard
3222 Hawthorne
Page 220

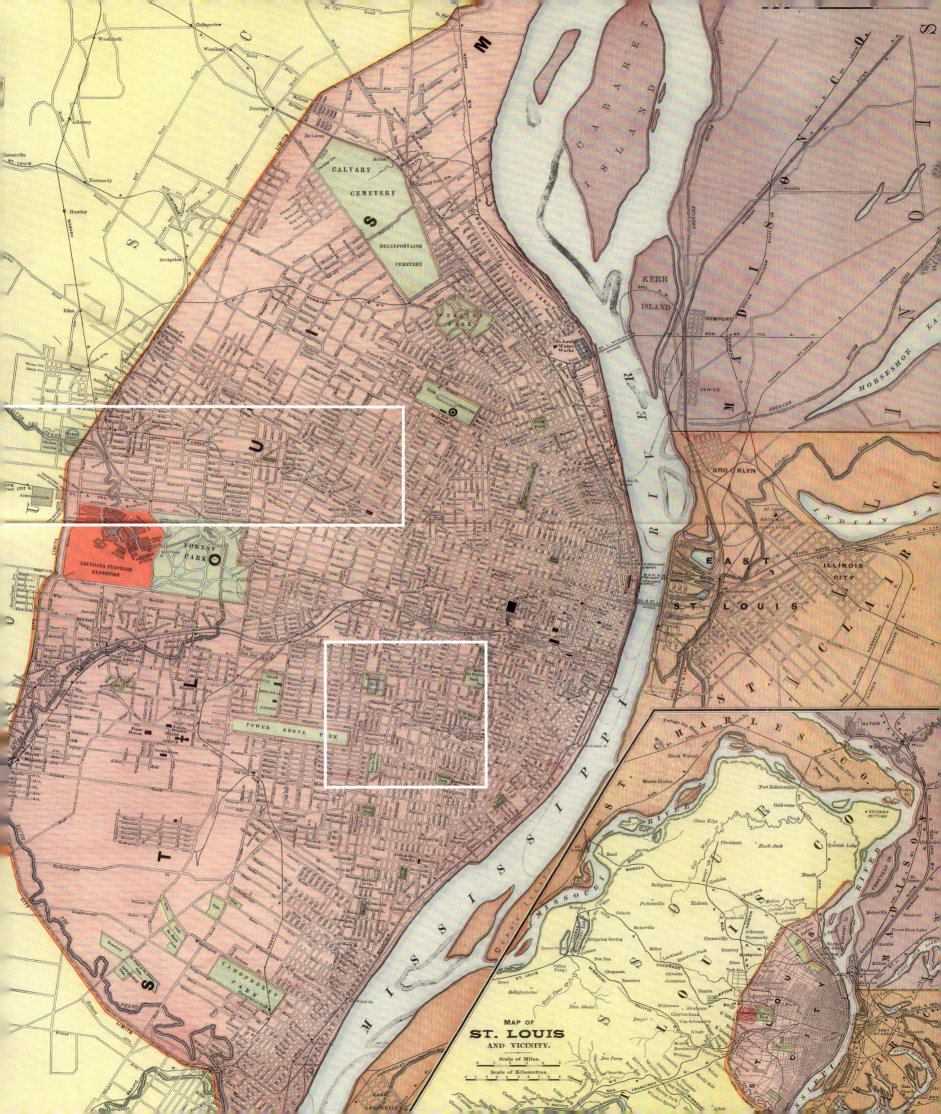

S. Jefferson Avenue
2244 S. Jefferson
Page 221

Kensington Avenue
5201 Kensington
Page 222

5205 Kensington
Page 223

5207 Kensington
Page 224

5209 Kensington
Page 225

5211 Kensington
Page 226

5215-5217 Kensington
Page 227

5219 Kensington
Page 228

5221 Kensington
Page 229

5223 Kensington
Page 230

5225 Kensington
Page 231

5227 Kensington
Page 232

5229 Kensington
Page 233

5231 Kensington
Page 234

5235-5237 Kensington
Page 235

Kingsbury Avenue
5931-5933 Kingsbury
Page 236

6040-6042 Kingsbury
Page 237

6041-6043 Kingsbury
Page 238

6045-6047 Kingsbury
Page 239

6139 Kingsbury
Page 240

6192 Kingsbury
Page 241

Lafayette Avenue
3228 Lafayette
Page 242

3232 Lafayette
Page 243

3236 Lafayette
Page 244

3240 Lafayette
Page 245

3244 Lafayette
Page 246

Lewis Place
39 Lewis
Page 247

Lindell Boulevard
4326 Lindell
Page 248

5225 Lindell
Page 249

Maple Avenue
5190 Maple
Page 250

5194 Maple
Page 251

5240 Maple
Page 252

5241 Maple
Page 253

5250 Maple
Page 254

5258 Maple
Page 255

5266 Maple
Page 256

5268 Maple
Page 257

5312 Maple
Page 258

5314 Maple
Page 259

5415 Maple
Page 260

5611 Maple
Page 261

Maple Avenue continued
5614-5616 Maple
Page 262

5618-5620 Maple
Page 263

5935-5937 Maple
Page 264

Dr. Martin Luther King Drive
4849 Dr. Martin Luther King
Page 265

4851 Dr. Martin Luther King
Page 266

4853-4855-4857 Dr. Martin Luther King
Page 267

4859 Dr. Martin Luther King
Page 268

4861 Dr. Martin Luther King
Page 269

McPherson Avenue
6163 McPherson
Page 270

6168 McPherson
Page 271

6170 McPherson
Page 272

6171 McPherson
Page 273

6174 McPherson
Page 274

6178 McPherson
Page 274

6179 McPherson
Page 274

6181 McPherson
Page 277

6182 McPherson
Page 278

6186 McPherson
Page 279

McPherson Avenue continued
6188 McPherson
Page 280

6306 McPherson
Page 281

North Drive
6256-6258 North
Page 282

6303 North
Page 283

6305 North
Page 284

6307 North
Page 285

6309 North
Page 286

6403 North
Page 287

6410 North
Page 288

6411 North
Page 289

6412 North
Page 290

6415 North
Page 291

6416 North
Page 292

6418 North
Page 293

6419 North
Page 294

Page Boulevard
5210-5212 Page
Page 295

5430-5434 Page
Page 296

Park Avenue
3119 Park
Page 297

3121 Park
Page 298

Pershing Avenue
6209 Pershing
Page 299

Pershing Place
4620 Pershing
Page 300

4624 Pershing
Page 301

Pestalozzi Street
3520-3522 Pestalozzi
Page 302

West Pine Boulevard
4233 West Pine
Page 303

Portland Place
5184 Portland
Page 304

Raymond Avenue
5008 Raymond
Page 305

5018 Raymond
Page 306

5031 Raymond
Page 307

5035 Raymond
Page 308

5060 Raymond
Page 309

5075 Raymond
Page 310

5133 Raymond
Page 311

5167 Raymond
Page 312

5226 Raymond
Page 313

5233 Raymond
Page 314

5237 Raymond
Page 315

5243 Raymond
Page 316

Ridge Avenue
5312 Ridge
Page 317

5314 Ridge
Page 318

5320 Ridge
Page 319

5322 Ridge
Page 320

Russell Blvd
2326 Russell
Page 321

3667 Russell
Page 322

3669 Russell
Page 323

Shenandoah Avenue
3665 Shenandoah
Page 324

Skinker Boulevard
500 Skinker
Page 325

520 Skinker
Page 326

Thornby Place
6 Thornby
Page 327

Union Boulevard
1320-1322 Union
Page 328

1324-1326 Union
Page 329

1328-1330 Union
Page 330

1336 Union
Page 331

1338 Union
Page 332

1342 Union
Page 333

1344 Union
Page 334

Union Boulevard continued

1384-1386 Union
Page 335

1387 Union
Page 336

1388-1390 Union
Page 337

1391 Union
Page 338

1395 Union
Page 339

1397 Union
Page 340

1399 Union
Page 341

Utah Place

3627 Utah
Page 342

Vernon Avenue

5039 Vernon
Page 343

5043 Vernon
Page 344

5045 Vernon
Page 345

5169 Vernon
Page 346

5195 Vernon
Page 347

5227 Vernon
Page 348

5231 Vernon
Page 349

5233 Vernon
Page 350

5237 Vernon
Page 351

5243 Vernon
Page 352

5247 Vernon
Page 353

5248 Vernon
Page 354

5249 Vernon
Page 355

Vernon Avenue continued

5252 Vernon
Page 356

5253 Vernon
Page 357

5255 Vernon
Page 358

5256 Vernon
Page 359

5259 Vernon
Page 360

5263 Vernon
Page 361

5359 Vernon
Page 362

5363 Vernon
Page 363

5616-5618 Vernon
Page 364

5620-5622 Vernon
Page 365

Washington Avenue

6224 Washington
Page 366

6309 Washington
Page 367

6311 Washington
Page 368

6317 Washington
Page 369

6353 Washington
Page 370

Washington Boulevard

5916-18 Washington
Page 371

6101 Washington
Page 372

6102-6104 Washington
Page 373

6108-6110 Washington
Page 374

6109-6111 Washington
Page 375

6114-6116 Washington
Page 376

Washington Boulevard continued

6115-6117 Washington
Page 377

6120-6122 Washington
Page 378

6126-6128 Washington
Page 379

6130 Washington
Page 380

6134 Washington
Page 381

6144 Washington
Page 382

6145 Washington
Page 383

6148 Washington
Page 384

6149 Washington
Page 385

6151 Washington
Page 386

6152 Washington
Page 387

6154 Washington
Page 388

6155 Washington
Page 389

6158 Washington
Page 390

6159 Washington
Page 391

6160 Washington
Page 392

6163 Washington
Page 393

6164 Washington
Page 394

6167 Washington
Page 395

6169 Washington
Page 396

6173 Washington
Page 397

6174 Washington
Page 398

6177 Washington
Page 399

Washington Boulevard continued

6178 Washington
Page 400

6182 Washington
Page 401

6186 Washington
Page 402

6190 Washington
Page 403

Washington Place

5088 Washington
Page 404

5090 Washington
Page 405

5129 Washington
Page 406

5133 Washington
Page 407

5137 Washington
Page 408

Waterman Avenue

6217 Waterman
Page 409

6307 Waterman
Page 410

Waterman Boulevard

5073 Waterman
Page 411

5212 Waterman
Page 412

5227 Waterman
Page 413

5229 Waterman
Page 414

5241-5243 Waterman
Page 415

5740 Waterman
Page 416

Wells Avenue

5334 Wells Avenue
Page 417

Westminster Place

4614 Westminster
Page 418

4616 Westminster
Page 419

4622 Westminster
Page 420

4721 Westminster
Page 421

4749 Westminster
Page 422

5250 Westminster
Page 423

6121 Westminster
Page 424

6123 Westminster
Page 425

6124 Westminster
Page 426

6127 Westminster
Page 427

6128 Westminster
Page 428

6132 Westminster
Page 429

6136 Westminster
Page 430

6140 Westminster
Page 431

6142 Westminster
Page 432

6146 Westminster
Page 433

6150 Westminster
Page 434

6154 Westminster
Page 435

6155 Westminster
Page 436

6158 Westminster
Page 437

6159 Westminster
Page 438

6160 Westminster
Page 439

6163 Westminster
Page 440

Westminster Place continued

6164 Westminster
Page 441

6165 Westminster
Page 442

6168 Westminster
Page 443

6169 Westminster
Page 444

6172 Westminster
Page 445

6173 Westminster
Page 446

6174 Westminster
Page 447

6175 Westminster
Page 448

6178 Westminster
Page 449

6179 Westminster
Page 450

6181 Westminster
Page 451

6182 Westminster
Page 452

6185 Westminster
Page 453

6186 Westminster
Page 454

6188 Westminster
Page 455

6189 Westminster
Page 456

6192 Westminster
Page 457

Westmoreland Drive

7327 Westmoreland
Page 458

Westmoreland Place

52 Westmoreland
Page 459

2144

ALLEN AVENUE

ABOVE Photo by Reed R. Radcliffe, 2022.

DAILY RECORD NO.
287

APPEARED IN THE DAILY RECORD
11/02/1902

OWNER
Valentine Krenze

BUILDER
A. A. Fischer

DESCRIPTION
2-story flat; 26 feet × 43 feet

BROKEN FRIEZE
Yes

PART OF A STREETSCAPE
No

NEIGHBORHOOD
● McKinley Heights

SIDE OF THE STREET
South

STATUS IN 2021
Occupied

2629
ALLEN AVENUE

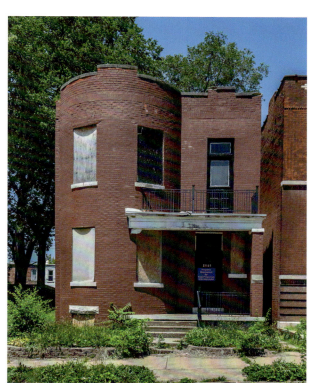

BUILDING PERMIT DATE
12/10/1895

OWNER
A. A. Fischer

BUILDER
A. A. Fischer

DESCRIPTION
2-story dwelling; 32 feet × 31 feet, 4.8 inches

BROKEN FRIEZE
No

PART OF A STREETSCAPE
Yes, 1 of 2 side by side (west to east: 2629, 2631)

NEIGHBORHOOD
● Fox Park

SIDE OF THE STREET
North

STATUS IN 2021
Condemned

TOP
Photo by Reed R. Radcliffe, 2022.

LEFT
Photo by Nancy Moore Hamilton, 2001.

DIRECTORY OF A. A. FISCHER BUILDS | 129

2631

ALLEN AVENUE

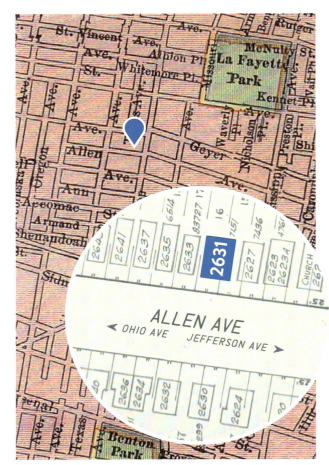

BUILDING PERMIT DATE
12/10/1895

OWNER
A. A. Fischer

BUILDER
A. A. Fischer

DESCRIPTION
2-story dwelling; 32 feet × 31 feet, 4.8 inches

BROKEN FRIEZE
No

PART OF A STREETSCAPE
Yes, 1 of 2 side by side (west to east: 2629, 2631)

NEIGHBORHOOD
● Fox Park

SIDE OF THE STREET
North

STATUS IN 2021
Razed in 2018

TOP
David Rumsey Map Collection, David Rumsey Map Center, Stanford Libraries at Stanford University.

CIRCLE
St. Louis Building Department Atlases, 1943–1946.
St. Louis Public Library.

LEFT
Photo by Nancy Moore Hamilton, 2001.

906-904

AUBERT AVENUE
This structure's original address was 902-904 Aubert Avenue.

ABOVE Photo by Reed R. Radcliffe, 2022.

DAILY RECORD NO.
956

APPEARED IN THE DAILY RECORD
09/20/1902

OWNER
A. A. Fischer Architectural & Building Company

BUILDER
A. A. Fischer Architectural & Building Company

DESCRIPTION
2-story flat; 23.5 feet × 42.3 feet; $7,000

BROKEN FRIEZE
Yes

PART OF A STREETSCAPE
Yes, 1 of 3 (west to east: 910, 908, 906-904)

NEIGHBORHOOD
● Fountain Park

SIDE OF THE STREET
East

STATUS IN 2021
Occupied

908

AUBERT AVENUE
This structure's original address was 906 Aubert Avenue.

ABOVE Photo by Reed R. Radcliffe, 2022.

DAILY RECORD NO.
159

APPEARED IN THE DAILY RECORD
10/14/1902

OWNER
A. A. Fischer Architectural & Building Company

BUILDER
A. A. Fischer Architectural & Building Company

DESCRIPTION
2-story flat; 26 feet × 43 feet

BROKEN FRIEZE
Yes

PART OF A STREETSCAPE
Yes, 1 of 3 (west to east: 910, 908, 906-904)

NEIGHBORHOOD
● Fountain Park

SIDE OF THE STREET
East

STATUS IN 2021
Occupied

910

AUBERT AVENUE
This structure's original address was 908 Aubert Avenue.

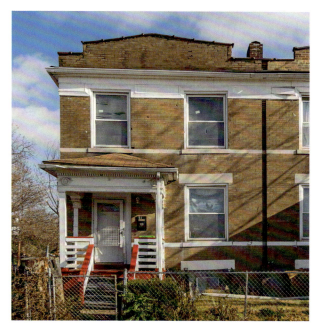

ABOVE Photo by Reed R. Radcliffe, 2022.

BUILDING PERMIT NO.
D-7159

BUILDING PERMIT DATE
10/15/1902

DAILY RECORD NO.
159

APPEARED IN THE DAILY RECORD
10/17/1902

OWNER
A. A. Fischer Architectural & Building Company

ARCHITECT
A. A. Fischer Architectural & Building Company

BUILDER
A. A. Fischer Architectural & Building Company

DESCRIPTION
2-story brick flat; 26 feet × 43 feet

BROKEN FRIEZE
Yes

PART OF A STREETSCAPE
Yes, 1 of 3 (west to east: 910, 908, 906-904)

NEIGHBORHOOD
● Fountain Park

SIDE OF THE STREET
East

STATUS IN 2021
Occupied

3855-57

BOTANICAL AVENUE

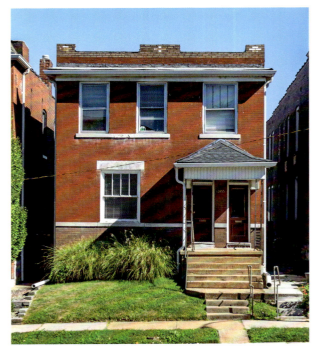

ABOVE Photo by Reed R. Radcliffe, 2022.

BUILDING PERMIT DATE
08/30/1902

DAILY RECORD NO.
824

APPEARED IN THE DAILY RECORD
08/30/1902

OWNER
John Hahn

BUILDER
A. A. Fischer Architectural & Building Company

DESCRIPTION
2-story flat; 23.5 feet × 42.3 feet; $3,750

BROKEN FRIEZE
No

PART OF A STREETSCAPE
No

NEIGHBORHOOD
● Shaw

SIDE OF THE STREET
North

STATUS IN 2021
Occupied

5095
CABANNE AVENUE

ABOVE
Photo by Reed R. Radcliffe, 2022.

RIGHT
Photo provided by Landmarks Association of St. Louis, 1980.

DAILY RECORD NO.
179

APPEARED IN THE DAILY RECORD
03/23/1904

OWNER
A. A. Fischer Architectural & Building Company

ARCHITECT
A. A. Fischer Architectural & Building Company

BUILDER
A. A. Fischer Architectural & Building Company

DESCRIPTION
2-story residence; 36 feet × 33 feet; $5,000

BROKEN FRIEZE
No

PART OF A STREETSCAPE
No

NEIGHBORHOOD
● Academy

SIDE OF THE STREET
North

STATUS IN 2021
Occupied

5201

CABANNE AVENUE

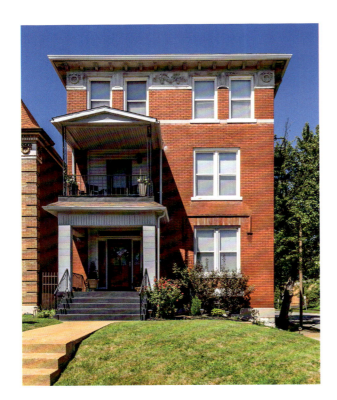

DAILY RECORD NO.
4698

APPEARED IN THE DAILY RECORD
08/04/1905

HOUSE NUMBER CERTIFICATE
08/02/1905

OWNER
A. A. Fischer

BUILDER
A. A. Fischer Architectural & Building Company

DESCRIPTION
3-story dwelling; 26 feet × 36 feet

BROKEN FRIEZE
Yes

PART OF A STREETSCAPE
Yes, 1 of 7 (west to east: 5223, 5219, 5215, 5211, 5209, 5205, 5201)

NEIGHBORHOOD
● Academy

SIDE OF THE STREET
North

STATUS IN 2021
Occupied

TOP
Photo by Reed R. Radcliffe, 2022.

LEFT
Photo by Lynn Josse for Landmarks Association of St. Louis, 2001.

5205

CABANNE AVENUE

ABOVE
Photo by Reed R. Radcliffe, 2022.

RIGHT
Photo by Lynn Josse for Landmarks Association of St. Louis, 2001.

BUILDING PERMIT NO.
E-4699

BUILDING PERMIT DATE
08/03/1905

DAILY RECORD NO.
4699

APPEARED IN THE DAILY RECORD
08/04/1905

BUILDER NO.
4699

APPEARED IN THE BUILDER
Aug. 1905

OWNER
A. A. Fischer

BUILDER
A. A. Fischer Architectural & Building Company

DESCRIPTION
2-story dwelling; 32 × 32 feet

BROKEN FRIEZE
Yes

PART OF A STREETSCAPE
Yes, 1 of 7 (west to east: 5223, 5219, 5215, 5211, 5209, 5205, 5201)

NEIGHBORHOOD
● Academy

SIDE OF THE STREET
North

STATUS IN 2021
Occupied

5209

CABANNE AVENUE

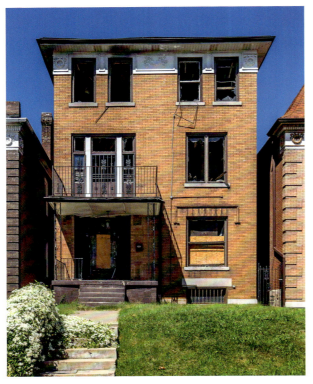

ABOVE
Photo by Reed R. Radcliffe, 2022.

RIGHT
Photo provided by Landmarks Association of St. Louis, 1980.

***DAILY RECORD* NO.**
4700

APPEARED IN THE *DAILY RECORD*
08/04/1905

***BUILDER* NO.**
4699

APPEARED IN THE *BUILDER*
Aug. 1905

HOUSE NUMBER CERTIFICATE
08/02/1905

OWNER
A. A. Fischer

BUILDER
A. A. Fischer Architectural & Building Company

DESCRIPTION
3-story residence; 25 feet × 35 feet

BROKEN FRIEZE
Yes

PART OF A STREETSCAPE
Yes, 1 of 7 (west to east: 5223, 5219, 5215, 5211, 5209, 5205, 5201)

NEIGHBORHOOD
● Academy

SIDE OF THE STREET
North

STATUS IN 2021
Occupied

5211

CABANNE AVENUE

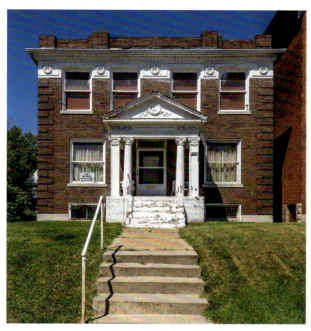

ABOVE
Photo by Reed R. Radcliffe, 2022.

RIGHT
Photo provided by Landmarks Association of St. Louis, 1980.

BUILDING PERMIT NO.
E-4699

BUILDING PERMIT DATE
08/03/1905

DAILY RECORD NO.
4699

APPEARED IN THE DAILY RECORD
08/04/1905

BUILDER NO.
4699

APPEARED IN THE BUILDER
08/1905

OWNER
A. A. Fischer

BUILDER
A. A. Fischer Architectural & Building Company

DESCRIPTION
2-story dwelling; 32 feet × 32 feet

BROKEN FRIEZE
Yes

PART OF A STREETSCAPE
Yes, 1 of 7 (west to east: 5223, 5219, 5215, 5211, 5209, 5205, 5201)

NEIGHBORHOOD
● Academy

SIDE OF THE STREET
North

STATUS IN 2021
Occupied

5215

CABANNE AVENUE

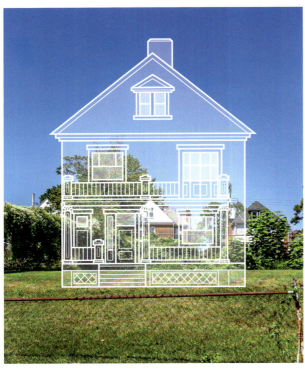

ABOVE Photo by Reed R. Radcliffe, 2022.

DAILY RECORD NO.
4831

APPEARED IN THE DAILY RECORD
08/17/1905

BUILDER NO.
4831

APPEARED IN THE BUILDER
Sept. 1905

OWNER
A. A. Fischer

ARCHITECT
A. A. Fischer Architectural & Building Company

BUILDER
A. A. Fischer Architectural & Building Company

DESCRIPTION
2-story dwelling; 40 feet × 33 feet

BROKEN FRIEZE
Unknown

PART OF A STREETSCAPE
Yes, 1 of 7 (west to east: 5223, 5219, 5215, 5211, 5209, 5205, 5201)

NEIGHBORHOOD
● Academy

SIDE OF THE STREET
North

STATUS IN 2021
Razed

5219
CABANNE AVENUE

ABOVE Photo by Reed R. Radcliffe, 2022.

DAILY RECORD NO.
4832

APPEARED IN THE DAILY RECORD
08/17/1905

BUILDER NO.
4832

APPEARED IN THE BUILDER
Sept. 1905

OWNER
A. A. Fischer

ARCHITECT
A. A. Fischer Architectural & Building Company

BUILDER
A. A. Fischer Architectural & Building Company

DESCRIPTION
2-story dwelling; 32 feet × 32 feet

BROKEN FRIEZE
Unknown

PART OF A STREETSCAPE
Yes, 1 of 7 (west to east: 5223, 5219, 5215, 5211, 5209, 5205, 5201)

NEIGHBORHOOD
● Academy

SIDE OF THE STREET
North

STATUS IN 2021
Razed

5223
CABANNE AVENUE

TOP Photo by Reed R. Radcliffe, 2022.
BOTTOM Photo provided by Landmarks Association of St. Louis, 1980.

DAILY RECORD NO.
4831

APPEARED IN THE DAILY RECORD
08/17/1905

HOUSE NUMBER CERTIFICATE
08/16/1905

OWNER
A. A. Fischer

ARCHITECT
A. A. Fischer Architectural & Building Company

BUILDER
A. A. Fischer Architectural & Building Company

DESCRIPTION
2-story dwelling; 40 feet × 33 feet

BROKEN FRIEZE
Yes

PART OF A STREETSCAPE
Yes, 1 of 7 (west to east: 5223, 5219, 5215, 5211, 5209, 5205, 5201)

NEIGHBORHOOD
● Academy

SIDE OF THE STREET
North

STATUS IN 2021
Occupied

5226

CABANNE AVENUE

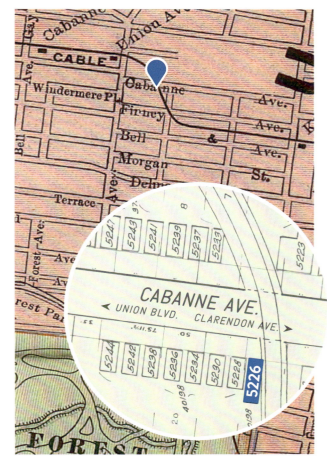

ABOVE
David Rumsey Map Collection, David Rumsey Map Center, Stanford Libraries at Stanford University.

CIRCLE
St. Louis Building Department Atlases, 1943–1946.
St. Louis Public Library.

DAILY RECORD NO.
633

APPEARED IN THE DAILY RECORD
02/15/1907

REALTY RECORD AND BUILDER NO.
633

APPEARED IN THE REALTY RECORD AND BUILDER
02/07/1907

OWNER
A. A. Fischer Realty Company

ARCHITECT
A. A. Fischer Realty Company

BUILDER
A. A. Fischer Realty Company

DESCRIPTION
2-story flat; 24 feet × 44 feet; $4,500

BROKEN FRIEZE
Unknown

PART OF A STREETSCAPE
Yes, 1 of 8 (west to east: 5244, 5242, 5238, 5236, 5234, 5230, 5228, 5226)

NEIGHBORHOOD
● Academy

SIDE OF THE STREET
South

STATUS IN 2021
Razed

5228

CABANNE AVENUE

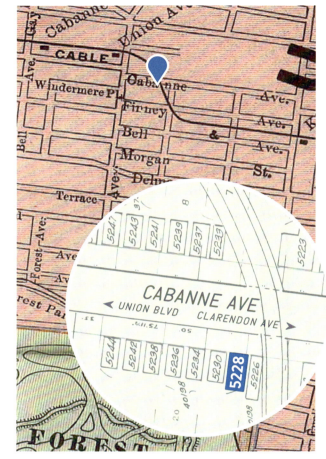

ABOVE
David Rumsey Map Collection, David Rumsey Map Center, Stanford Libraries at Stanford University.

CIRCLE
St. Louis Building Department Atlases, 1943–1946.
St. Louis Public Library.

DAILY RECORD NO.
634

APPEARED IN THE DAILY RECORD
02/15/1907

REALTY RECORD AND BUILDER NO.
634

APPEARED IN THE REALTY RECORD AND BUILDER
02/07/1907

OWNER
A. A. Fischer Realty Company

ARCHITECT
A. A. Fischer Realty Company

BUILDER
A. A. Fischer Realty Company

DESCRIPTION
2-story dwelling; 24 feet × 33 feet

BROKEN FRIEZE
Unknown

PART OF A STREETSCAPE
Yes, 1 of 8 (west to east: 5244, 5242, 5238, 5236, 5234, 5230, 5228, 5226)

NEIGHBORHOOD
● Academy

SIDE OF THE STREET
South

STATUS IN 2021
Razed

5230

CABANNE AVENUE

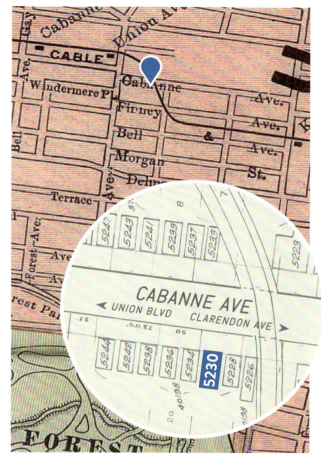

ABOVE
David Rumsey Map Collection, David Rumsey Map Center, Stanford Libraries at Stanford University.

CIRCLE
St. Louis Building Department Atlases, 1943–1946.
St. Louis Public Library.

DAILY RECORD NO.
634

APPEARED IN THE DAILY RECORD
02/15/1907

REALTY RECORD AND BUILDER NO.
634

APPEARED IN THE REALTY RECORD AND BUILDER
02/07/1907

OWNER
A. A. Fischer Realty Company

ARCHITECT
A. A. Fischer Realty Company

BUILDER
A. A. Fischer Realty Company

DESCRIPTION
2-story dwelling; 24 feet × 33 feet

BROKEN FRIEZE
Unknown

PART OF A STREETSCAPE
Yes, 1 of 8 (west to east: 5244, 5242, 5238, 5236, 5234, 5230, 5228, 5226)

NEIGHBORHOOD
● Academy

SIDE OF THE STREET
South

STATUS IN 2021
Razed

5233
CABANNE AVENUE

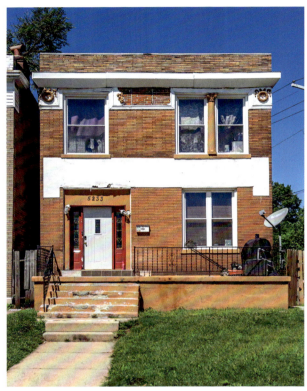

ABOVE
Photo by Reed R. Radcliffe, 2022.

RIGHT
Photo provided by Landmarks Association of St. Louis, 1980.

BUILDING PERMIT NO.
E-6551

BUILDING PERMIT DATE
02/13/1906

DAILY RECORD NO.
6551

APPEARED IN THE DAILY RECORD
02/14/1906

HOUSE NUMBER CERTIFICATE
02/13/1906

OWNER
A. A. Fischer Architectural & Building Company

ARCHITECT
A. A. Fischer Architectural & Building Company

BUILDER
A. A. Fischer Architectural & Building Company

DESCRIPTION
2-story dwelling; 23 feet × 33 feet

BROKEN FRIEZE
Yes

PART OF A STREETSCAPE
Yes, 1 of 9 (west to east: 5253, 5251, 5249, 5247, 5243, 5241, 5239, 5237, 5233)

NEIGHBORHOOD
● Academy

SIDE OF THE STREET
North

STATUS IN 2021
Occupied

5234

CABANNE AVENUE

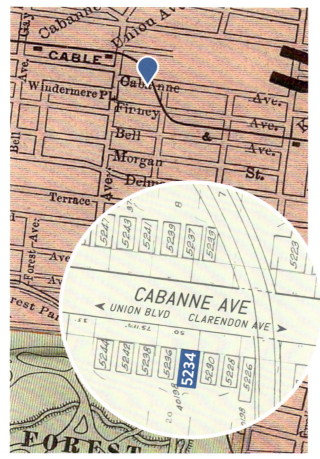

ABOVE
David Rumsey Map Collection, David Rumsey Map Center, Stanford Libraries at Stanford University.

CIRCLE
St. Louis Building Department Atlases, 1943–1946.
St. Louis Public Library.

DAILY RECORD NO.
634

APPEARED IN THE DAILY RECORD
02/15/1907

REALTY RECORD AND BUILDER NO.
634

APPEARED IN THE REALTY RECORD AND BUILDER
02/07/1907

OWNER
A. A. Fischer Realty Company

ARCHITECT
A. A. Fischer Realty Company

BUILDER
A. A. Fischer Realty Company

DESCRIPTION
2-story dwelling; 24 feet × 33 feet

BROKEN FRIEZE
Unknown

PART OF A STREETSCAPE
Yes, 1 of 8 (west to east: 5244, 5242, 5238, 5236, 5234, 5230, 5228, 5226)

NEIGHBORHOOD
● Academy

SIDE OF THE STREET
South

STATUS IN 2021
Razed

5236

CABANNE AVENUE

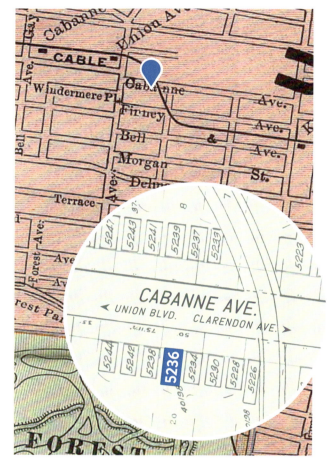

ABOVE
David Rumsey Map Collection, David Rumsey Map Center, Stanford Libraries at Stanford University.

CIRCLE
St. Louis Building Department Atlases, 1943–1946.
St. Louis Public Library.

DAILY RECORD NO.
634

APPEARED IN THE *DAILY RECORD*
02/15/1907

REALTY RECORD AND BUILDER NO.
634

APPEARED IN THE *REALTY RECORD AND BUILDER*
02/07/1907

OWNER
A. A. Fischer Realty Company

ARCHITECT
A. A. Fischer Realty Company

BUILDER
A. A. Fischer Realty Company

DESCRIPTION
2-story dwelling; 24 feet × 33 feet

BROKEN FRIEZE
Unknown

PART OF A STREETSCAPE
Yes, 1 of 8 (west to east: 5244, 5242, 5238, 5236, 5234, 5230, 5228, 5226)

NEIGHBORHOOD
● Academy

SIDE OF THE STREET
South

STATUS IN 2021
Razed

5237

CABANNE AVENUE

ABOVE
Photo by Reed R. Radcliffe, 2022.

RIGHT
Photo provided by Landmarks Association of St. Louis, 1980.

BUILDING PERMIT NO.
E-6551

BUILDING PERMIT DATE
02/13/1906

DAILY RECORD NO.
6551

APPEARED IN THE DAILY RECORD
02/14/1906

HOUSE NUMBER CERTIFICATE
02/13/1906

OWNER
A. A. Fischer Architectural & Building Company

ARCHITECT
A. A. Fischer Architectural & Building Company

BUILDER
A. A. Fischer Architectural & Building Company

DESCRIPTION
2-story dwelling; 23 feet × 33 feet

BROKEN FRIEZE
Yes

PART OF A STREETSCAPE
Yes, 1 of 9 (west to east: 5253, 5251, 5249, 5247, 5243, 5241, 5239, 5237, 5233)

NEIGHBORHOOD
● Academy

SIDE OF THE STREET
North

STATUS IN 2021
Occupied, but in moderate disrepair

5238

CABANNE AVENUE

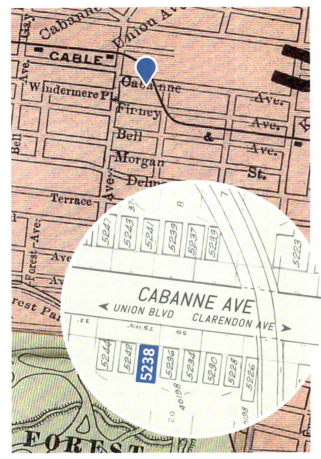

ABOVE
David Rumsey Map Collection, David Rumsey Map Center, Stanford Libraries at Stanford University.

CIRCLE
St. Louis Building Department Atlases, 1943–1946.
St. Louis Public Library.

DAILY RECORD **NO.**
634

APPEARED IN THE *DAILY RECORD*
02/15/1907

REALTY RECORD AND BUILDER **NO.**
634

APPEARED IN THE *REALTY RECORD AND BUILDER*
02/07/1907

OWNER
A. A. Fischer Realty Company

ARCHITECT
A. A. Fischer Realty Company

BUILDER
A. A. Fischer Realty Company

DESCRIPTION
2-story dwelling; 24 feet × 33 feet

BROKEN FRIEZE
Unknown

PART OF A STREETSCAPE
Yes, 1 of 8 (west to east: 5244, 5242, 5238, 5236, 5234, 5230, 5228, 5226)

NEIGHBORHOOD
● Academy

SIDE OF THE STREET
South

STATUS IN 2021
Razed

5239
CABANNE AVENUE

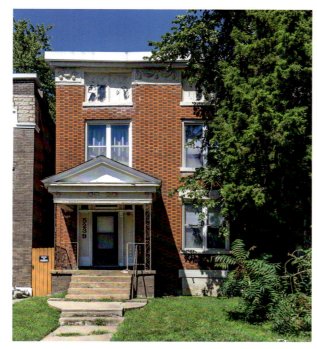

TOP Photo by Reed R. Radcliffe, 2022.
BOTTOM LEFT Photo provided by Landmarks Association of St. Louis, 1980.
BOTTOM RIGHT Photo by Lori Berdak Miller, 2022.

DAILY RECORD NO.
6550

APPEARED IN THE DAILY RECORD
02/14/1906

HOUSE NUMBER CERTIFICATE
02/13/1906

OWNER
A. A. Fischer Realty Company

ARCHITECT
A. A. Fischer Realty Company

BUILDER
A. A. Fischer Realty Company

DESCRIPTION
2-story dwelling; 24 feet × 32 feet

BROKEN FRIEZE
Yes

PART OF A STREETSCAPE
Yes, 1 of 9 (west to east: 5253, 5251, 5249, 5247, 5243, 5241, 5239, 5237, 5233)

NEIGHBORHOOD
● Academy

SIDE OF THE STREET
North

STATUS IN 2021
Occupied

5241

CABANNE AVENUE

ABOVE
Photo by Reed R. Radcliffe, 2022.

RIGHT
Photo provided by Landmarks Association of St. Louis, 1980.

BUILDING PERMIT NO.
E-6551

BUILDING PERMIT DATE
02/13/1906

DAILY RECORD NO.
6551

APPEARED IN THE DAILY RECORD
02/14/1906

HOUSE NUMBER CERTIFICATE
02/13/1906

OWNER
A. A. Fischer Architectural & Building Company

ARCHITECT
A. A. Fischer Architectural & Building Company

BUILDER
A. A. Fischer Architectural & Building Company

DESCRIPTION
2-story dwelling; 23 feet × 33 feet

BROKEN FRIEZE
Yes

PART OF A STREETSCAPE
Yes, 1 of 9 (west to east: 5253, 5251, 5249, 5247, 5243, 5241, 5239, 5237, 5233)

NEIGHBORHOOD
● Academy

SIDE OF THE STREET
North

STATUS IN 2021
Occupied

5242
CABANNE AVENUE

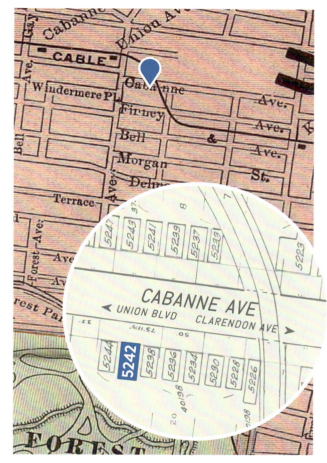

ABOVE
David Rumsey Map Collection, David Rumsey Map Center, Stanford Libraries at Stanford University.

CIRCLE
St. Louis Building Department Atlases, 1943–1946.
St. Louis Public Library.

DAILY RECORD NO.
634

APPEARED IN THE DAILY RECORD
02/15/1907

REALTY RECORD AND BUILDER NO.
634

APPEARED IN THE REALTY RECORD AND BUILDER
02/07/1907

OWNER
A. A. Fischer Realty Company

ARCHITECT
A. A. Fischer Realty Company

BUILDER
A. A. Fischer Realty Company

DESCRIPTION
2-story dwelling; 24 feet × 33 feet

BROKEN FRIEZE
Unknown

PART OF A STREETSCAPE
Yes, 1 of 8 (west to east: 5244, 5242, 5238, 5236, 5234, 5230, 5228, 5226)

NEIGHBORHOOD
● Academy

SIDE OF THE STREET
South

STATUS IN 2021
Razed

5243

CABANNE AVENUE

ABOVE
Photo by Reed R. Radcliffe, 2022.
RIGHT
Photo provided by Landmarks Association of St. Louis, 1980.

DAILY RECORD NO.
6550

APPEARED IN THE *DAILY RECORD*
02/14/1906

HOUSE NUMBER CERTIFICATE
02/13/1906

OWNER
A. A. Fischer Realty Company

ARCHITECT
A. A. Fischer Realty Company

BUILDER
A. A. Fischer Realty Company

DESCRIPTION
2-story dwelling; 24 feet × 32 feet

BROKEN FRIEZE
Yes

PART OF A STREETSCAPE
Yes, 1 of 9 (west to east: 5253, 5251, 5249, 5247, 5243, 5241, 5239, 5237, 5233)

NEIGHBORHOOD
● Academy

SIDE OF THE STREET
North

STATUS IN 2021
Occupied

5244
CABANNE AVENUE

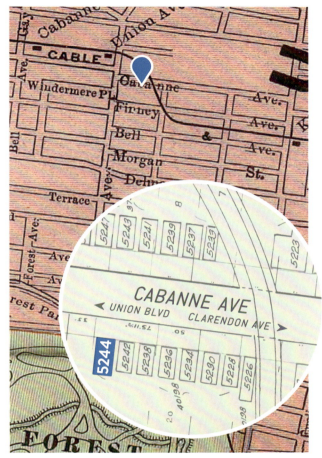

ABOVE
David Rumsey Map Collection, David Rumsey Map Center, Stanford Libraries at Stanford University.

CIRCLE
St. Louis Building Department Atlases, 1943–1946.
St. Louis Public Library.

DAILY RECORD NO.
634

APPEARED IN THE DAILY RECORD
02/15/1907

REALTY RECORD AND BUILDER NO.
634

APPEARED IN THE REALTY RECORD AND BUILDER
02/07/1907

OWNER
A. A. Fischer Realty Company

ARCHITECT
A. A. Fischer Realty Company

BUILDER
A. A. Fischer Realty Company

DESCRIPTION
2-story dwelling; 24 feet × 33 feet

BROKEN FRIEZE
Unknown

PART OF A STREETSCAPE
Yes, 1 of 8 (west to east: 5244, 5242, 5238, 5236, 5234, 5230, 5228, 5226)

NEIGHBORHOOD
● Academy

SIDE OF THE STREET
South

STATUS IN 2021
Razed

5247

CABANNE AVENUE

ABOVE
Photo by Reed R. Radcliffe, 2022.

RIGHT
Photo provided by Landmarks Association of St. Louis, 1980.

BUILDING PERMIT NO.
E-6551

BUILDING PERMIT DATE
02/13/1906

DAILY RECORD NO.
6551

APPEARED IN THE DAILY RECORD
02/14/1906

HOUSE NUMBER CERTIFICATE
02/13/1906

OWNER
A. A. Fischer Architectural & Building Company

ARCHITECT
A. A. Fischer Architectural & Building Company

BUILDER
A. A. Fischer Architectural & Building Company

DESCRIPTION
2-story dwelling; 24 feet × 32 feet

BROKEN FRIEZE
Yes

PART OF A STREETSCAPE
Yes, 1 of 9 (west to east: 5253, 5251, 5249, 5247, 5243, 5241, 5239, 5237, 5233)

NEIGHBORHOOD
● Academy

SIDE OF THE STREET
North

STATUS IN 2021
Occupied

NOTE Described in an advertisement paid for by A. A. Fischer in the *St. Louis Post-Dispatch* on September 13, 1908, as "Owner has left city, offers his handsome 8-room house, built by this company eighteen months ago, at a sacrifice."

5249
CABANNE AVENUE

ABOVE
Photo by Reed R. Radcliffe, 2022.

RIGHT
Photo provided by Landmarks Association of St. Louis, 1980.

DAILY RECORD NO.
6550

APPEARED IN THE DAILY RECORD
02/14/1906

HOUSE NUMBER CERTIFICATE
02/13/1906

OWNER
A. A. Fischer Realty Company

ARCHITECT
A. A. Fischer Realty Company

BUILDER
A. A. Fischer Realty Company

DESCRIPTION
2-story dwelling; 24 feet × 32 feet

BROKEN FRIEZE
No

PART OF A STREETSCAPE
Yes, 1 of 9 (west to east: 5253, 5251, 5249, 5247, 5243, 5241, 5239, 5237, 5233)

NEIGHBORHOOD
● Academy

SIDE OF THE STREET
North

STATUS IN 2021
Occupied

5251

CABANNE AVENUE

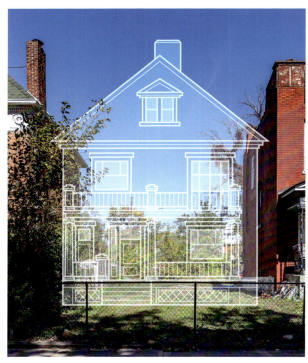

ABOVE Photo by Reed R. Radcliffe, 2022.

BUILDING PERMIT NO.
E-6551

BUILDING PERMIT DATE
02/13/1906

DAILY RECORD NO.
6551

APPEARED IN THE DAILY RECORD
02/14/1906

HOUSE NUMBER CERTIFICATE
02/13/1906

OWNER
A. A. Fischer Realty Company/
A. A. Fischer Architectural & Building Company

ARCHITECT
A. A. Fischer Realty Company/
A. A. Fischer Architectural & Building Company

BUILDER
A. A. Fischer Realty Company

DESCRIPTION
2-story dwelling; 24 feet × 32 feet

BROKEN FRIEZE
Unknown

PART OF A STREETSCAPE
Yes, 1 of 9 (west to east: 5253, 5251, 5249, 5247, 5243, 5241, 5239, 5237, 5233)

NEIGHBORHOOD
● Academy

SIDE OF THE STREET
North

STATUS IN 2021
Razed

5253
CABANNE AVENUE

DAILY RECORD NO.
6550

APPEARED IN THE DAILY RECORD
02/14/1906

HOUSE NUMBER CERTIFICATE
02/13/1906

OWNER
A. A. Fischer Realty Company

ARCHITECT
A. A. Fischer Realty Company

BUILDER
A. A. Fischer Realty Company

DESCRIPTION
2-story dwelling; 24 feet × 32 feet

BROKEN FRIEZE
Yes

PART OF A STREETSCAPE
Yes, 1 of 9 (west to east: 5253, 5251, 5249, 5247, 5243, 5241, 5239, 5237, 5233)

NEIGHBORHOOD
● Academy

SIDE OF THE STREET
North

STATUS IN 2021
Occupied

TOP
Photo by Reed R. Radcliffe, 2022.

LEFT
Photo provided by Landmarks Association of St. Louis, 1980.

5514
CABANNE AVENUE

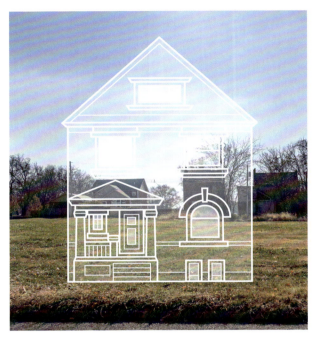

ABOVE Photo by Reed R. Radcliffe, 2022.

DAILY RECORD NO.
4136

APPEARED IN THE DAILY RECORD
June 1905

APPEARED IN THE BUILDER
June 1905

APPEARED IN THE REALTY RECORD
June 1905

HOUSE NUMBER CERTIFICATE
06/08/1905

OWNER
A. A. Fischer/A. A. Fischer Architectural & Building Company

ARCHITECT
A. A. Fischer/A. A. Fischer Architectural & Building Company

BUILDER
A. A. Fischer/A. A. Fischer Architectural & Building Company

DESCRIPTION
3-story apartment; 50 feet × 58 feet; $20,000

BROKEN FRIEZE
Unknown

PART OF A STREETSCAPE
Possibly 1 of 2 side by side (west to east: 5520, 5514)

NEIGHBORHOOD
● West End

SIDE OF THE STREET
South

STATUS IN 2021
Razed in 1997

5520

CABANNE AVENUE

5520 Cabanne Avenue may or may not have stood directly next to 5514 Cabanne Avenue.
It is possible that a separate structure stood between them.

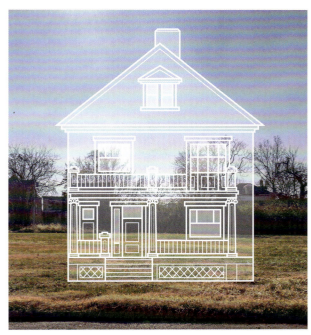

ABOVE Photo by Reed R. Radcliffe, 2022.

REALTY RECORD AND BUILDER NO.
1624

APPEARED IN THE REALTY RECORD AND BUILDER
Sept. 1909

OWNER
Dobyne Realty & Investment Co.

ARCHITECT
A. A. Fischer Realty Company

BUILDER
A. A. Fischer Realty Company

DESCRIPTION
3-story apartment house; 36 feet × 62 feet; $10,000

BROKEN FRIEZE
Unknown

PART OF A STREETSCAPE
Possibly 1 of 2 side by side (west to east: 5520, 5514)

NEIGHBORHOOD
● West End

SIDE OF THE STREET
South

STATUS IN 2021
Razed

6254
CABANNE AVENUE

ABOVE City of University City building permit, 1922. The Archives of the University City Public Library.

BUILDING PERMIT NO.
1827

BUILDING PERMIT DATE
06/03/1922

DAILY RECORD NO.
1827

APPEARED IN THE DAILY RECORD
06/13/1922

OWNER
A. A. Fischer

BUILDER
A. A. Fischer

DESCRIPTION
2-story, 4-family brick tenement; $8,000

BROKEN FRIEZE
Unknown

PART OF A STREETSCAPE
Yes, originally 1 of 11 (west to east: 6306, 6304, 6300, 6272, 6270, 6268, 6264, 6262, 6258, 6256, 6254)

NEIGHBORHOOD
● University City

SIDE OF THE STREET
South

STATUS IN 2021
Razed

6256
CABANNE AVENUE

ABOVE City of University City building permit, 1922. The Archives of the University City Public Library.

BUILDING PERMIT NO.
1828

BUILDING PERMIT DATE
06/03/1922

DAILY RECORD NO.
1828

APPEARED IN THE DAILY RECORD
06/13/1922

OWNER
A. A. Fischer

BUILDER
A. A. Fischer

DESCRIPTION
1-story brick bungalow; 22 feet × 30 feet

BROKEN FRIEZE
Unknown

PART OF A STREETSCAPE
Yes, originally 1 of 11 (west to east: 6306, 6304, 6300, 6272, 6270, 6268, 6264, 6262, 6258, 6256, 6254)

NEIGHBORHOOD
● University City

SIDE OF THE STREET
South

STATUS IN 2021
Razed

DIRECTORY OF A. A. FISCHER BUILDS | 163

6258

CABANNE AVENUE

ABOVE Photo by Reed R. Radcliffe, 2022.

BUILDING PERMIT NO.
1828

BUILDING PERMIT DATE
06/03/1922

DAILY RECORD NO.
1828

APPEARED IN THE DAILY RECORD
06/13/1922

OWNER
A. A. Fischer/Vina Brehe and A. A. Fischer

BUILDER
A. A. Fischer

DESCRIPTION
1-story brick bungalow; $3,500

BROKEN FRIEZE
No

PART OF A STREETSCAPE
Yes, originally 1 of 11 (west to east: 6306, 6304, 6300, 6272, 6270, 6268, 6264, 6262, 6258, 6256, 6254)

NEIGHBORHOOD
● University City

SIDE OF THE STREET
South

STATUS IN 2021
Occupied

6262

CABANNE AVENUE

ABOVE City of University City building permit, 1922. The Archives of the University City Public Library.

BUILDING PERMIT NO.
1828

BUILDING PERMIT DATE
06/03/1922

DAILY RECORD NO.
1828

APPEARED IN THE DAILY RECORD
06/13/1922

OWNER
A. A. Fischer/Vina Brehe and A. A. Fischer

BUILDER
A. A. Fischer

DESCRIPTION
Single-family residence; 1-story brick bungalow; $3,500

BROKEN FRIEZE
Unknown

PART OF A STREETSCAPE
Yes, originally 1 of 11 (west to east: 6306, 6304, 6300, 6272, 6270, 6268, 6264, 6262, 6258, 6256, 6254)

NEIGHBORHOOD
● University City

SIDE OF THE STREET
Southwest

STATUS IN 2021
Razed

DIRECTORY OF A. A. FISCHER BUILDS | 165

6264

CABANNE AVENUE

ABOVE Photo by Reed R. Radcliffe, 2022.

BUILDING PERMIT NO.
1828

BUILDING PERMIT DATE
06/03/1922

DAILY RECORD NO.
1828

APPEARED IN THE DAILY RECORD
06/13/1922

OWNER
A. A. Fischer/Vina Brehe and A. A. Fischer

BUILDER
A. A. Fischer

DESCRIPTION
1-story brick bungalow; $3,500

BROKEN FRIEZE
Unknown

PART OF A STREETSCAPE
Yes, originally 1 of 11 (west to east: 6306, 6304, 6300, 6272, 6270, 6268, 6264, 6262, 6258, 6256, 6254)

NEIGHBORHOOD
● University City

SIDE OF THE STREET
South

STATUS IN 2021
Occupied

6268

CABANNE AVENUE

ABOVE City of University City building permit, 1922. The Archives of the University City Public Library.

BUILDING PERMIT NO.
1835

BUILDING PERMIT DATE
06/05/1922

DAILY RECORD NO.
1835

APPEARED IN THE DAILY RECORD
06/13/1922

OWNER
R. A. Fischer

BUILDER
R. A. Fischer

DESCRIPTION
1-story brick bungalow; 28 feet × 35 feet; $4,000

BROKEN FRIEZE
Unknown

PART OF A STREETSCAPE
Yes, originally 1 of 11 (west to east: 6306, 6304, 6300, 6272, 6270, 6268, 6264, 6262, 6258, 6256, 6254)

NEIGHBORHOOD
● University City

SIDE OF THE STREET
South

STATUS IN 2021
Razed

6270
CABANNE AVENUE

TOP Photo by Reed R. Radcliffe, 2022.
BOTTOM Photo by Esley Hamilton for Landmarks Association of St. Louis, 1982.

BUILDING PERMIT NO.
1663

BUILDING PERMIT DATE
01/16/1922

BUILDER
R. A. Fischer

DESCRIPTION
Single-family residence; brick bungalow

BROKEN FRIEZE
No

PART OF A STREETSCAPE
Yes, originally 1 of 11 (west to east: 6306, 6304, 6300, 6272, 6270, 6268, 6264, 6262, 6258, 6256, 6254)

NEIGHBORHOOD
● University City

SIDE OF THE STREET
South

STATUS IN 2021
Occupied

6272

CABANNE AVENUE

ABOVE Photo by Reed R. Radcliffe, 2022.

BUILDING PERMIT NO.
1647

BUILDING PERMIT DATE
12/05/1921

OWNER
Joe Badolato

BUILDER
R. A. Fischer

DESCRIPTION
Single-family residence

BROKEN FRIEZE
No

PART OF A STREETSCAPE
Yes, originally 1 of 11 (west to east: 6306, 6304, 6300, 6272, 6270, 6268, 6264, 6262, 6258, 6256, 6254)

NEIGHBORHOOD
● University City

SIDE OF THE STREET
South

STATUS IN 2021
Occupied

6300
CABANNE AVENUE

ABOVE Photo by Reed R. Radcliffe, 2022.

BUILDING PERMIT NO.
1835

BUILDING PERMIT DATE
06/05/1922

DAILY RECORD NO.
1835

APPEARED IN THE DAILY RECORD
06/13/1922

OWNER
R. A. Fischer

BUILDER
R. A. Fischer

DESCRIPTION
1-story brick bungalow; 28 feet × 35 feet; $4,000

BROKEN FRIEZE
No

PART OF A STREETSCAPE
Yes, originally 1 of 11 (west to east: 6306, 6304, 6300, 6272, 6270, 6268, 6264, 6262, 6258, 6256, 6254)

NEIGHBORHOOD
● University City

SIDE OF THE STREET
South

STATUS IN 2021
Occupied

6304

CABANNE AVENUE

ABOVE Photo by Reed R. Radcliffe, 2022.

BUILDING PERMIT NO.
1835

BUILDING PERMIT DATE
06/05/1922

DAILY RECORD NO.
1835

APPEARED IN THE DAILY RECORD
06/13/1922

OWNER
R. A. Fischer

BUILDER
R. A. Fischer

DESCRIPTION
1-story brick bungalow; 28 feet × 35 feet; $4,000

BROKEN FRIEZE
No

PART OF A STREETSCAPE
Yes, originally 1 of 11 (west to east: 6306, 6304, 6300, 6272, 6270, 6268, 6264, 6262, 6258, 6256, 6254)

NEIGHBORHOOD
● University City

SIDE OF THE STREET
South

STATUS IN 2021
Occupied

6305

CABANNE AVENUE

City of University City

Building Commissioner's Office

No. 2548 University City, Mo. May 3 1924

Permission is hereby granted to Ella K. Bergermann

To construct 2 Sty. Bri. Apt. building on front part of

Lot No. 2 + 3, Block No. 10, Subdivision N. Parkview.

House No. 6305 Cabanne in the City of

University City, in accordance with the provisions of the city ordinances and

application No. 2548 filed by A. A. Fischer with the Building

Commissioner, said building to be used as Class 'C' Res

Estimated cost, - - $ 20,000.00

Fee, - - - - $ 10.50 This permit expires Nov. 3, 1924

Inspection fee, - - $ 12.00

Boiler Inspection fee - $ 1.00

Total, - - - $ 23.50

Building Commissioner.

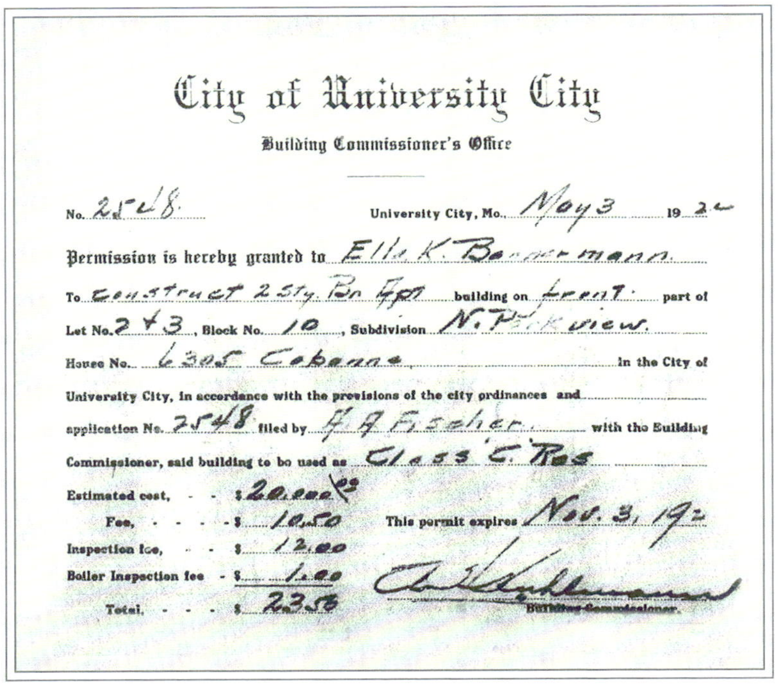

ABOVE City of University City building permit, 1924. The Archives of the University City Public Library.

BUILDING PERMIT NO.
2548

BUILDING PERMIT DATE
05/03/1924

DAILY RECORD NO.
2548

APPEARED IN THE *DAILY RECORD*
05/24/1924

ARCHITECT
A. A. Fischer

BUILDER
A. A. Fischer

DESCRIPTION
2-story brick apartment building; 38 feet × 83 feet; $20,000

BROKEN FRIEZE
Unknown

PART OF A STREETSCAPE
No

NEIGHBORHOOD
● University City

SIDE OF THE STREET
North

STATUS IN 2021
Razed

6306

CABANNE AVENUE

ABOVE City of University City building permit, 1922. The Archives of the University City Public Library.

BUILDING PERMIT NO.
1827

BUILDING PERMIT DATE
06/03/1922

DAILY RECORD NO.
1827

APPEARED IN THE DAILY RECORD
06/13/1922

OWNER
A. A. Fischer

BUILDER
A. A. Fischer

DESCRIPTION
2-story, 4-family brick tenement; 29 feet × 34 feet; $8,000

BROKEN FRIEZE
Unknown

PART OF A STREETSCAPE
Yes, originally 1 of 11 (west to east: 6306, 6304, 6300, 6272, 6270, 6268, 6264, 6262, 6258, 6256, 6254)

NEIGHBORHOOD
● University City

SIDE OF THE STREET
South

STATUS IN 2021
Razed

6407

CABANNE AVENUE

City of University City

Building Commissioner's Office

No. 1535 University City, Mo., 15 19 21

Permission is hereby granted to

To building on part of

Lot No. 3, Block No. 11, Subdivision

House No. 6407 Cabanne in the City of

University City, in accordance with the provisions of the city ordinances and

application No. filed by A. A. Fischer with the Building

Commissioner, said building to be used as

Estimated cost, . . . $ 3500

Fee, ... $ 2.50

Inspection fee, . . . $ 5.00

Boiler inspection fee, . $ 1.00

Total, ... $ 8.50

This permit expires

Building Commissioner.

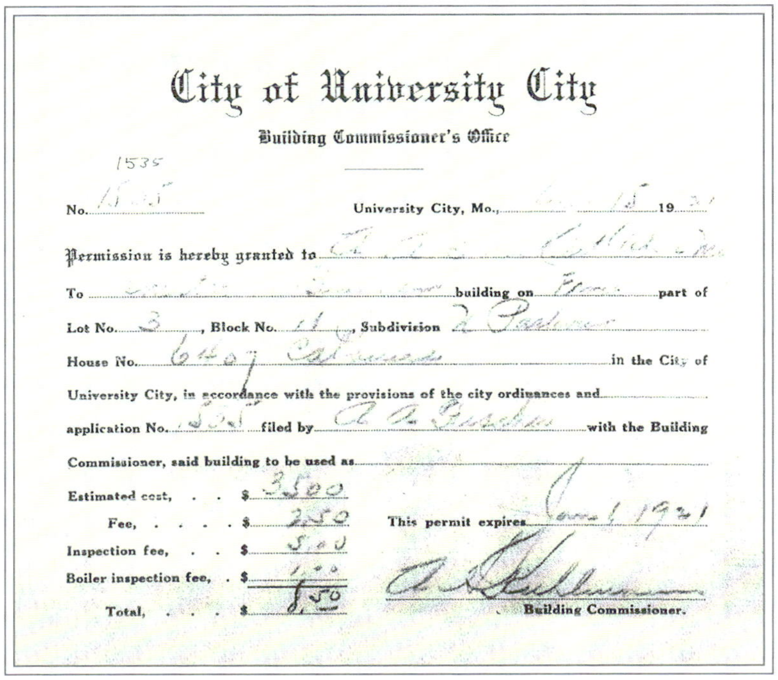

ABOVE City of University City building permit, 1921. The Archives of the University City Public Library.

BUILDING PERMIT NO.
1535

BUILDING PERMIT DATE
08/15/1921

OWNER
Alice Mayes

BUILDER
A. A. Fischer

DESCRIPTION
2-story, 4-family brick tenement; 29 feet × 34 feet; $8,000

BROKEN FRIEZE
Unknown

PART OF A STREETSCAPE
No

NEIGHBORHOOD
● University City

SIDE OF THE STREET
North

STATUS IN 2021
Razed

5968

WEST CABANNE PLACE

TOP Photo by Reed R. Radcliffe, 2022.
BOTTOM Photo by Jane Porter for Landmarks Association of St. Louis, 1980.

APPEARED IN THE *DAILY RECORD*
11/28/1906

***REALTY RECORD AND BUILDER* NO.**
12

APPEARED IN THE *REALTY RECORD AND BUILDER*
12/06/1906

OWNER
Robert L. Lund, care of Roberts, Johnson & Rand Shoe Co.

ARCHITECT
A. A. Fischer Architectural & Building Company

BUILDER
A. A. Fischer Architectural & Building Company

DESCRIPTION
2-story dwelling; 40 feet × 37 feet; $10,000

BROKEN FRIEZE
Yes

PART OF A STREETSCAPE
Yes, 1 of 3 (west to east: 6006, 6002, 5968)

NEIGHBORHOOD
● West End

SIDE OF THE STREET
South

STATUS IN 2021
Occupied

NOTE The 1979 National Register of Historic Places Inventory nomination for the West Cabanne Place Historic District describes this home as follows: "This 1906 house (Photo no. 14) is the only one in West Cabanne Place to reflect the profuse use elsewhere in St. Louis of terra cotta ornament and one of three West Cabanne Place houses by the prolific St. Louis builder A. A. Fischer. Of yellow brick with white trim, it has a massive, pedimented two story portico with two fluted Corinthian columns. A heavy garlanded and wreathed cornice frieze is partially interrupted by the second story windows. The roof parapet, with stone coping, has lost the two terracotta panels which ornamented it, but a terra cotta cartouche remains below at a centered second story balcony. The house was built for Robert Lund, who was at one time superintendent for the important Roberts, Johnson & Rand Shoe Company, and later general manager of the Lambert Pharmacal Company and Vice President of the National Association of Manufacturers. The family owned the house until 1953."

6002

WEST CABANNE PLACE

TOP Photo by Reed R. Radcliffe, 2022.
BOTTOM Photo by Jane Porter for Landmarks Association of St. Louis, 1980.

DAILY RECORD NO.
1596

REALTY RECORD AND BUILDER NO.
1596

APPEARED IN THE REALTY RECORD AND BUILDER
Sept. 1909

OWNER
Mrs. Jennie Dobyne Mahler

ARCHITECT
A. A. Fischer Realty Company

BUILDER
A. A. Fischer Realty Company

DESCRIPTION
3-story dwelling; 35 feet × 39 feet; $8,000

BROKEN FRIEZE
No

PART OF A STREETSCAPE
Yes, 1 of 3 (west to east: 6006, 6002, 5968)

NEIGHBORHOOD
● West End

SIDE OF THE STREET
South

STATUS IN 2021
Occupied

NOTE The 1979 National Register of Historic Places Inventory nomination for the West Cabanne Place Historic District describes this home as follows: "Built by [A. A.] Fischer [in 1909], this house . . . is of three full stories, with a shallow red tile mansard roof of wide angles and pronounced eaves with pairs of massive, dark-stained wood brackets on the façade only. Of rosy brick, it has bold window lintels and a belt course of contrasting stone."

6006

WEST CABANNE PLACE

TOP Photo by Reed R. Radcliffe, 2022.
BOTTOM Photo by Nancy Moore Hamilton, 2001.

DAILY RECORD NO.
1595

REALTY RECORD AND BUILDER NO.
1595

APPEARED IN THE REALTY RECORD AND BUILDER
Sept. 1909

OWNER
J. B. Dobyne

ARCHITECT
A. A. Fischer Realty Company

BUILDER
A. A. Fischer Realty Company

DESCRIPTION
2.5-story dwelling; 35 feet × 39 feet; $8,000

BROKEN FRIEZE
No

PART OF A STREETSCAPE
Yes, 1 of 3 (west to east: 6006, 6002, 5968)

NEIGHBORHOOD
● West End

SIDE OF THE STREET
South

STATUS IN 2021
Occupied

NOTE The 1979 National Register of Historic Places Inventory nomination for the West Cabanne Place Historic District describes this home as follows: "Massive design elements and textured materials are combined in this 1909 house by A. A. Fischer.... With its deep, belled mansard roof of red tile, the house might be described as 'modern French,' but the textures of the dark stained wood trim and porch pediment contrasting with the rosy brick walls and tile roof, and the rectangular patterning of window members relate it also to the Arts & Crafts houses, with their borrowings from Japanese and European architecture. The entrance porch is supported by two square brickwork columns with Corinthian capitals. There is a glassed, one-story conservatory on the east side of the house. Built for James B. Dobyne, President of the Champion Shoe Machinery Company and of a realty company."

5007
CATES AVENUE

ABOVE Photo by Reed R. Radcliffe, 2022.
RIGHT Photo provided by Landmarks Association of St. Louis, 1980.

DAILY RECORD NO.
781

APPEARED IN THE DAILY RECORD
07/30/1903

OWNER
A. A. Fischer Architectural & Building Company

ARCHITECT
A. A. Fischer Architectural & Building Company

BUILDER
A. A. Fischer Architectural & Building Company

DESCRIPTION
Brick flats; 23.8 feet × 35 feet

BROKEN FRIEZE
Yes

PART OF A STREETSCAPE
Yes, 1 of 2 side by side (west to east: 5009, 5007)

NEIGHBORHOOD
● Academy

SIDE OF THE STREET
North

STATUS IN 2021
Occupied

5009

CATES AVENUE

ABOVE Photo by Reed R. Radcliffe, 2022.
RIGHT Photo provided by Landmarks Association of St. Louis, 1980.

DAILY RECORD NO.
781

APPEARED IN THE DAILY RECORD
07/30/1903

OWNER
A. A. Fischer Architectural & Building Company

ARCHITECT
A. A. Fischer Architectural & Building Company

BUILDER
A. A. Fischer Architectural & Building Company

DESCRIPTION
Brick flats; 23.8 feet × 35 feet

BROKEN FRIEZE
Yes

PART OF A STREETSCAPE
Yes, 1 of 2 side by side (west to east: 5009, 5007)

NEIGHBORHOOD
● Academy

SIDE OF THE STREET
North

STATUS IN 2021
Occupied

5034-5036

CATES AVENUE
This structure's original address was 5036 Fairmount Avenue.

ABOVE
Photo by Reed R. Radcliffe, 2022.

RIGHT
Photo provided by Landmarks Association of St. Louis, 1980.

DAILY RECORD NO.
475

APPEARED IN THE DAILY RECORD
11/07/1903

BUILDER NO.
475

APPEARED IN THE BUILDER
11/16/1903

OWNER
A. A. Fischer/A. A. Fischer Architectural & Building Company

BUILDER
A. A. Fischer/A. A. Fischer Architectural & Building Company

DESCRIPTION
2-story flat; $4,500

BROKEN FRIEZE
Yes

PART OF A STREETSCAPE
Yes, 1 of 2 side by side (west to east: 5038, 5034-5036)

NEIGHBORHOOD
● Academy

SIDE OF THE STREET
South

STATUS IN 2021
Occupied

5038

CATES AVENUE

This structure's original address was 5038 Fairmount Avenue.

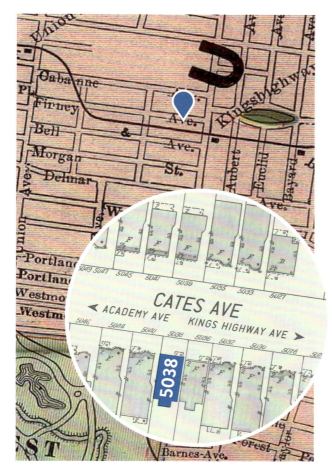

DAILY RECORD NO.
475

APPEARED IN THE *DAILY RECORD*
11/07/1903

OWNER
A. A. Fischer/A. A. Fischer Architectural & Building Company

BUILDER
A. A. Fischer Architectural & Building Company

DESCRIPTION
2-story flat; $4,500

BROKEN FRIEZE
Yes

PART OF A STREETSCAPE
Yes, 1 of 2 side by side (west to east: 5038, 5034-5036)

NEIGHBORHOOD
● Academy

SIDE OF THE STREET
South

STATUS IN 2021
Razed in 2016

TOP
David Rumsey Map Collection, David Rumsey Map Center, Stanford Libraries at Stanford University.

CIRCLE
Sanborn Fire Insurance Map from Saint Louis, Independent City, Missouri. Vol. 6, 1909.

LEFT
Photo provided by Landmarks Association of St. Louis, 1980.

DIRECTORY OF A. A. FISCHER BUILDS

5107

CATES AVENUE

This structure's original address was 5107 Fairmount Avenue.

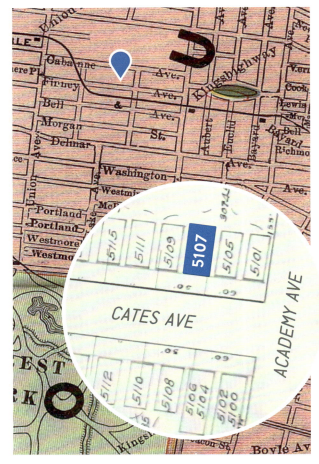

ABOVE
David Rumsey Map Collection, David Rumsey Map Center, Stanford Libraries at Stanford University.

CIRCLE
St. Louis Building Department Atlases, 1943–1946.
St. Louis Public Library

BUILDER NO.
781

APPEARED IN THE BUILDER
08/03/1903

APPEARED IN THE DAILY RECORD
Aug. 1903

OWNER
A. A. Fischer Architectural & Building Company

ARCHITECT
A. A. Fischer Architectural & Building Company

BUILDER
A. A. Fischer Architectural & Building Company

DESCRIPTION
Brick flat; 23.8 feet × 35 feet

BROKEN FRIEZE
Unknown

PART OF A STREETSCAPE
Yes, 1 of 2 side by side (west to east: 5109, 5107)

NEIGHBORHOOD
● Academy

SIDE OF THE STREET
North

STATUS IN 2021
Razed

5109

CATES AVENUE

This structure's original address was 5109 Fairmount Avenue.

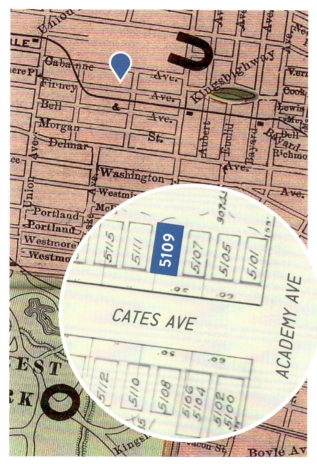

ABOVE
David Rumsey Map Collection, David Rumsey Map Center, Stanford Libraries at Stanford University.

CIRCLE
St. Louis Building Department Atlases, 1943–1946.
St. Louis Public Library

BUILDER NO.
781

APPEARED IN THE BUILDER
08/03/1903

APPEARED IN THE DAILY RECORD
Aug. 1903

OWNER
A. A. Fischer Architectural & Building Company

ARCHITECT
A. A. Fischer Architectural & Building Company

BUILDER
A. A. Fischer Architectural & Building Company

DESCRIPTION
Brick flat; 23.8 feet × 35 feet

BROKEN FRIEZE
Unknown

PART OF A STREETSCAPE
Yes, 1 of 2 side by side (west to east: 5109, 5107)

NEIGHBORHOOD
● Academy

SIDE OF THE STREET
North

STATUS IN 2021
Razed

5153-5155A
CATES AVENUE

ABOVE
Photo by Lori Berdak Miller, 2021.

RIGHT
Photo provided by Landmarks Association of St. Louis, 1980.

DAILY RECORD NO.
703

APPEARED IN THE DAILY RECORD
02/04/1903

OWNER
A. A. Fischer Architectural & Building Company

BUILDER
A. A. Fischer Architectural & Building Company

DESCRIPTION
2-story dwelling; 26.5 feet × 36 feet; $3,500

BROKEN FRIEZE
Yes

PART OF A STREETSCAPE
Yes, 1 of 10 (west to east: 5179-5181, 5177, 5175, 5171, 5169, 5165, 5163, 5159, 5157, 5153-5155A)

NEIGHBORHOOD
● Academy

SIDE OF THE STREET
North

STATUS IN 2021
Occupied

5157
CATES AVENUE

ABOVE
Photo by Reed R. Radcliffe, 2022.

RIGHT
Photo provided by Landmarks Association of St. Louis, 1980.

DAILY RECORD NO.
703

APPEARED IN THE DAILY RECORD
02/04/1903

OWNER
A. A. Fischer Architectural & Building Company

BUILDER
A. A. Fischer Architectural & Building Company

DESCRIPTION
2-story dwelling; 26.5 feet × 36 feet; $3,500

BROKEN FRIEZE
Yes

PART OF A STREETSCAPE
Yes, 1 of 10 (west to east: 5179-5181, 5177, 5175, 5171, 5169, 5165, 5163, 5159, 5157, 5153-5155A)

NEIGHBORHOOD
● Academy

SIDE OF THE STREET
North

STATUS IN 2021
Occupied

5159
CATES AVENUE

ABOVE Photo by Reed R. Radcliffe, 2022.

DAILY RECORD NO.
703

APPEARED IN THE DAILY RECORD
02/04/1903

HOUSE NUMBER SLIP
02/02/1903

OWNER
A. A. Fischer Architectural & Building Company

BUILDER
A. A. Fischer Architectural & Building Company

DESCRIPTION
2-story dwelling; 26.5 feet × 36 feet; $3,500

BROKEN FRIEZE
Yes

PART OF A STREETSCAPE
Yes, 1 of 10 (west to east: 5179-5181, 5177, 5175, 5171, 5169, 5165, 5163, 5159, 5157, 5153-5155A)

NEIGHBORHOOD
● Academy

SIDE OF THE STREET
North

STATUS IN 2021
Restored

5163

CATES AVENUE

ABOVE Photo by Reed R. Radcliffe, 2022.

DAILY RECORD NO.
703

APPEARED IN THE DAILY RECORD
02/04/1903

HOUSE NUMBER SLIP
02/02/1903

OWNER
A. A. Fischer Architectural & Building Company

BUILDER
A. A. Fischer Architectural & Building Company

DESCRIPTION
2-story dwelling; 26.5 feet × 36 feet; $3,500

BROKEN FRIEZE
Yes

PART OF A STREETSCAPE
Yes, 1 of 10 (west to east: 5179-5181, 5177, 5175, 5171, 5169, 5165, 5163, 5159, 5157, 5153-5155A)

NEIGHBORHOOD
● Academy

SIDE OF THE STREET
North

STATUS IN 2021
Occupied

5165
CATES AVENUE

ABOVE
Photo by Reed R. Radcliffe, 2022.

RIGHT
Photo provided by Landmarks Association of St. Louis, 1980.

DAILY RECORD NO.
703

APPEARED IN THE DAILY RECORD
02/04/1903

HOUSE NUMBER SLIP
02/02/1903

OWNER
A. A. Fischer Architectural & Building Company

BUILDER
A. A. Fischer Architectural & Building Company

DESCRIPTION
2-story dwelling; 26.5 feet × 36 feet; $3,500

BROKEN FRIEZE
Yes

PART OF A STREETSCAPE
Yes, 1 of 10 (west to east: 5179-5181, 5177, 5175, 5171, 5169, 5165, 5163, 5159, 5157, 5153-5155A)

NEIGHBORHOOD
● Academy

SIDE OF THE STREET
North

STATUS IN 2021
Occupied

5169

CATES AVENUE

ABOVE
Photo by Reed R. Radcliffe, 2022.

RIGHT
Photo by Lynn Josse for Landmarks Association of St. Louis, 2001.

DAILY RECORD NO.
558

APPEARED IN THE DAILY RECORD
01/06/1903

HOUSE NUMBER SLIP
01/05/1903

OWNER
A. A. Fischer Architectural & Building Company

BUILDER
A. A. Fischer Architectural & Building Company

DESCRIPTION
2-story dwelling; 25.3 feet × 34.3 feet; $4,000

BROKEN FRIEZE
Yes

PART OF A STREETSCAPE
Yes, 1 of 10 (west to east: 5179-5181, 5177, 5175, 5171, 5169, 5165, 5163, 5159, 5157, 5153-5155A)

NEIGHBORHOOD
● Academy

SIDE OF THE STREET
North

STATUS IN 2021
Occupied

5171

CATES AVENUE

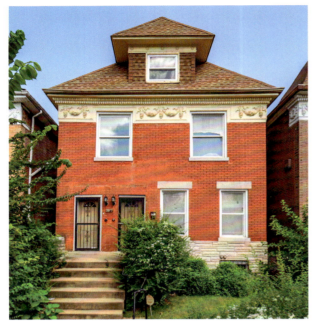

ABOVE
Photo by Reed R. Radcliffe, 2022.

RIGHT
Photo by Lynn Josse for Landmarks Association of St. Louis, 2001.

DAILY RECORD NO.
558

APPEARED IN THE DAILY RECORD
01/06/1903

HOUSE NUMBER SLIP
01/05/1903

OWNER
A. A. Fischer Architectural & Building Company

BUILDER
A. A. Fischer Architectural & Building Company

DESCRIPTION
2-story dwelling; 25.3 feet × 34.3 feet; $4,000

BROKEN FRIEZE
Yes

PART OF A STREETSCAPE
Yes, 1 of 10 (west to east: 5179-5181, 5177, 5175, 5171, 5169, 5165, 5163, 5159, 5157, 5153-5155A)

NEIGHBORHOOD
● Academy

SIDE OF THE STREET
North

STATUS IN 2021
Occupied

5175
CATES AVENUE

ABOVE
Photo by Reed R. Radcliffe, 2022.

RIGHT
Photo by Lynn Josse for Landmarks Association of St. Louis, 2001.

DAILY RECORD NO.
558

APPEARED IN THE DAILY RECORD
01/06/1903

HOUSE NUMBER SLIP
01/05/1903

OWNER
A. A. Fischer Architectural & Building Company

BUILDER
A. A. Fischer Architectural & Building Company

DESCRIPTION
2-story dwelling; 25.3 feet × 34.3 feet; $4,000

BROKEN FRIEZE
Yes

PART OF A STREETSCAPE
Yes, 1 of 10 (west to east: 5179-5181, 5177, 5175, 5171, 5169, 5165, 5163, 5159, 5157, 5153-5155A)

NEIGHBORHOOD
● Academy

SIDE OF THE STREET
North

STATUS IN 2021
Occupied

5177

CATES AVENUE

ABOVE
Photo by Reed R. Radcliffe, 2022.

RIGHT
Photo provided by Landmarks Association of St. Louis, 1980.

DAILY RECORD **NO.**
558

APPEARED IN THE *DAILY RECORD*
01/06/1903

HOUSE NUMBER SLIP
01/05/1903

OWNER
A. A. Fischer Architectural & Building Company

BUILDER
A. A. Fischer Architectural & Building Company

DESCRIPTION
2-story dwelling; 25.3 feet × 34.3 feet; $4,000

BROKEN FRIEZE
Yes

PART OF A STREETSCAPE
Yes, 1 of 10 (west to east: 5179-5181, 5177, 5175, 5171, 5169, 5165, 5163, 5159, 5157, 5153-5155A)

NEIGHBORHOOD
● Academy

SIDE OF THE STREET
North

STATUS IN 2021
Occupied

5179-5181
CATES AVENUE

ABOVE
Photo by Reed R. Radcliffe, 2022.

RIGHT
Photo by Lynn Josse for Landmarks Association of St. Louis, 2001.

DAILY RECORD NO.
558

APPEARED IN THE DAILY RECORD
01/06/1903

OWNER
A. A. Fischer Architectural & Building Company

BUILDER
A. A. Fischer Architectural & Building Company

DESCRIPTION
2-story dwelling; 25.3 feet × 34.3 feet; $4,000

BROKEN FRIEZE
Yes

PART OF A STREETSCAPE
Yes, 1 of 10 (west to east: 5179-5181, 5177, 5175, 5171, 5169, 5165, 5163, 5159, 5157, 5153-5155A)

NEIGHBORHOOD
● Academy

SIDE OF THE STREET
North

STATUS IN 2021
Occupied

DIRECTORY OF A. A. FISCHER BUILDS | 193

5965-5967

CATES AVENUE

This structure's original address was 5967 Cates Avenue.

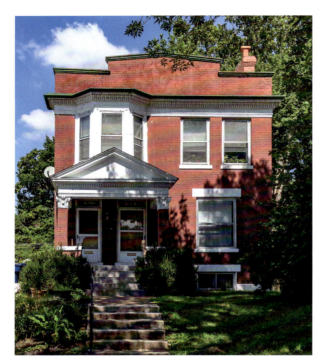

TOP Photo by Reed R. Radcliffe, 2022.
BOTTOM Photo provided by Landmarks Association of St. Louis, 1980.

BUILDING PERMIT NO.
F-1330

DAILY RECORD NO.
1330

APPEARED IN THE DAILY RECORD
04/05/1907

REALTY RECORD AND BUILDER NO.
1330

APPEARED IN THE REALTY RECORD AND BUILDER
04/07/1907

OWNER
A. A. Fischer Realty Company

ARCHITECT
A. A. Fischer Realty Company

BUILDER
A. A. Fischer Realty Company

DESCRIPTION
2-story flats; 26 feet × 48 feet; $4,500

BROKEN FRIEZE
No

PART OF A STREETSCAPE
Yes, 1 of 2 side by side (5967, 5969)

NEIGHBORHOOD
● West End

SIDE OF THE STREET
North

STATUS IN 2021
Occupied

5971-5973

CATES AVENUE
This structure's original address was 5969 Cates Avenue

TOP Photo by Reed R. Radcliffe, 2022.
BOTTOM Photo provided by Landmarks Association of St. Louis, 1980.

BUILDING PERMIT NO.
F-1497

REALTY RECORD AND BUILDER NO.
1497

APPEARED IN THE REALTY RECORD AND BUILDER
05/07/1907

APPEARED IN THE DAILY RECORD
04/16/1907

OWNER
A. A. Fischer Realty Company

ARCHITECT
A. A. Fischer Realty Company

BUILDER
A. A. Fischer Realty Company

DESCRIPTION
2-story flat; 24 feet × 45 feet; $4,000

BROKEN FRIEZE
No

PART OF A STREETSCAPE
Yes, 1 of 2 side by side (5967, 5969)

NEIGHBORHOOD
● West End

SIDE OF THE STREET
North

STATUS IN 2021
Occupied

NOTE Described in a real estate listing in the *St. Louis Post-Dispatch* on September 13, 1908, as "a new 11-room flat; attractive features are the separate entrance scheme, paneled living-room and wide-columned reception hall; Dutch dining-rooms, attractively treated. Rooms are perfect for light and ventilation; tiled bathrooms, marble sinks and steel girders."

6003
CATES AVENUE

TOP Photo by Lori Berdak Miller, 2021.
BOTTOM Photo by Nancy Moore Hamilton, 2001.

BUILDING PERMIT NO.
F-1170

DAILY RECORD NO.
1170

APPEARED IN THE DAILY RECORD
03/25/1907

REALTY RECORD AND BUILDER NO.
1170

APPEARED IN THE REALTY RECORD AND BUILDER
04/07/1907

OWNER
A. A. Fischer Realty Company

ARCHITECT
A. A. Fischer Realty Company

BUILDER
A. A. Fischer Realty Company

DESCRIPTION
2-story dwelling; 25 feet × 33 feet

BROKEN FRIEZE
Yes

PART OF A STREETSCAPE
Yes, 1 of 2 side by side (6003, 6007)

NEIGHBORHOOD
● West End

SIDE OF THE STREET
North

STATUS IN 2021
Occupied

6007
CATES AVENUE

TOP Photo by Reed R. Radcliffe, 2022.
BOTTOM Photo by Nancy Moore Hamilton, 2001.

BUILDING PERMIT NO.
F-8654

BUILDING PERMIT DATE
01/24/1909

DAILY RECORD NO.
8654

APPEARED IN THE DAILY RECORD
01/26/1909

OWNER
A. A. Fischer/A. A. Fischer Architectural & Building Company

ARCHITECT
A. A. Fischer Architectural & Building Company

BUILDER
A. A. Fischer

BROKEN FRIEZE
No

PART OF A STREETSCAPE
Yes, 1 of 2 side by side (6003, 6007)

NEIGHBORHOOD
● West End

SIDE OF THE STREET
North

STATUS IN 2021
Restored

6029
CATES AVENUE

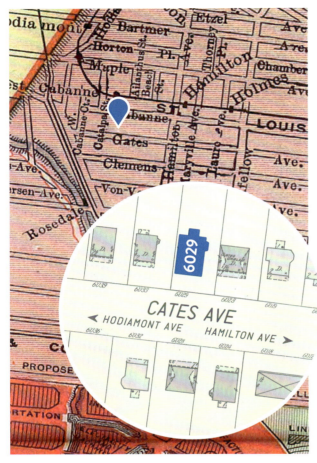

ABOVE
David Rumsey Map Collection, David Rumsey Map Center, Stanford Libraries at Stanford University.

CIRCLE
Sanborn Fire Insurance Map from Saint Louis, Independent City, Missouri. Vol. 6, 1909.

BUILDING PERMIT NO.
D-8879

APPEARED IN THE *BUILDER*
08/24/1903

DAILY RECORD **NO.**
879

APPEARED IN THE *DAILY RECORD*
08/17/1903

OWNER
A. A. Fischer Architectural & Building Company

ARCHITECT
A. A. Fischer Architectural & Building Company

BUILDER
A. A. Fischer Architectural & Building Company

DESCRIPTION
2-story residence; 25 feet, 2 inches × 35 feet; $4,000

BROKEN FRIEZE
Unknown

PART OF A STREETSCAPE
No

NEIGHBORHOOD
● West End

SIDE OF THE STREET
North

STATUS IN 2021
Razed

5575

CHAMBERLAIN AVENUE

ABOVE Photos by Reed R. Radcliffe, 2022.

DAILY RECORD NO.
589

APPEARED IN THE DAILY RECORD
03/05/1902

OWNER
A. A. Fischer

BUILDER
A. A. Fischer

DESCRIPTION
2-story dwelling; 31.5 feet × 35 feet

BROKEN FRIEZE
Yes

PART OF A STREETSCAPE
Yes, 1 of 2 side by side (5575, 5579)

NEIGHBORHOOD
● West End

SIDE OF THE STREET
North

STATUS IN 2021
Occupied

5579

CHAMBERLAIN AVENUE

ABOVE Photo by Reed R. Radcliffe, 2022.

DAILY RECORD NO.
589

APPEARED IN THE *DAILY RECORD*
03/05/1902

OWNER
A. A. Fischer

BUILDER
A. A. Fischer

DESCRIPTION
2-story dwelling; 31.5 feet × 35 feet

BROKEN FRIEZE
Yes

PART OF A STREETSCAPE
Yes, 1 of 2 side by side (5575, 5579)

NEIGHBORHOOD
● West End

SIDE OF THE STREET
North

STATUS IN 2021
Occupied

915

CLARENDON AVENUE

ABOVE Photo by Reed R. Radcliffe, 2022.

DAILY RECORD NO.
2200

APPEARED IN THE DAILY RECORD
11/29/1904

OWNER
A. A. Fischer Architectural & Building Company

BUILDER
A. A. Fischer Architectural & Building Company

DESCRIPTION
2-story dwelling; 20 feet × 33 feet

BROKEN FRIEZE
Originally, yes; as of 2021, no

PART OF A STREETSCAPE
Yes, 1 of 3 (north to south 919, 917, 915)

NEIGHBORHOOD
● Academy

SIDE OF THE STREET
West

STATUS IN 2021
Occupied

917
CLARENDON AVENUE

ABOVE
Photo by Reed R. Radcliffe, 2022.

RIGHT
Photo provided by Landmarks Association of St. Louis, 1980.

DAILY RECORD NO.
2200

APPEARED IN THE *DAILY RECORD*
11/29/1904

OWNER
A. A. Fischer Architectural & Building Company

BUILDER
A. A. Fischer Architectural & Building Company

DESCRIPTION
2-story dwelling; 20 feet × 33 feet

BROKEN FRIEZE
Yes

PART OF A STREETSCAPE
Yes, 1 of 3 (north to south: 919, 917, 915)

NEIGHBORHOOD
● Academy

SIDE OF THE STREET
West

STATUS IN 2021
Occupied

919
CLARENDON AVENUE

ABOVE
Photo by Reed R. Radcliffe, 2022.

RIGHT
Photo provided by Landmarks Association of St. Louis, 1980.

DAILY RECORD NO.
2200

APPEARED IN THE DAILY RECORD
11/29/1904

OWNER
A. A. Fischer Architectural & Building Company

BUILDER
A. A. Fischer Architectural & Building Company

DESCRIPTION
2-story dwelling; 20 feet × 33 feet

BROKEN FRIEZE
No

PART OF A STREETSCAPE
Yes, 1 of 3 (north to south: 919, 917, 915)

NEIGHBORHOOD
● Academy

SIDE OF THE STREET
West

STATUS IN 2021
Occupied

5725-5727
CLEMENS AVENUE

HOUSE NUMBER SLIP
07/22/1907

DESCRIPTION
1 house; 26 feet wide

BROKEN FRIEZE
No

PART OF A STREETSCAPE
No

NEIGHBORHOOD
● West End

SIDE OF THE STREET
North

STATUS IN 2021
Occupied

TOP
Photo by Lori Berdak Miller, 2021.

LEFT
Photo by Nancy Moore Hamilton, 2001.

3815
CLEVELAND AVENUE

ABOVE Photo by Reed R. Radcliffe, 2022.

DAILY RECORD NO.
511

APPEARED IN THE *DAILY RECORD*
12/18/1902

OWNER
Cleveland Realty & Building Company

BUILDER
Cleveland Realty & Building Company

DESCRIPTION
2-story dwelling; 25 feet × 34.5 feet; $3,500

BROKEN FRIEZE
Yes

PART OF A STREETSCAPE
Yes, 1 of 5 (west to east: 3825, 3823, 3821, 3817, 3815)

NEIGHBORHOOD
● Shaw

SIDE OF THE STREET
North

STATUS IN 2021
Restored

3817

CLEVELAND AVENUE

DAILY RECORD NO.
511

APPEARED IN THE DAILY RECORD
12/18/1902

OWNER
Cleveland Realty & Building Company

BUILDER
Cleveland Realty & Building Company

DESCRIPTION
2-story dwelling; 25 feet × 34.5 feet; $3,500

BROKEN FRIEZE
No

PART OF A STREETSCAPE
Yes, 1 of 5 (west to east: 3825, 3823, 3821, 3817, 3815)

NEIGHBORHOOD
● Shaw

SIDE OF THE STREET
North

STATUS IN 2021
Occupied

TOP
Photo by Reed R. Radcliffe, 2022.

LEFT
Photo by Lori Berdak Miller, 2021.

3821

CLEVELAND AVENUE

DAILY RECORD NO.
511

APPEARED IN THE DAILY RECORD
12/18/1902

OWNER
Cleveland Realty & Building Company

BUILDER
Cleveland Realty & Building Company

DESCRIPTION
2-story dwelling; 25 feet × 34.5 feet; $3,500

BROKEN FRIEZE
Yes

PART OF A STREETSCAPE
Yes, 1 of 5 (west to east: 3825, 3823, 3821, 3817, 3815)

NEIGHBORHOOD
● Shaw

SIDE OF THE STREET
North

STATUS IN 2021
Restored

TOP
Photo by Reed R. Radcliffe, 2022.
LEFT
Photo by Joan Young, 2006.

3823

CLEVELAND AVENUE

DAILY RECORD NO.
511

APPEARED IN THE DAILY RECORD
12/18/1902

OWNER
Cleveland Realty & Building Company

BUILDER
Cleveland Realty & Building Company

DESCRIPTION
2-story dwelling; 25 feet × 34.5 feet; $3,500

BROKEN FRIEZE
Currently, no; originally, most likely, yes

PART OF A STREETSCAPE
Yes, 1 of 5 (west to east: 3825, 3823, 3821, 3817, 3815)

NEIGHBORHOOD
● Shaw

SIDE OF THE STREET
North

STATUS IN 2021
Occupied

TOP
Photo by Reed R. Radcliffe, 2022.

LEFT
Photo by Joan Young, 2006.

3825

CLEVELAND AVENUE

DAILY RECORD NO.
511

APPEARED IN THE DAILY RECORD
12/18/1902

OWNER
Cleveland Realty & Building Company

BUILDER
Cleveland Realty & Building Company

DESCRIPTION
2-story dwelling; 25 feet × 34.5 feet; $3,500

BROKEN FRIEZE
Yes

PART OF A STREETSCAPE
Yes, 1 of 5 (west to east: 3825, 3823, 3821, 3817, 3815)

NEIGHBORHOOD
● Shaw

SIDE OF THE STREET
North

STATUS IN 2021
Restored

TOP
Photo by Reed R. Radcliffe, 2022.

LEFT
Photo by Joan Young, 2006.

3253

COPELIN AVENUE

DAILY RECORD NO.
780

APPEARED IN THE DAILY RECORD
07/30/1903

OWNER
Charles A. Lange

ARCHITECT
A. A. Fischer Architectural & Building Company

BUILDER
A. A. Fischer Architectural & Building Company

DESCRIPTION
2-story brick dwelling; 35 feet × 37 feet; $6,000

BROKEN FRIEZE
Unknown

PART OF A STREETSCAPE
No

NEIGHBORHOOD
● Compton Heights

SIDE OF THE STREET
North

STATUS IN 2021
Razed

ABOVE
David Rumsey Map Collection, David Rumsey Map Center, Stanford Libraries at Stanford University.

CIRCLE
St. Louis Building Department Atlases, 1943–1946.
St. Louis Public Library.

7320

DORSET AVENUE

BUILDING PERMIT NO.
4722

BUILDING PERMIT DATE
04/04/1929

BUILDING PERMIT FILED BY
A. A. Fischer

DESCRIPTION
1-story brick residence

BROKEN FRIEZE
No

PART OF A STREETSCAPE
No

NEIGHBORHOOD
● University City

SIDE OF THE STREET
South

STATUS IN 2021
Restored

TOP AND CENTER
Photos by Reed R. Radcliffe, 2022.

BOTTOM
Photo by Nancy Moore Hamilton, 2000.

5032-5034

ENRIGHT AVENUE

This structure's original address was 5032-32A Enright Avenue.

ABOVE
Photo by Reed R. Radcliffe, 2022.

RIGHT
Photo provided by Landmarks Association of St. Louis, 1980.

BUILDING PERMIT NO.
D-8107

BUILDING PERMIT DATE
04/07/1903

DAILY RECORD NO.
107

APPEARED IN THE DAILY RECORD
04/08/1903

OWNER
A. A. Fischer Building & Architectural Company

ARCHITECT
A. A. Fischer Building & Architectural Company

BUILDER
A. A. Fischer Building & Architectural Company

DESCRIPTION
2-story flats; 26.5 feet × 45 feet

BROKEN FRIEZE
Yes

PART OF A STREETSCAPE
No

NEIGHBORHOOD
● Academy

SIDE OF THE STREET
South

STATUS IN 2021
Occupied

3655

FLORA PLACE

ABOVE Photo by Reed R. Radcliffe, 2022.

BUILDING PERMIT NO.
D-9616

BUILDING PERMIT DATE
12/03/1903

APPEARED IN THE *BUILDER*
12/14/1903

***DAILY RECORD* NO.**
616

APPEARED IN THE *DAILY RECORD*
Dec. 1903

OWNER
C. A. Stevenson

ARCHITECT
A. A. Fischer

BUILDER
A. A. Fischer Architectural & Building Company

DESCRIPTION
2-story residence; 46 feet × 46 feet; $17,000

BROKEN FRIEZE
Yes

PART OF A STREETSCAPE
No

NEIGHBORHOOD
● Shaw

SIDE OF THE STREET
North

STATUS IN 2021
Restored

3832

FLORA PLACE

ABOVE
Photo by Reed R. Radcliffe, 2022.

RIGHT
Photo by Nancy Moore Hamilton, 2000.

DAILY RECORD NO.
889

THE *BUILDER* NO.
889

APPEARED IN THE *BUILDER*
July 1904

OWNER
Mrs. Emilie Barthels

ARCHITECT
A. A. Fischer Architectural & Building Company

BUILDER
A. A. Fischer Architectural & Building Company

DESCRIPTION
2-story dwelling; 28 feet × 50 feet

BROKEN FRIEZE
No

PART OF A STREETSCAPE
No

NEIGHBORHOOD
● Shaw

SIDE OF THE STREET
South

STATUS IN 2021
Restored

3924

FLORA PLACE

REALTY RECORD AND BUILDER NO.
4348

APPEARED IN THE REALTY RECORD AND BUILDER
Feb. 1908

OWNER
A. A. Fischer Realty Company

ARCHITECT
A. A. Fischer Architectural & Building Company

BUILDER
A. A. Fischer Architectural & Building Company

DESCRIPTION
2-story dwelling; 25 feet × 35 feet; $5,000

BROKEN FRIEZE
No

PART OF A STREETSCAPE
No

NEIGHBORHOOD
● Shaw

SIDE OF THE STREET
South

STATUS IN 2021
Restored

TOP AND BOTTOM
Photos by Reed R. Radcliffe, 2022.

3441

HALLIDAY AVENUE

BUILDING PERMIT NO.
E-3639

BUILDING PERMIT DATE
04/26/1905

DAILY RECORD NO.
3639

APPEARED IN THE DAILY RECORD
04/27/1905

OWNER
M. W. Feldman and Marian V. Feldman

ARCHITECT
A. A. Fischer/A. A. Fischer Architectural & Building Company

BUILDER
A. A. Fischer/A. A. Fischer Architectural & Building Company

DESCRIPTION
2-story brick dwelling; 27 feet × 36 feet

BROKEN FRIEZE
Yes

PART OF A STREETSCAPE
No

NEIGHBORHOOD
● Tower Grove East

SIDE OF THE STREET
North

STATUS IN 2021
Restored

TOP AND BOTTOM
Photos by Reed R. Radcliffe, 2022.

3525-3527
HALLIDAY AVENUE

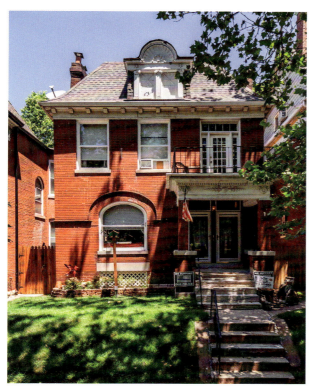

ABOVE
Photo by Reed R. Radcliffe, 2022.

RIGHT
Photo by Nancy Moore Hamilton, 2000.

DAILY RECORD NO.
3633

APPEARED IN THE DAILY RECORD
04/27/1905

OWNER
A. H. Witte

ARCHITECT
A. A. Fischer Architectural & Building Company

BUILDER
A. A. Fischer Architectural & Building Company

DESCRIPTION
2-story flats; 29 feet × 55 feet

BROKEN FRIEZE
No

PART OF A STREETSCAPE
Yes, 1 of 2 side by side (3525-3527, 3529-3531)

NEIGHBORHOOD
● Tower Grove East

SIDE OF THE STREET
North

STATUS IN 2021
Occupied

3529-3531

HALLIDAY AVENUE

ABOVE
Photo by Reed R. Radcliffe, 2022.

RIGHT
Photo by Nancy Moore Hamilton, 2000.

DAILY RECORD NO.
3633

APPEARED IN THE DAILY RECORD
04/27/1905

OWNER
A. H. Witte

ARCHITECT
A. A. Fischer Architectural & Building Company

BUILDER
A. A. Fischer Architectural & Building Company

DESCRIPTION
2-story flats; 29 feet × 55 feet

BROKEN FRIEZE
No

PART OF A STREETSCAPE
Yes, 1 of 2 side by side (3525-3527, 3529-3531)

NEIGHBORHOOD
● Tower Grove East

SIDE OF THE STREET
North

STATUS IN 2021
Restored

3631

HARTFORD STREET

BUILDING PERMIT NO.
F-5913

BUILDING PERMIT DATE
05/29/1908

REALTY RECORD AND BUILDER NO.
5913

APPEARED IN THE REALTY RECORD AND BUILDER
June 1908

OWNER
A. A. Fischer Realty Company

ARCHITECT
A. A. Fischer Realty Company

BUILDER
A. A. Fischer Realty Company

DESCRIPTION
2.5-story dwelling; 25 feet × 35 feet; $5,000

BROKEN FRIEZE
Yes

PART OF A STREETSCAPE
No

NEIGHBORHOOD
● Tower Grove East

SIDE OF THE STREET
North

STATUS IN 2021
Restored

TOP
Photo by Reed R. Radcliffe, 2022.

LEFT
Photo by Lori Berdak Miller, 2022.

3222

HAWTHORNE BOULEVARD

DAILY RECORD NO.
4911

APPEARED IN THE DAILY RECORD
08/24/1905

OWNER
Henry Scheer

ARCHITECT
A. A. Fischer Architectural & Building Company

BUILDER
A. A. Fischer Architectural & Building Company

DESCRIPTION
2-story dwelling; 40 feet × 36 feet

BROKEN FRIEZE
Yes

PART OF A STREETSCAPE
No

NEIGHBORHOOD
● Compton Heights

SIDE OF THE STREET
South

STATUS IN 2021
Restored

TOP, CENTER AND BOTTOM
Photos by Reed R. Radcliffe, 2022.

2244

S. JEFFERSON AVENUE

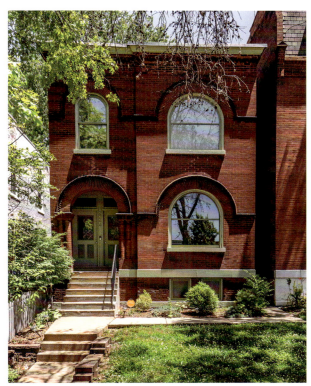

BUILDING PERMIT NO.
B-9531

BUILDING PERMIT DATE
07/09/1894

APPEARED IN THE *DAILY RECORD*
07/10/1894

OWNER
A. A. Fischer

BUILDER
A. A. Fischer

DESCRIPTION
1 house, 22 feet wide

BROKEN FRIEZE
No

PART OF A STREETSCAPE
No

NEIGHBORHOOD
● McKinley Heights

SIDE OF THE STREET
East

STATUS IN 2021
Restored

TOP
Photo by Reed R. Radcliffe, 2022.

LEFT
Photo by Nancy Moore Hamilton, 2001.

NOTE The first time Fischer's name appears on a building permit is July 10, 1894, for this property. This house is considered the very first Fischer structure.

5201
KENSINGTON AVENUE

ABOVE Photo by Reed R. Radcliffe, 2022.

DAILY RECORD NO.
1887

APPEARED IN THE DAILY RECORD
10/22/1904

HOUSE NUMBER CERTIFICATE
10/21/1904

OWNER
A. A. Fischer Architectural & Building Company

BUILDER
A. A. Fischer Architectural & Building Company

DESCRIPTION
2-story dwelling; 23 feet × 35 feet

BROKEN FRIEZE
Yes

PART OF A STREETSCAPE
Yes, originally 1 of 14 (west to east: 5235-5237, 5231, 5229, 5227, 5225, 5223, 5221, 5219, 5215-5217, 5211, 5209, 5207, 5205, 5201)

NEIGHBORHOOD
● Academy

SIDE OF THE STREET
North

STATUS IN 2021
Occupied

5205

KENSINGTON AVENUE

ABOVE Photo by Reed R. Radcliffe, 2022.

DAILY RECORD NO.
1887

APPEARED IN THE DAILY RECORD
10/22/1904

HOUSE NUMBER CERTIFICATE
10/21/1904

OWNER
A. A. Fischer Architectural & Building Company

BUILDER
A. A. Fischer Architectural & Building Company

DESCRIPTION
2-story dwelling; 23 feet × 35 feet

BROKEN FRIEZE
Unknown

PART OF A STREETSCAPE
Yes, originally 1 of 14 (west to east: 5235-5237, 5231, 5229, 5227, 5225, 5223, 5221, 5219, 5215-5217, 5211, 5209, 5207, 5205, 5201)

NEIGHBORHOOD
● Academy

SIDE OF THE STREET
North

STATUS IN 2021
Razed

5207

KENSINGTON AVENUE

TOP Photo by Reed R. Radcliffe, 2022.
BOTTOM Photo by Lori Berdak Miller, 2022.

***DAILY RECORD* NO.**
1887

APPEARED IN THE *DAILY RECORD*
10/22/1904

HOUSE NUMBER CERTIFICATE
10/21/1904

OWNER
A. A. Fischer Architectural & Building Company

BUILDER
A. A. Fischer Architectural & Building Company

DESCRIPTION
2-story dwelling; 23 feet × 35 feet

BROKEN FRIEZE
Yes

PART OF A STREETSCAPE
Yes, originally 1 of 14 (west to east: 5235-5237, 5231, 5229, 5227, 5225, 5223, 5221, 5219, 5215-5217, 5211, 5209, 5207, 5205, 5201)

NEIGHBORHOOD
● Academy

SIDE OF THE STREET
North

STATUS IN 2021
Occupied

5209
KENSINGTON AVENUE

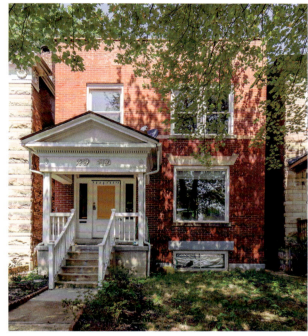

ABOVE Photo by Reed R. Radcliffe, 2022.

DAILY RECORD NO.
1887

APPEARED IN THE DAILY RECORD
10/22/1904

HOUSE NUMBER CERTIFICATE
10/21/1904

OWNER
A. A. Fischer Architectural & Building Company

BUILDER
A. A. Fischer Architectural & Building Company

DESCRIPTION
2-story dwelling; 23 feet × 35 feet

BROKEN FRIEZE
No

PART OF A STREETSCAPE
Yes, originally 1 of 14 (west to east: 5235-5237, 5231, 5229, 5227, 5225, 5223, 5221, 5219, 5215-5217, 5211, 5209, 5207, 5205, 5201)

NEIGHBORHOOD
● Academy

SIDE OF THE STREET
North

STATUS IN 2021
Occupied

5211
KENSINGTON AVENUE

ABOVE Photo by Reed R. Radcliffe, 2022.

DAILY RECORD NO.
1887

APPEARED IN THE DAILY RECORD
10/22/1904

HOUSE NUMBER CERTIFICATE
10/21/1904

OWNER
A. A. Fischer Architectural & Building Company

BUILDER
A. A. Fischer Architectural & Building Company

DESCRIPTION
2-story dwelling; 23 feet × 35 feet

BROKEN FRIEZE
Yes

PART OF A STREETSCAPE
Yes, originally 1 of 14 (west to east: 5235-5237, 5231, 5229, 5227, 5225, 5223, 5221, 5219, 5215-5217, 5211, 5209, 5207, 5205, 5201)

NEIGHBORHOOD
● Academy

SIDE OF THE STREET
North

STATUS IN 2021
Occupied

5215-5217

KENSINGTON AVENUE

ABOVE Photo by Reed R. Radcliffe, 2022.

DAILY RECORD NO.
346

APPEARED IN THE DAILY RECORD
04/13/1904

APPEARED IN THE BUILDER
May 1904

HOUSE NUMBER CERTIFICATE
04/12/1904

OWNER
A. A. Fischer Architectural & Building Company

ARCHITECT
A. A. Fischer Architectural & Building Company

BUILDER
A. A. Fischer Architectural & Building Company

DESCRIPTION
2-story flat

BROKEN FRIEZE
Yes

PART OF A STREETSCAPE
Yes, originally 1 of 14 (west to east: 5235-5237, 5231, 5229, 5227, 5225, 5223, 5221, 5219, 5215-5217, 5211, 5209, 5207, 5205, 5201)

NEIGHBORHOOD
● Academy

SIDE OF THE STREET
North

STATUS IN 2021
Condemned

5219

KENSINGTON AVENUE

ABOVE Photo by Reed R. Radcliffe, 2022.

DAILY RECORD NO.
346

APPEARED IN THE DAILY RECORD
04/13/1904

APPEARED IN THE BUILDER
May 1904

HOUSE NUMBER CERTIFICATE
04/12/1904

OWNER
A. A. Fischer Architectural & Building Company

ARCHITECT
A. A. Fischer Architectural & Building Company

BUILDER
A. A. Fischer Architectural & Building Company

DESCRIPTION
2-story flat

BROKEN FRIEZE
Unknown

PART OF A STREETSCAPE
Yes, originally 1 of 14 (west to east: 5235-5237, 5231, 5229, 5227, 5225, 5223, 5221, 5219, 5215-5217, 5211, 5209, 5207, 5205, 5201)

NEIGHBORHOOD
● Academy

SIDE OF THE STREET
North

STATUS IN 2021
Razed

5221
KENSINGTON AVENUE

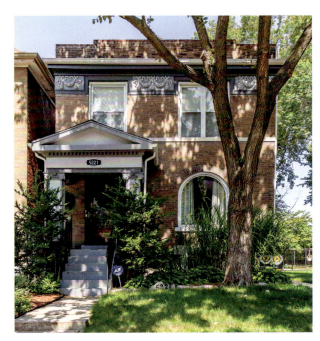

ABOVE Photo by Reed R. Radcliffe, 2022.

DAILY RECORD NO.
346

APPEARED IN THE DAILY RECORD
04/13/1904

APPEARED IN THE BUILDER
May 1904

HOUSE NUMBER CERTIFICATE
04/12/1904

OWNER
A. A. Fischer Architectural & Building Company

ARCHITECT
A. A. Fischer Architectural & Building Company

BUILDER
A. A. Fischer Architectural & Building Company

DESCRIPTION
2-story flat

BROKEN FRIEZE
Yes

PART OF A STREETSCAPE
Yes, originally 1 of 14 (west to east: 5235-5237, 5231, 5229, 5227, 5225, 5223, 5221, 5219, 5215-5217, 5211, 5209, 5207, 5205, 5201)

NEIGHBORHOOD
● Academy

SIDE OF THE STREET
North

STATUS IN 2021
Restored

5223

KENSINGTON AVENUE

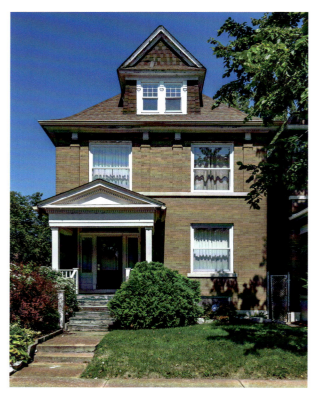

ABOVE Photo by Reed R. Radcliffe, 2022.

DAILY RECORD NO.
346

APPEARED IN THE DAILY RECORD
04/13/1904

APPEARED IN THE BUILDER
May 1904

HOUSE NUMBER CERTIFICATE
04/12/1904

OWNER
A. A. Fischer Architectural & Building Company

ARCHITECT
A. A. Fischer Architectural & Building Company

BUILDER
A. A. Fischer Architectural & Building Company

DESCRIPTION
2-story flat

BROKEN FRIEZE
No

PART OF A STREETSCAPE
Yes, originally 1 of 14 (west to east: 5235-5237, 5231, 5229, 5227, 5225, 5223, 5221, 5219, 5215-5217, 5211, 5209, 5207, 5205, 5201)

NEIGHBORHOOD
● Academy

SIDE OF THE STREET
North

STATUS IN 2021
Occupied

5225
KENSINGTON AVENUE

ABOVE Photo by Reed R. Radcliffe, 2022.

DAILY RECORD NO.
346

APPEARED IN THE *DAILY RECORD*
04/13/1904

APPEARED IN THE *BUILDER*
May 1904

HOUSE NUMBER CERTIFICATE
04/12/1904

OWNER
A. A. Fischer Architectural & Building Company

ARCHITECT
A. A. Fischer Architectural & Building Company

BUILDER
A. A. Fischer Architectural & Building Company

DESCRIPTION
2-story flat

BROKEN FRIEZE
Unknown

PART OF A STREETSCAPE
Yes, originally 1 of 14 (west to east: 5235-5237, 5231, 5229, 5227, 5225, 5223, 5221, 5219, 5215-5217, 5211, 5209, 5207, 5205, 5201)

NEIGHBORHOOD
● Academy

SIDE OF THE STREET
North

STATUS IN 2021
Razed

5227
KENSINGTON AVENUE

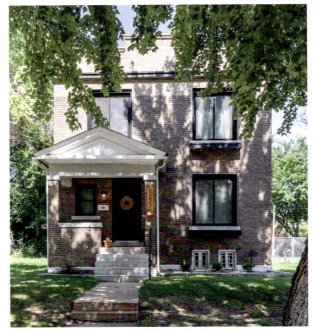

ABOVE
Photo by Reed R. Radcliffe, 2022.

RIGHT
Photo by Lori Berdak Miller, 2022.

DAILY RECORD NO.
346

APPEARED IN THE DAILY RECORD
04/13/1904

APPEARED IN THE BUILDER
May 1904

HOUSE NUMBER CERTIFICATE
04/12/1904

OWNER
A. A. Fischer Architectural & Building Company

ARCHITECT
A. A. Fischer Architectural & Building Company

BUILDER
A. A. Fischer Architectural & Building Company

DESCRIPTION
2-story flat

BROKEN FRIEZE
Currently, no; originally, likely

PART OF A STREETSCAPE
Yes, originally 1 of 14 (west to east: 5235-5237, 5231, 5229, 5227, 5225, 5223, 5221, 5219, 5215-5217, 5211, 5209, 5207, 5205, 5201)

NEIGHBORHOOD
● Academy

SIDE OF THE STREET
North

STATUS IN 2021
Occupied

5229
KENSINGTON AVENUE

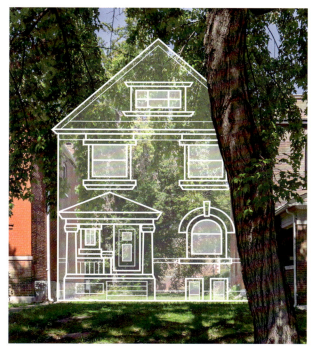

ABOVE Photo by Reed R. Radcliffe, 2022.

DAILY RECORD NO.
346

APPEARED IN THE DAILY RECORD
04/13/1904

APPEARED IN THE BUILDER
May 1904

HOUSE NUMBER CERTIFICATE
04/12/1904

OWNER
A. A. Fischer Architectural & Building Company

ARCHITECT
A. A. Fischer Architectural & Building Company

BUILDER
A. A. Fischer Architectural & Building Company

DESCRIPTION
2-story flat

BROKEN FRIEZE
Unknown

PART OF A STREETSCAPE
Yes, originally 1 of 14 (west to east: 5235-5237, 5231, 5229, 5227, 5225, 5223, 5221, 5219, 5215-5217, 5211, 5209, 5207, 5205, 5201)

NEIGHBORHOOD
● Academy

SIDE OF THE STREET
North

STATUS IN 2021
Razed

5231

KENSINGTON AVENUE

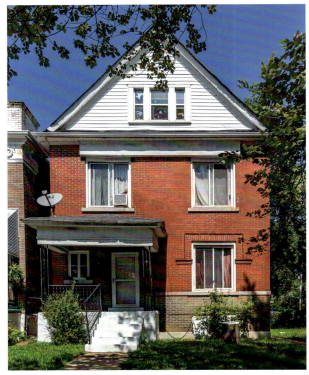

ABOVE
Photo by Reed R. Radcliffe, 2022.

RIGHT
Photo by Lynn Josse for Landmarks Association of St. Louis, 2002.

DAILY RECORD NO.
346

APPEARED IN THE DAILY RECORD
04/13/1904

APPEARED IN THE BUILDER
May 1904

HOUSE NUMBER CERTIFICATE
04/12/1904

OWNER
A. A. Fischer Architectural & Building Company

ARCHITECT
A. A. Fischer Architectural & Building Company

BUILDER
A. A. Fischer Architectural & Building Company

DESCRIPTION
2-story flat

BROKEN FRIEZE
No

PART OF A STREETSCAPE
Yes, originally 1 of 14 (west to east: 5235-5237, 5231, 5229, 5227, 5225, 5223, 5221, 5219, 5215-5217, 5211, 5209, 5207, 5205, 5201)

NEIGHBORHOOD
● Academy

SIDE OF THE STREET
North

STATUS IN 2021
Occupied

5235-5237
KENSINGTON AVENUE

ABOVE
Photo by Reed R. Radcliffe, 2022.

RIGHT
Photo by Lynn Josse for Landmarks Association of St. Louis, 2002.

DAILY RECORD NO.
346

APPEARED IN THE DAILY RECORD
04/13/1904

APPEARED IN THE BUILDER
May 1904

HOUSE NUMBER CERTIFICATE
04/12/1904

OWNER
A. A. Fischer Architectural & Building Company

ARCHITECT
A. A. Fischer Architectural & Building Company

BUILDER
A. A. Fischer Architectural & Building Company

DESCRIPTION
2-story flat

BROKEN FRIEZE
Yes

PART OF A STREETSCAPE
Yes, originally 1 of 14 (west to east: 5235-5237, 5231, 5229, 5227, 5225, 5223, 5221, 5219, 5215-5217, 5211, 5209, 5207, 5205, 5201)

NEIGHBORHOOD
● Academy

SIDE OF THE STREET
North

STATUS IN 2021
Occupied

5931-5933
KINGSBURY AVENUE

ABOVE Photo by Reed R. Radcliffe, 2022.

BUILDING PERMIT NO.
G-6503

BUILDING PERMIT DATE
11/16/1910

REALTY RECORD AND BUILDER NO.
6503

APPEARED IN THE REALTY RECORD AND BUILDER
Nov. 1910

OWNER
A. A. Fischer Realty Company

ARCHITECT
A. A. Fischer Realty Company

BUILDER
A. A. Fischer/A. A. Fischer Realty Company

DESCRIPTION
3-story brick tenement; 58 feet × 42 feet; $10,000

BROKEN FRIEZE
Yes

PART OF A STREETSCAPE
No

NEIGHBORHOOD
● Skinker DeBaliviere

SIDE OF THE STREET
North

STATUS IN 2021
Occupied

6040-6042

KINGSBURY AVENUE

Building permit records indicate this structure's address was 6040-6042 Kingsbury Place.

ABOVE Photo by Reed R. Radcliffe, 2022.

BUILDING PERMIT NO.
G-847

BUILDING PERMIT DATE
06/24/1909

DAILY RECORD NO.
847

REALTY RECORD AND BUILDER NO.
847

APPEARED IN THE REALTY RECORD AND BUILDER
July 1909

OWNER
A. A. Fischer Realty Company

ARCHITECT
A. A. Fischer Realty Company

BUILDER
A. A. Fischer Realty Company

DESCRIPTION
3-story tenement;
52 feet × 33 feet; $8,000

BROKEN FRIEZE
No

PART OF A STREETSCAPE
No

NEIGHBORHOOD
● Skinker DeBaliviere

SIDE OF THE STREET
South

STATUS IN 2021
Restored

6041–6043
KINGSBURY AVENUE

ABOVE Photo by Reed R. Radcliffe, 2022.

BUILDING PERMIT NO.
G-2371

BUILDING PERMIT DATE
10/30/1909

DAILY RECORD NO.
2371

REALTY RECORD AND BUILDER NO.
2371

APPEARED IN THE *REALTY RECORD AND BUILDER*
Nov. 1909

OWNER
A. A. Fischer Realty Company

ARCHITECT
A. A. Fischer Realty Company

BUILDER
A. A. Fischer Realty Company

DESCRIPTION
3-story apartment building; 55 feet × 33 feet; $8,000

BROKEN FRIEZE
No

PART OF A STREETSCAPE
Yes, 1 of 2 apartment buildings side by side (west to east: 6045-6047, 6041-6043)

NEIGHBORHOOD
● Skinker DeBaliviere

SIDE OF THE STREET
North

STATUS IN 2021
Restored

6045-6047
KINGSBURY AVENUE

ABOVE Photo by Reed R. Radcliffe, 2022.

BUILDING PERMIT NO.
G-2371

BUILDING PERMIT DATE
10/30/1909

DAILY RECORD NO.
2371

REALTY RECORD AND BUILDER NO.
2371

APPEARED IN THE REALTY RECORD AND BUILDER
Nov. 1909

OWNER
A. A. Fischer Realty Company

ARCHITECT
A. A. Fischer Realty Company

BUILDER
A. A. Fischer Realty Company

DESCRIPTION
3-story apartment building; 55 feet × 33 feet; $8,000

BROKEN FRIEZE
No

PART OF A STREETSCAPE
Yes, 1 of 2 apartment buildings side by side (west to east: 6045-6047, 6041-6043)

NEIGHBORHOOD
● Skinker DeBaliviere

SIDE OF THE STREET
North

STATUS IN 2021
Restored

6139
KINGSBURY AVENUE

ABOVE Photo by Reed R. Radcliffe, 2022.

REALTY RECORD AND BUILDER NO.
8033

APPEARED IN THE REALTY RECORD AND BUILDER
Dec. 1908

HOUSE NUMBER SLIP
11/18/1908

OWNER
Mr. and Mrs. H. L. McGuire

ARCHITECT
A. A. Fischer Architectural & Building Company

BUILDER
A. A. Fischer Architectural & Building Company

DESCRIPTION
2-story dwelling; 36 feet × 55 feet; $6,500

BROKEN FRIEZE
Yes

PART OF A STREETSCAPE
No

NEIGHBORHOOD
● Skinker DeBaliviere

SIDE OF THE STREET
North

STATUS IN 2021
Restored

6192

KINGSBURY AVENUE

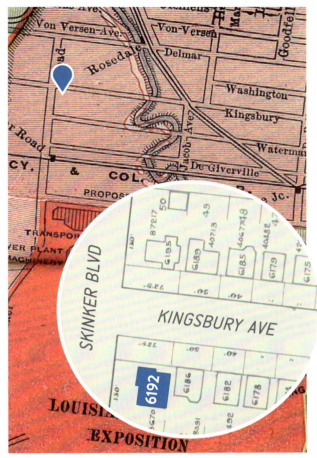

ABOVE
David Rumsey Map Collection, David Rumsey Map Center, Stanford Libraries at Stanford University.

CIRCLE
St. Louis Building Department Atlases, 1943–1946.
St. Louis Public Library.

BUILDING PERMIT NO.
F-5829

BUILDING PERMIT DATE
05/21/1908

DAILY RECORD NO.
5829

APPEARED IN THE DAILY RECORD
05/22/1908

REALTY RECORD AND BUILDER NO.
5829

APPEARED IN THE REALTY RECORD AND BUILDER
May 1908

OWNER
A. H. Frederick

ARCHITECT
A. A. Fischer Realty Company

BUILDER
A. A. Fischer Realty Company

DESCRIPTION
2.5-story dwelling; 39 feet × 33 feet; $10,000

BROKEN FRIEZE
Unknown

PART OF A STREETSCAPE
No

NEIGHBORHOOD
● Skinker DeBaliviere

SIDE OF THE STREET
South

STATUS IN 2021
Razed

3228

LAFAYETTE AVENUE

ABOVE Photo by Reed R. Radcliffe, 2022.

DAILY RECORD NO.
2353

APPEARED IN THE DAILY RECORD
12/24/1904

BUILDER
Cleveland Realty & Building Company

OWNER
Cleveland Realty & Building Company

DESCRIPTION
2-story dwelling; 26 feet × 36 feet

BROKEN FRIEZE
No

PART OF A STREETSCAPE
Yes, originally 1 of 5 (west to east: 3244, 3240, 3234-3236, 3232, 3228)

NEIGHBORHOOD
● The Gate District

SIDE OF THE STREET
South

STATUS IN 2021
Occupied

3232
LAFAYETTE AVENUE

DAILY RECORD NO.
2353

APPEARED IN THE DAILY RECORD
12/24/1904

BUILDER
Cleveland Realty & Building Company

OWNER
Cleveland Realty & Building Company

DESCRIPTION
2-story dwelling; 26 feet × 36 feet

BROKEN FRIEZE
No

PART OF A STREETSCAPE
Yes, originally 1 of 5 (west to east: 3244, 3240, 3234-3236, 3232, 3228)

NEIGHBORHOOD
● The Gate District

SIDE OF THE STREET
South

STATUS IN 2021
Occupied

TOP
Photo by Reed R. Radcliffe, 2022.

LEFT
Photo by Joan Young, 2006.

3236

LAFAYETTE AVENUE
This structure's original address was 3234 Lafayette Avenue.

ABOVE Photo by Reed R. Radcliffe, 2022.

DAILY RECORD NO.
2353

APPEARED IN THE DAILY RECORD
12/24/1904

BUILDER
Cleveland Realty & Building Company

OWNER
Cleveland Realty & Building Company

DESCRIPTION
2-story dwelling; 26 feet × 36 feet

BROKEN FRIEZE
No

PART OF A STREETSCAPE
Yes, originally 1 of 5 (west to east: 3244, 3240, 3234-3236, 3232, 3228)

NEIGHBORHOOD
● The Gate District

SIDE OF THE STREET
South

STATUS IN 2021
Occupied

3240
LAFAYETTE AVENUE

DAILY RECORD NO.
2353

APPEARED IN THE DAILY RECORD
12/24/1904

BUILDER
Cleveland Realty & Building Company

OWNER
Cleveland Realty & Building Company

BROKEN FRIEZE
Yes

PART OF A STREETSCAPE
Yes, originally 1 of 5 (west to east: 3244, 3240, 3234-3236, 3232, 3228)

NEIGHBORHOOD
● The Gate District

SIDE OF THE STREET
South

STATUS IN 2021
Restored

TOP
Photo by Reed R. Radcliffe, 2022.

LEFT
Photo by Joan Young, 2006.

3244
LAFAYETTE AVENUE

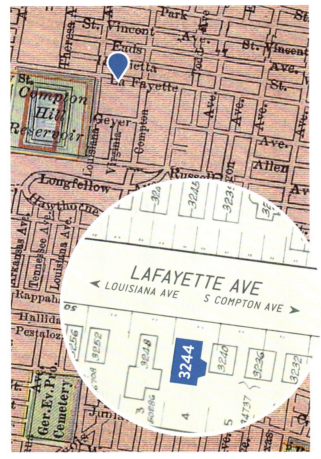

ABOVE
David Rumsey Map Collection, David Rumsey Map Center, Stanford Libraries at Stanford University.

CIRCLE
St. Louis Building Department Atlases, 1943–1946.
St. Louis Public Library.

DAILY RECORD NO.
2353

APPEARED IN THE DAILY RECORD
12/24/1904

BUILDER
Cleveland Realty & Building Company

OWNER
Cleveland Realty & Building Company

DESCRIPTION
2-story dwelling; 26 feet × 36 feet

BROKEN FRIEZE
Unknown

PART OF A STREETSCAPE
Yes, originally 1 of 5 (west to east: 3244, 3240, 3234-3236, 3232, 3228)

NEIGHBORHOOD
● The Gate District

SIDE OF THE STREET
South

STATUS IN 2021
Razed

39

LEWIS PLACE
This structure's original address was 4617 Lewis Place.

TOP Photo by Reed R. Radcliffe, 2022.
BOTTOM LEFT Photo by Nancy Moore Hamilton, 2001.
BOTTOM RIGHT Photo by Mimi Stiritz for Landmarks Association of St. Louis, 1979.

BUILDING PERMIT NO.
E-3637

BUILDING PERMIT DATE
04/26/1905

"USE" PER BUILDING PERMIT
Brick 2-story and attic residence

COST PER BUILDING PERMIT
$7,000

DAILY RECORD NO.
3637

APPEARED IN THE DAILY RECORD
04/27/1905

OWNER
Edith Rogers

ARCHITECT
A. A. Fischer Architectural & Building Company

BUILDER
A. A. Fischer Architectural & Building Company

DESCRIPTION
2-story dwelling; 23 feet × 36 feet

BROKEN FRIEZE
Yes

PART OF A STREETSCAPE
No

NEIGHBORHOOD
● Lewis Place

SIDE OF THE STREET
North

STATUS IN 2021
Restored

NOTE Since 1980 this structure has been recognized as part of the Lewis Place Historic District. Its nomination to the National Register of Historic Places describes it as "Architect/contractor A. A. Fischer's 1906 design . . . exhibits characteristics familiar in his work on other West End private streets. A hallmark of Fischer's style is his flair for combining materials of varied texture and color in a formal composition replete with historical detail. Here, courses of rock-faced and smooth stone alternate on the façade; white terracotta garlands and wreaths are liberally applied at the cornice line and a shell motif ornaments the porch and dormer pediments; polished rose granite columns support classical capitals."

4326

LINDELL BOULEVARD

ABOVE Photo by Lori Berdak Miller, 2022.

REALTY RECORD AND BUILDER NO.
7251

APPEARED IN THE *REALTY RECORD AND BUILDER*
05/06/1906

OWNER
Jennie S. Garvey

ARCHITECT
A. A. Fischer Architectural & Building Company

BUILDER
A. A. Fischer Architectural & Building Company

DESCRIPTION
3-story apartment building; 34 feet × 66 feet; $15,000

BROKEN FRIEZE
No

PART OF A STREETSCAPE
No

NEIGHBORHOOD
● Central West End

SIDE OF THE STREET
South

STATUS IN 2021
Occupied

5225
LINDELL BOULEVARD

ABOVE Photo by Reed R. Radcliffe, 2022.

APPEARED IN THE *BUILDER*
Aug. 1904

***BUILDER* NO.**
1071

APPEARED IN THE *DAILY RECORD*
07/23/1904

OWNER
A. A. Fischer Architectural & Building Company

ARCHITECT
A. A. Fischer Architectural & Building Company

BUILDER
A. A. Fischer Architectural & Building Company

DESCRIPTION
2-story dwelling; 32 feet × 33 feet; $15,000

BROKEN FRIEZE
Yes

PART OF A STREETSCAPE
No

NEIGHBORHOOD
● Central West End

SIDE OF THE STREET
North

STATUS IN 2021
Restored

5190

MAPLE AVENUE

ABOVE Photo by Reed R. Radcliffe, 2022.

BUILDING PERMIT NO.
D-3817

BUILDING PERMIT DATE
04/09/1901

"USE" PER BUILDING PERMIT
2-story brick dwelling

DAILY RECORD NO.
817

APPEARED IN THE DAILY RECORD
04/10/1901

OWNER
A. A. Fischer

ARCHITECT
A. A. Fischer

BUILDER
A. A. Fischer

DESCRIPTION
2-story brick dwelling

BROKEN FRIEZE
Yes

PART OF A STREETSCAPE
Yes, 1 of 2 side by side (west to east: 5194, 5190)

NEIGHBORHOOD
● Academy

SIDE OF THE STREET
South

STATUS IN 2021
Condemned

5194

MAPLE AVENUE

ABOVE Photo by Reed R. Radcliffe, 2022.

BUILDING PERMIT NO.
D-3817

BUILDING PERMIT DATE
04/09/1901

DAILY RECORD NO.
817

APPEARED IN THE DAILY RECORD
04/10/1901

OWNER
A. A. Fischer

ARCHITECT
A. A. Fischer

BUILDER
A. A. Fischer

DESCRIPTION
2-story brick dwelling

BROKEN FRIEZE
Yes

PART OF A STREETSCAPE
Yes, 1 of 2 side by side (west to east: 5194, 5190)

NEIGHBORHOOD
● Academy

SIDE OF THE STREET
South

STATUS IN 2021
Occupied

5240
MAPLE AVENUE

ABOVE
David Rumsey Map Collection, David Rumsey Map Center, Stanford Libraries at Stanford University.

CIRCLE
St. Louis Building Department Atlases, 1943–1946.
St. Louis Public Library.

BUILDING PERMIT NO.
6653

BUILDING PERMIT DATE
03/26/1897

APPEARED IN THE *DAILY RECORD*
03/27/1897

OWNER
A. A. Fischer

BUILDER
A. A. Fischer

DESCRIPTION
2.5-story dwelling

BROKEN FRIEZE
Unknown

PART OF A STREETSCAPE
No

NEIGHBORHOOD
● Academy

SIDE OF THE STREET
South

STATUS IN 2021
Razed

5241

MAPLE AVENUE

ABOVE Photo by Reed R. Radcliffe, 2022.

BUILDING PERMIT NO.
D-3818

BUILDING PERMIT DATE
04/09/1901

DAILY RECORD NO.
818

APPEARED IN THE DAILY RECORD
04/10/1901

OWNER
A. A. Fischer/A. A. Fischer Architectural & Building Company

ARCHITECT
A. A. Fischer Architectural & Building Company

BUILDER
A. A. Fischer/A. A. Fischer Architectural & Building Company

DESCRIPTION
2-story brick dwelling; 31.5 feet × 35 feet; $4,000

BROKEN FRIEZE
Yes

PART OF A STREETSCAPE
No

NEIGHBORHOOD
● Academy

SIDE OF THE STREET
North

STATUS IN 2021
Occupied

5250

MAPLE AVENUE

This structure's original address was 5252 Maple Avenue.

BUILDING PERMIT NO.
D-4266

BUILDING PERMIT DATE
06/19/1901

DAILY RECORD NO.
226

APPEARED IN THE DAILY RECORD
06/21/1901

OWNER
A. A. Fischer Architectural & Building Company

ARCHITECT
A. A. Fischer

BUILDER
A. A. Fischer

DESCRIPTION
2.5-story brick dwelling

BROKEN FRIEZE
Yes

PART OF A STREETSCAPE
No

NEIGHBORHOOD
● Academy

SIDE OF THE STREET
South

STATUS IN 2021
Occupied

TOP Photo by Reed R. Radcliffe, 2022.
BOTTOM Photo by Lynn Josse for Landmarks Association of St. Louis, 2002.

5258

MAPLE AVENUE

ABOVE Photo by Reed R. Radcliffe, 2022.

BUILDING PERMIT NO.
D-4266

BUILDING PERMIT DATE
06/19/1901

DAILY RECORD NO.
226

APPEARED IN THE DAILY RECORD
06/21/1901

OWNER
A. A. Fischer Architectural & Building Company

ARCHITECT
A. A. Fischer

BUILDER
A. A. Fischer

DESCRIPTION
2.5-story brick dwelling

BROKEN FRIEZE
Yes

PART OF A STREETSCAPE
No

NEIGHBORHOOD
● Academy

SIDE OF THE STREET
South

STATUS IN 2021
Under renovation

NOTE The Mount Cabanne–Raymond Place Historic District nomination describes this home as follows: "[It adheres to] late 19th and 20th Century Revival Styles . . . 2 stories high and 2 bays wide. Steep hips meet in T-shape asphalt shingle roof. Limestone façade alternates thin & thick courses of rough-faced stone. Upper windows separated by pilaster. Projecting porch left. Frieze has applied swags. The building appears to be in good condition."

5266

MAPLE AVENUE

ABOVE Photo by Reed R. Radcliffe, 2022.

BUILDING PERMIT NO.
D-3692

BUILDING PERMIT DATE
03/18/1901

DAILY RECORD NO.
692

APPEARED IN THE DAILY RECORD
03/20/1901

OWNER
A. A. Fischer

ARCHITECT
A. A. Fischer

BUILDER
A. A. Fischer

DESCRIPTION
2.5-story brick dwelling; 27.5 feet × 40 feet; $4,000

BROKEN FRIEZE
No

PART OF A STREETSCAPE
Yes, 1 of 2 side by side (west to east: 5268, 5266)

NEIGHBORHOOD
● Academy

SIDE OF THE STREET
South

STATUS IN 2021
Restored

NOTE Although this building was at one time condemned, according to the City of St. Louis's online Address and Property Search portal, its owners invested upward of $240,000 into restoring the property in 2020 and 2021 alone. Its restoration followed the restoration of the property next door at 5268 Maple Avenue.

5268

MAPLE AVENUE

ABOVE Photo by Reed R. Radcliffe, 2022.

BUILDING PERMIT NO.
D-3692

BUILDING PERMIT DATE
03/18/1901

DAILY RECORD NO.
692

APPEARED IN THE DAILY RECORD
03/20/1901

OWNER
A. A. Fischer

ARCHITECT
A. A. Fischer

BUILDER
A. A. Fischer

DESCRIPTION
2-story dwelling; 27.5 feet × 40 feet; $4,000

BROKEN FRIEZE
No

PART OF A STREETSCAPE
Yes, 1 of 2 side by side (west to east: 5268, 5266)

NEIGHBORHOOD
● Academy

SIDE OF THE STREET
South

STATUS IN 2021
Restored

NOTE Like its neighbor to the east at 5266 Maple Avenue, 5268 Maple Avenue was at one time condemned but has been restored. According to the City of St. Louis's online Address and Property Search portal, more than $280,000 was invested in this property between 2019 and 2021.

5312

MAPLE AVENUE

ABOVE Photo by Reed R. Radcliffe, 2022.

APPEARED IN THE *DAILY RECORD*
10/13/1898

OWNER
A. A. Fischer

BUILDER
A. A. Fischer

DESCRIPTION
Dwelling; 26 feet × 36 feet

BROKEN FRIEZE
No

PART OF A STREETSCAPE
Yes, 1 of 2 side by side (west to east: 5314, 5312)

NEIGHBORHOOD
● Visitation Park

SIDE OF THE STREET
South

STATUS IN 2021
Occupied

5314

MAPLE AVENUE

ABOVE Photo by Reed R. Radcliffe, 2022.

APPEARED IN THE *DAILY RECORD*
10/13/1898

OWNER
A. A. Fischer

BUILDER
A. A. Fischer

DESCRIPTION
Dwelling; 26 feet × 36 feet

BROKEN FRIEZE
No

PART OF A STREETSCAPE
Yes, 1 of 2 side by side (west to east: 5314, 5312)

NEIGHBORHOOD
● Visitation Park

SIDE OF THE STREET
South

STATUS IN 2021
Occupied

5415

MAPLE AVENUE

ABOVE Photo by Reed R. Radcliffe, 2022.

BUILDING PERMIT NO.
E-3333

DAILY RECORD NO.
3333

APPEARED IN THE DAILY RECORD
04/06/1905

OWNER
Henry J. Goebbels

ARCHITECT
A. A. Fischer/A. A. Fischer Architectural & Building Company

BUILDER
A. A. Fischer/A. A. Fischer Architectural & Building Company

DESCRIPTION
2-story dwelling; 27 feet × 36 feet

BROKEN FRIEZE
Yes

PART OF A STREETSCAPE
No

NEIGHBORHOOD
● West End

SIDE OF THE STREET
North

STATUS IN 2021
Occupied

5611

MAPLE AVENUE

ABOVE Photo by Lori Berdak Miller, 2021.

BUILDING PERMIT NO.
E-4135

BUILDING PERMIT DATE
06/08/1905

DAILY RECORD NO.
4135

APPEARED IN THE *REALTY RECORD AND BUILDER*
June 1905

OWNER
A. A. Fischer/A. A. Fischer Architectural & Building Company

ARCHITECT
A. A. Fischer/A. A. Fischer Architectural & Building Company

BUILDER
A. A. Fischer/A. A. Fischer Architectural & Building Company

DESCRIPTION
2-story brick dwelling; 26 feet × 35 feet; $4,600

BROKEN FRIEZE
Yes

PART OF A STREETSCAPE
No

NEIGHBORHOOD
● West End

SIDE OF THE STREET
North

STATUS IN 2021
Occupied

5614-5616

MAPLE AVENUE

ABOVE
Photo by Reed R. Radcliffe, 2022.

RIGHT
Photo by Nancy Moore Hamilton, 2001.

BUILDING PERMIT NO.
4748

DAILY RECORD NO.
4748

APPEARED IN THE DAILY RECORD
08/08/1905

APPEARED IN THE BUILDER
Aug. 1905

OWNER
A. A. Fischer/A. A. Fischer Architectural & Building Company

ARCHITECT
A. A. Fischer Architectural & Building Company

BUILDER
A. A. Fischer Architectural & Building Company

DESCRIPTION
2-story flat; 28 feet × 47 feet

BROKEN FRIEZE
Yes

PART OF A STREETSCAPE
Yes, 1 of 2 side by side (west to east: 5618-5620, 5614-5616)

NEIGHBORHOOD
● West End

SIDE OF THE STREET
South

STATUS IN 2021
Occupied

5618-5620

MAPLE AVENUE

ABOVE
Photo by Reed R. Radcliffe, 2022.

RIGHT
Photo by Nancy Moore Hamilton, 2001.

DAILY RECORD NO.
4748

APPEARED IN THE DAILY RECORD
08/08/1905

APPEARED IN THE BUILDER
Aug. 1905

OWNER
A. A. Fischer Architectural & Building Company

ARCHITECT
A. A. Fischer/A. A. Fischer Architectural & Building Company

BUILDER
A. A. Fischer/A. A. Fischer Architectural & Building Company

DESCRIPTION
2-story flat; 28 feet × 47 feet

BROKEN FRIEZE
Yes

PART OF A STREETSCAPE
Yes, 1 of 2 side by side (west to east: 5618-5620, 5614-5616)

NEIGHBORHOOD
● West End

SIDE OF THE STREET
South

STATUS IN 2021
Occupied

5935-5937
MAPLE AVENUE

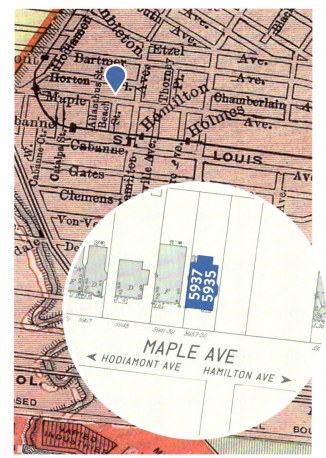

DAILY RECORD NO.
1705

APPEARED IN THE DAILY RECORD
10/04/1904

APPEARED IN THE BUILDER
Oct. 1904

OWNER
A. A. Fischer Architectural & Building Company

ARCHITECT
A. A. Fischer Architectural & Building Company

BUILDER
A. A. Fischer Architectural & Building Company

DESCRIPTION
2-story flat; 26 feet × 44 feet

BROKEN FRIEZE
Yes

PART OF A STREETSCAPE
No

NEIGHBORHOOD
● West End

SIDE OF THE STREET
North

STATUS IN 2021
Razed in 2020

TOP
David Rumsey Map Collection, David Rumsey Map Center, Stanford Libraries at Stanford University.

CIRCLE
Sanborn Fire Insurance Map from Saint Louis, Independent City, Missouri. Vol. 6, 1909.

LEFT
Photo by Nancy Moore Hamilton, 2001.

4849

DR. MARTIN LUTHER KING DRIVE
Dr. Martin Luther King Drive was formerly known as Easton Avenue.

ABOVE
Photo by Reed R. Radcliffe, 2022.

RIGHT
Photo by Nancy Moore Hamilton, 2001.

DAILY RECORD NO.
9570

APPEARED IN THE DAILY RECORD
08/22/1911

OWNER
Herman Laube

ARCHITECT
Roland Fischer

BUILDER
Herman Laube

DESCRIPTION
2-story store and tenement; 20 feet × 50 feet

BROKEN FRIEZE
No

PART OF A STREETSCAPE
Yes, 1 of 5 (west/north to east/south: 4861, 4859, 4853-55-57, 4851, 4849)

NEIGHBORHOOD
● Kingsway East

SIDE OF THE STREET
North/East

STATUS IN 2021
Occupied

NOTE Herman Laube, owner and builder of this property, was the manager of Builders' Manufacturing & Supply Company. A. A. Fischer was part-owner of this business.

4851

DR. MARTIN LUTHER KING DRIVE

Dr. Martin Luther King Drive was formerly known as Easton Avenue.

ABOVE
Photo by Reed R. Radcliffe, 2022.

RIGHT
Photo by Nancy Moore Hamilton, 2001.

DAILY RECORD NO.
5729

APPEARED IN THE DAILY RECORD
11/08/1905

OWNER
A. A. Fischer Architectural & Building Company

ARCHITECT
A. A. Fischer Architectural & Building Company

BUILDER
A. A. Fischer Architectural & Building Company

DESCRIPTION
2-story store and dwelling

BROKEN FRIEZE
Yes

PART OF A STREETSCAPE
Yes, built as 1 of 4 (west/north to east/south: 4861, 4859, 4853-55-57, 4851). A fifth Fischer structure was added to the streetscape at 4849 in 1911.

NEIGHBORHOOD
● Kingsway East

SIDE OF THE STREET
North

STATUS IN 2021
Occupied

4853-4855-4857

DR. MARTIN LUTHER KING DRIVE

Dr. Martin Luther King Drive was formerly known as Easton Avenue.

ABOVE Photo by Reed R. Radcliffe, 2022.

DAILY RECORD NO.
5728

APPEARED IN THE DAILY RECORD
11/08/1905

APPEARED IN THE BUILDER
Nov. 1905

OWNER
A. A. Fischer Architectural & Building Company

ARCHITECT
A. A. Fischer Architectural & Building Company

BUILDER
A. A. Fischer Architectural & Building Company

DESCRIPTION
Double 2-story store and dwelling; 44 feet × 42 feet

BROKEN FRIEZE
Unknown

PART OF A STREETSCAPE
Yes, built as 1 of 4 (west/north to east/south: 4861, 4859, 4853-55-57, 4851). A fifth Fischer structure was added to the streetscape at 4849 in 1911.

NEIGHBORHOOD
● Kingsway East

SIDE OF THE STREET
North

STATUS IN 2021
Razed in 1989

4859

DR. MARTIN LUTHER KING DRIVE
Dr. Martin Luther King Drive was formerly known as Easton Avenue.

ABOVE
Photo by Reed R. Radcliffe, 2022.

RIGHT
Photo by Nancy Moore Hamilton, 2001.

DAILY RECORD NO.
5718

APPEARED IN THE DAILY RECORD
11/07/1905

OWNER
A. A. Fischer Architectural & Building Company

BUILDER
A. A. Fischer Architectural & Building Company

DESCRIPTION
2-story store and flats; 24 feet × 40 feet

BROKEN FRIEZE
Yes

PART OF A STREETSCAPE
Yes, built as 1 of 4 (west/north to east/south: 4861, 4859, 4853-55-57, 4851). A fifth Fischer structure was added to the streetscape at 4849 in 1911.

NEIGHBORHOOD
● Kingsway East

SIDE OF THE STREET
North

STATUS IN 2021
Condemned

4861

DR. MARTIN LUTHER KING DRIVE

Dr. Martin Luther King Drive was formerly known as Easton Avenue.

ABOVE
Photo by Reed R. Radcliffe, 2022.

RIGHT
Photo by Nancy Moore Hamilton, 2001.

DAILY RECORD NO.
5718

APPEARED IN THE DAILY RECORD
11/07/1905

OWNER
A. A. Fischer Architectural & Building Company

BUILDER
A. A. Fischer Architectural & Building Company

DESCRIPTION
2-story store and flat; 24 feet × 40 feet

BROKEN FRIEZE
Yes

PART OF A STREETSCAPE
Yes, built as 1 of 4 (west/north to east/south: 4861, 4859, 4853-55-57, 4851). A fifth Fischer structure was added to the streetscape at 4849 in 1911.

NEIGHBORHOOD
● Kingsway East

SIDE OF THE STREET
North

STATUS IN 2021
Condemned

6163

McPHERSON AVENUE

ABOVE
Photo by Reed R. Radcliffe, 2022.

RIGHT
Photo by Nancy Moore Hamilton, 2001.

DAILY RECORD NO.
3646

APPEARED IN THE DAILY RECORD
10/10/1907

OWNER
Cleveland Realty & Building Company

ARCHITECT
Cleveland Realty & Building Company

BUILDER
Cleveland Realty & Building Company

DESCRIPTION
2-story dwelling; 25 feet × 35 feet

BROKEN FRIEZE
Yes

PART OF A STREETSCAPE
No

NEIGHBORHOOD
● Skinker DeBaliviere

SIDE OF THE STREET
North

STATUS IN 2021
Restored

NOTE In 1902, A. A. Fischer and Harry Mepham incorporated Cleveland Realty & Building Company, so structures built by this company are included in the official tally of Fischer structures.

6168

McPHERSON AVENUE

ABOVE Photo by Reed R. Radcliffe, 2022.

DAILY RECORD NO.
3470

APPEARED IN THE DAILY RECORD
09/25/1907

OWNER
Cleveland Realty & Building Company

ARCHITECT
Cleveland Realty & Building Company

BUILDER
Cleveland Realty & Building Company

DESCRIPTION
2-story dwelling; 25 feet × 35 feet

BROKEN FRIEZE
No

PART OF A STREETSCAPE
Yes, originally 1 of 7 (west to east: 6188, 6186, 6182, 6178, 6174, 6170, 6168)

NEIGHBORHOOD
● Skinker DeBaliviere

SIDE OF THE STREET
South

STATUS IN 2021
Occupied

NOTE Pulitzer Prize–winning playwright William Inge lived here, ca. 1949.

6170

McPHERSON AVENUE

ABOVE Photo by Reed R. Radcliffe, 2022.

BUILDING PERMIT NO.
F-8438

BUILDING PERMIT DATE
12/30/1908

REALTY RECORD AND BUILDER NO.
8438

APPEARED IN THE REALTY RECORD AND BUILDER
01/1909

OWNER
A. A. Fischer Realty Company

ARCHITECT
A. A. Fischer Realty Company

BUILDER
A. A. Fischer Realty Company

DESCRIPTION
2-story dwelling; 30 feet × 32 feet; $5,000

BROKEN FRIEZE
No

PART OF A STREETSCAPE
Yes, originally 1 of 7 (west to east: 6188, 6186, 6182, 6178, 6174, 6170, 6168)

NEIGHBORHOOD
● Skinker DeBaliviere

SIDE OF THE STREET
South

STATUS IN 2021
Restored

6171
McPHERSON AVENUE

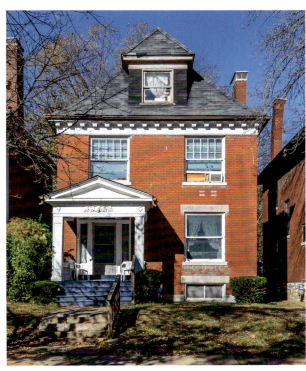

ABOVE Photo by Reed R. Radcliffe, 2022.

DAILY RECORD NO.
3646

APPEARED IN THE DAILY RECORD
10/10/1907

OWNER
Cleveland Realty & Building Company

ARCHITECT
Cleveland Realty & Building Company

BUILDER
Cleveland Realty & Building Company

DESCRIPTION
2-story dwelling; 25 feet × 35 feet

BROKEN FRIEZE
No

PART OF A STREETSCAPE
Yes, originally 1 of 3 (west to east: 6181, 6179, 6171; 6181 has been razed)

NEIGHBORHOOD
● Skinker DeBaliviere

SIDE OF THE STREET
North

STATUS IN 2021
Occupied

6174

McPHERSON AVENUE

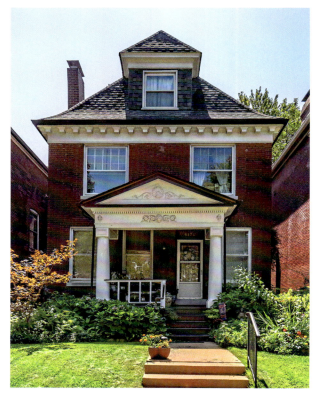

ABOVE Photo by Reed R. Radcliffe, 2022.

DAILY RECORD NO.
3470

APPEARED IN THE DAILY RECORD
09/25/1907

OWNER
Cleveland Realty & Building Company

ARCHITECT
Cleveland Realty & Building Company

BUILDER
Cleveland Realty & Building Company

DESCRIPTION
2-story dwelling; 25 feet × 35 feet

BROKEN FRIEZE
No

PART OF A STREETSCAPE
Yes, originally 1 of 7 (west to east: 6188, 6186, 6182, 6178, 6174, 6170, 6168)

NEIGHBORHOOD
● Skinker DeBaliviere

SIDE OF THE STREET
South

STATUS IN 2021
Occupied

6178

McPherson Avenue

TOP Photo by Reed R. Radcliffe, 2022.
BOTTOM Photo by Lori Berdak Miller, 2021.

BUILDING PERMIT NO.
F-8438

BUILDING PERMIT DATE
12/30/1908

REALTY RECORD AND BUILDER NO.
8438

APPEARED IN THE REALTY RECORD AND BUILDER
Jan. 1909

OWNER
A. A. Fischer Realty Company

ARCHITECT
A. A. Fischer Realty Company

BUILDER
A. A. Fischer Realty Company

DESCRIPTION
2-story dwelling; 30 feet × 32 feet; $5,000

BROKEN FRIEZE
No

PART OF A STREETSCAPE
Yes, originally 1 of 7 (west to east: 6188, 6186, 6182, 6178, 6174, 6170, 6168)

NEIGHBORHOOD
● Skinker DeBaliviere

SIDE OF THE STREET
South

STATUS IN 2021
Restored

6179

McPHERSON AVENUE

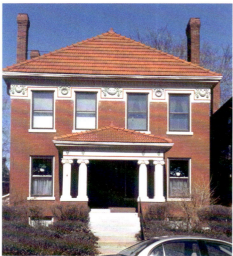

TOP Photo by Reed R. Radcliffe, 2022.
BOTTOM Photo by Nancy Moore Hamilton, 2001.

BUILDING PERMIT NO.
G-3499

BUILDING PERMIT DATE
03/10/1910

DAILY RECORD NO.
3499

APPEARED IN THE DAILY RECORD
03/11/1910

OWNER
A. A. Fischer Realty Company

ARCHITECT
A. A. Fischer Realty Company

BUILDER
A. A. Fischer Realty Company

DESCRIPTION
2-story brick dwelling

BROKEN FRIEZE
Yes

PART OF A STREETSCAPE
Yes, originally 1 of 3 (west to east: 6181, 6179, 6171; 6181 has been razed)

NEIGHBORHOOD
● Skinker DeBaliviere

SIDE OF THE STREET
North

STATUS IN 2021
Occupied

6181

McPHERSON AVENUE

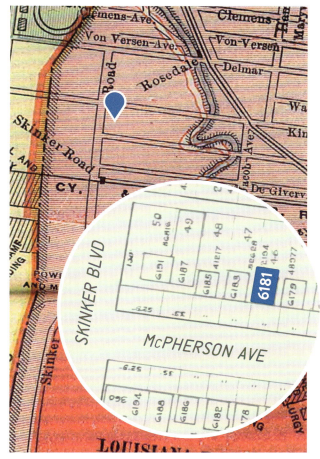

ABOVE
David Rumsey Map Collection, David Rumsey Map Center, Stanford Libraries at Stanford University.

CIRCLE
St. Louis Building Department Atlases, 1943–1946.
St. Louis Public Library.

DAILY RECORD NO.
3646

APPEARED IN THE DAILY RECORD
10/10/1907

OWNER
Cleveland Realty & Building Company

ARCHITECT
Cleveland Realty & Building Company

BUILDER
Cleveland Realty & Building Company

DESCRIPTION
2-story dwelling; 25 feet × 35 feet

BROKEN FRIEZE
Unknown

PART OF A STREETSCAPE
Yes, originally 1 of 3 (west to east: 6181, 6179, 6171; 6181 has been razed)

NEIGHBORHOOD
● Skinker DeBaliviere

SIDE OF THE STREET
North

STATUS IN 2021
Razed

6182

McPHERSON AVENUE

ABOVE Photo by Reed R. Radcliffe, 2022.

DAILY RECORD NO.
3470

APPEARED IN THE DAILY RECORD
09/25/1907

OWNER
Cleveland Realty & Building Company

ARCHITECT
Cleveland Realty & Building Company

BUILDER
Cleveland Realty & Building Company

DESCRIPTION
2-story dwelling; 25 feet × 35 feet

BROKEN FRIEZE
No

PART OF A STREETSCAPE
Yes, originally 1 of 7 (west to east: 6188, 6186, 6182, 6178, 6174, 6170, 6168)

NEIGHBORHOOD
● Skinker DeBaliviere

SIDE OF THE STREET
South

STATUS IN 2021
Restored

6186

McPHERSON AVENUE

ABOVE Photo by Reed R. Radcliffe, 2022.

BUILDING PERMIT NO.
F-8438

BUILDING PERMIT DATE
12/30/1908

REALTY RECORD AND BUILDER NO.
8438

APPEARED IN THE REALTY RECORD AND BUILDER
Jan. 1909

OWNER
A. A. Fischer Realty Company

ARCHITECT
A. A. Fischer Realty Company

BUILDER
A. A. Fischer Realty Company

DESCRIPTION
2-story dwelling; 30 feet × 32 feet; $5,000

BROKEN FRIEZE
Yes

PART OF A STREETSCAPE
Yes, originally 1 of 7 (west to east: 6188, 6186, 6182, 6178, 6174, 6170, 6168)

NEIGHBORHOOD
● Skinker DeBaliviere

SIDE OF THE STREET
South

STATUS IN 2021
Occupied

6188

McPHERSON AVENUE

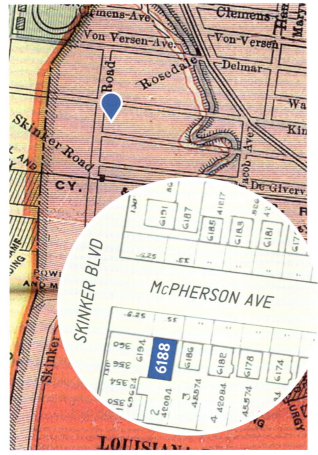

ABOVE
David Rumsey Map Collection, David Rumsey Map Center, Stanford Libraries at Stanford University.

CIRCLE
St. Louis Building Department Atlases, 1943–1946. St. Louis Public Library.

DAILY RECORD NO.
3470

APPEARED IN THE DAILY RECORD
09/25/1907

OWNER
Cleveland Realty & Building Company

ARCHITECT
Cleveland Realty & Building Company

BUILDER
Cleveland Realty & Building Company

DESCRIPTION
2-story dwelling; 25 feet × 35 feet; slate roofs, stove heat

BROKEN FRIEZE
Unknown

PART OF A STREETSCAPE
Yes, originally 1 of 7 (west to east: 6188, 6186, 6182, 6178, 6174, 6170, 6168)

NEIGHBORHOOD
● Skinker DeBaliviere

SIDE OF THE STREET
South

STATUS IN 2021
Razed

6306

McPHERSON AVENUE

DAILY RECORD NO.
1854

APPEARED IN THE DAILY RECORD
08/17/1908

OWNER
Mary Virginia Farrell

BUILDER
A. A. Fischer Realty Company

BROKEN FRIEZE
No

PART OF A STREETSCAPE
No

NEIGHBORHOOD
● Parkview subdivision of University City

SIDE OF THE STREET
South

STATUS IN 2021
Restored

TOP AND CENTER
Photos by Reed R. Radcliffe, 2022.

BOTTOM
Photo by Nancy Moore Hamilton, 2001.

6256-6258

NORTH DRIVE

City of University City

Building Commissioner's Office

No. 1837 University City, Mo., June 5 1922

Permission is hereby granted to A A Fischer

To Construct 2 sty 4 family Br. Tenement building on front part of

Lot No. 6, Block No. 70 Subdivision N. Parkview

House No. 6256-58 N. Drive in the City of

University City, in accordance with the provisions of the city ordinances and

application No. 1837 filed by A A Fischer with the Building

Commissioner, said building to be used as tenement

Estimated cost,	$ 7000
Fee,	$ 4.00
Inspection fee,	$ 6.00
Boiler inspection fee,	$ 1.00
Total,	$ 11.00

This permit expires Dec 5, 1922

Building Commissioner.

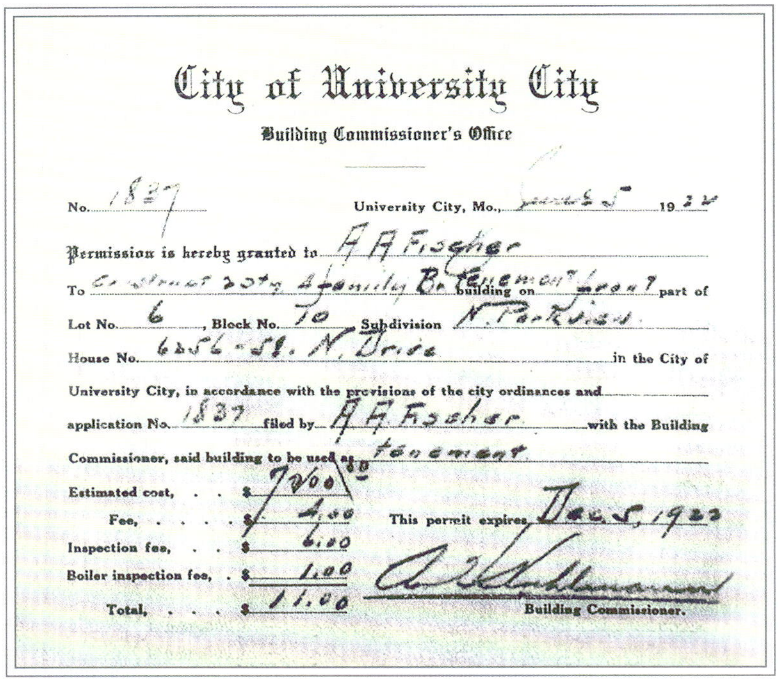

ABOVE City of University City building permit, 1922. The Archives of the University City Public Library.

BUILDING PERMIT NO.
1837

BUILDING PERMIT DATE
06/05/1922

***DAILY RECORD* NO.**
1837

APPEARED IN THE *DAILY RECORD*
06/13/1922

OWNER
A. A. Fischer

BUILDER
A. A. Fischer

DESCRIPTION
2-story, 4-family brick tenement; 29 feet × 34 feet; $7,000

BROKEN FRIEZE
Unknown

PART OF A STREETSCAPE
No

NEIGHBORHOOD
● University City

SIDE OF THE STREET
South

STATUS IN 2021
Razed

6303
NORTH DRIVE

ABOVE City of University City building permit, 1922. The Archives of the University City Public Library.

BUILDING PERMIT NO.
1816

BUILDING PERMIT DATE
05/23/1922

DAILY RECORD NO.
1816

APPEARED IN THE
DAILY RECORD
05/29/1922

OWNER
A. A. Fischer

BUILDER
A. A. Fischer

DESCRIPTION
1-story brick bungalow;
20 feet × 30 feet; $3,500

BROKEN FRIEZE
No

PART OF A STREETSCAPE
Yes, 1 of 4 (west to east: 6309, 6307, 6305, 6303)

NEIGHBORHOOD
● University City

SIDE OF THE STREET
North

STATUS IN 2021
Razed

6305

NORTH DRIVE

ABOVE City of University City building permit, 1922. The Archives of the University City Public Library.

BUILDING PERMIT NO.
1816

BUILDING PERMIT DATE
05/23/1922

DAILY RECORD NO.
1816

APPEARED IN THE *DAILY RECORD*
05/29/1922

OWNER
A. A. Fischer

BUILDER
A. A. Fischer

DESCRIPTION
1-story brick bungalow; 20 feet × 30 feet; $3,500

BROKEN FRIEZE
No

PART OF A STREETSCAPE
Yes, 1 of 4 (west to east: 6309, 6307, 6305, 6303)

NEIGHBORHOOD
● University City

SIDE OF THE STREET
North

STATUS IN 2021
Razed

ND
6307

NORTH DRIVE

ABOVE City of University City building permit, 1922. The Archives of the University City Public Library.

BUILDING PERMIT NO.
1816

BUILDING PERMIT DATE
05/23/1922

DAILY RECORD NO.
1816

APPEARED IN THE *DAILY RECORD*
05/29/1922

OWNER
A. A. Fischer

BUILDER
A. A. Fischer

DESCRIPTION
1-story brick bungalow; 20 feet × 30 feet; $3,500

BROKEN FRIEZE
No

PART OF A STREETSCAPE
Yes, 1 of 4 (west to east: 6309, 6307, 6305, 6303)

NEIGHBORHOOD
● University City

SIDE OF THE STREET
North

STATUS IN 2021
Razed

6309

NORTH DRIVE

ABOVE City of University City building permit, 1922. The Archives of the University City Public Library.

BUILDING PERMIT NO.
1816

BUILDING PERMIT DATE
05/23/1922

DAILY RECORD NO.
1816

APPEARED IN THE
DAILY RECORD
05/29/1922

OWNER
A. A. Fischer

BUILDER
A. A. Fischer

DESCRIPTION
1-story brick bungalow;
20 feet × 30 feet; $3,500

BROKEN FRIEZE
No

PART OF A STREETSCAPE
Yes, 1 of 4 (west to east: 6309, 6307, 6305, 6303)

NEIGHBORHOOD
● University City

SIDE OF THE STREET
North

STATUS IN 2021
Razed

6403

NORTH DRIVE

ABOVE City of University City building permit, 1922. The Archives of the University City Public Library.

BUILDING PERMIT NO.
1831

BUILDING PERMIT DATE
06/03/1922

***DAILY RECORD* NO.**
1831

APPEARED IN THE *DAILY RECORD*
06/13/1922

OWNER
A. A. Fischer

BUILDER
A. A. Fischer

DESCRIPTION
2-story, 4-family brick tenement; 29 feet × 34 feet; $7,000

BROKEN FRIEZE
Unknown

PART OF A STREETSCAPE
No

NEIGHBORHOOD
● University City

SIDE OF THE STREET
North

STATUS IN 2021
Razed

6410

NORTH DRIVE

ABOVE City of University City building permit, 1922. The Archives of the University City Public Library.

BUILDING PERMIT NO.
1830

BUILDING PERMIT DATE
06/03/1922

DAILY RECORD NO.
1831

APPEARED IN THE DAILY RECORD
06/13/1922

ARCHITECT
A. A. Fischer

BUILDER
A. A. Fischer

DESCRIPTION
2-story, 4-family brick tenement; 29 feet × 34 feet; $7,000

BROKEN FRIEZE
Unknown

PART OF A STREETSCAPE
Yes, 1 of 2 side by side (west to east: 6412, 6410)

NEIGHBORHOOD
● University City

SIDE OF THE STREET
South

STATUS IN 2021
Razed

6411

NORTH DRIVE

ABOVE City of University City building permit, 1921. The Archives of the University City Public Library.

BUILDING PERMIT NO.
1503

BUILDING PERMIT DATE
06/25/1921

BUILDER
A. A. Fischer

DESCRIPTION
1-story residence

BROKEN FRIEZE
Unknown

PART OF A STREETSCAPE
No

NEIGHBORHOOD
● University City

SIDE OF THE STREET
North

STATUS IN 2021
Razed

6412

NORTH DRIVE

ABOVE City of University City building permit, 1922. The Archives of the University City Public Library.

BUILDING PERMIT NO.
1830

BUILDING PERMIT DATE
06/03/1922

DAILY RECORD NO.
1831

APPEARED IN THE DAILY RECORD
06/13/1922

ARCHITECT
A. A. Fischer

BUILDER
A. A. Fischer

DESCRIPTION
2-story, 4-family brick tenement; 29 feet × 34 feet; $7,000

BROKEN FRIEZE
Unknown

PART OF A STREETSCAPE
Yes, 1 of 2 side by side (west to east: 6412, 6410)

NEIGHBORHOOD
● University City

SIDE OF THE STREET
South

STATUS IN 2021
Razed

6415

NORTH DRIVE

ABOVE City of University City building permit, 1922. The Archives of the University City Public Library.

BUILDING PERMIT NO.
1829

BUILDING PERMIT DATE
06/03/1922

DAILY RECORD NO.
1831

APPEARED IN THE DAILY RECORD
06/13/1922

ARCHITECT
A. A. Fischer

BUILDER
A. A. Fischer

DESCRIPTION
2-story, 4-family brick tenement; 29 feet × 34 feet; $7,000

BROKEN FRIEZE
Unknown

PART OF A STREETSCAPE
No

NEIGHBORHOOD
● University City

SIDE OF THE STREET
North

STATUS IN 2021
Razed

DIRECTORY OF A. A. FISCHER BUILDS | 291

6416

NORTH DRIVE

ABOVE City of University City building permit, 1922. The Archives of the University City Public Library.

BUILDING PERMIT NO.
1830

BUILDING PERMIT DATE
06/03/1922

DAILY RECORD NO.
1831

APPEARED IN THE DAILY RECORD
06/13/1922

ARCHITECT
A. A. Fischer

BUILDER
A. A. Fischer

DESCRIPTION
2-story, 4-family brick tenement; 29 feet × 34 feet; $7,000

BROKEN FRIEZE
Unknown

PART OF A STREETSCAPE
Yes, 1 of 2 side by side (west to east: 6418, 6416)

NEIGHBORHOOD
● University City

SIDE OF THE STREET
South

STATUS IN 2021
Razed

6418

NORTH DRIVE

ABOVE City of University City building permit, 1922. The Archives of the University City Public Library.

BUILDING PERMIT NO.
1830

BUILDING PERMIT DATE
06/03/1922

APPEARED IN THE *DAILY RECORD*
06/13/1922

ARCHITECT
A. A. Fischer

BUILDER
A. A. Fischer

DESCRIPTION
2-story, 4-family brick tenement; 29 feet × 34 feet; $7,000

BROKEN FRIEZE
Unknown

PART OF A STREETSCAPE
Yes, 1 of 2 side by side (west to east: 6418, 6416)

NEIGHBORHOOD
● University City

SIDE OF THE STREET
South

STATUS IN 2021
Razed

6419
NORTH DRIVE

ABOVE City of University City building permit, 1922. The Archives of the University City Public Library.

BUILDING PERMIT NO.
1829

BUILDING PERMIT DATE
06/03/1922

DAILY RECORD **NO.**
1831

APPEARED IN THE
DAILY RECORD
06/13/1922

ARCHITECT
A. A. Fischer

BUILDER
A. A. Fischer

DESCRIPTION
2-story, 4-family brick tenement; 29 feet × 34 feet; $7,000

BROKEN FRIEZE
Unknown

PART OF A STREETSCAPE
No

NEIGHBORHOOD
● University City

SIDE OF THE STREET
North

STATUS IN 2021
Razed

5210-5212

PAGE BOULEVARD

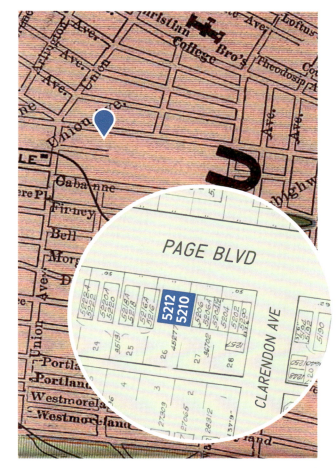

BUILDING PERMIT NO.
F-7977

BUILDING PERMIT DATE
11/12/1908

DAILY RECORD NO.
7977

APPEARED IN THE DAILY RECORD
11/13/1908

OWNER
A. A. Fischer Realty Company

ARCHITECT
A. A. Fischer Realty Company

BUILDER
A. A. Fischer Realty Company

DESCRIPTION
3-story apartments; 46 feet × 31 feet; $8,000

BROKEN FRIEZE
Unknown

PART OF A STREETSCAPE
No

NEIGHBORHOOD
● Academy

SIDE OF THE STREET
South

STATUS IN 2021
Razed in 2000

TOP
David Rumsey Map Collection, David Rumsey Map Center, Stanford Libraries at Stanford University.

CIRCLE
St. Louis Building Department Atlases, 1943–1946. St. Louis Public Library.

LEFT
Photo provided by Landmarks Association of St. Louis, 1980.

DIRECTORY OF A. A. FISCHER BUILDS | 295

5430-5434
PAGE BOULEVARD
This structure's original address was 5434 Page Boulevard.

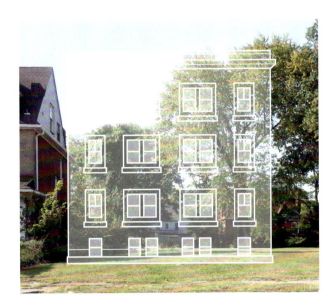

TOP Photo provided by City of St. Louis Address and Property Search, 2020.
BOTTOM Photo provided by City of St. Louis Address and Property Search, 2016.

BUILDING PERMIT NO.
C-5151

BUILDING PERMIT DATE
09/29/1924

DAILY RECORD NO.
5151

APPEARED IN THE DAILY RECORD
09/30/1924

ARCHITECT
A. A. Fischer

BUILDER
A. A. Fischer

DESCRIPTION
3-story brick tenement; 38 feet × 104 feet; $25,000

BROKEN FRIEZE
No

PART OF A STREETSCAPE
No

NEIGHBORHOOD
● West End

SIDE OF THE STREET
South

STATUS IN 2021
Razed

3119
PARK AVENUE

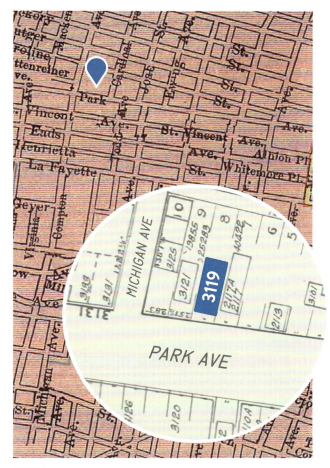

ABOVE
David Rumsey Map Collection, David Rumsey Map Center, Stanford Libraries at Stanford University.

CIRCLE
St. Louis Building Department Atlases, 1943–1946.
St. Louis Public Library.

BUILDING PERMIT NO.
C-3073

APPEARED IN THE *DAILY RECORD*
09/06/1895

OWNER
A. A. Fischer

BUILDER
A. A. Fischer

DESCRIPTION
2-story brick dwelling; 22 feet × 30 feet

BROKEN FRIEZE
Unknown, but unlikely

PART OF A STREETSCAPE
Yes, 1 of 2 side by side (west to east: 3121, 3119)

NEIGHBORHOOD
● The Gate District

SIDE OF THE STREET
North

STATUS IN 2021
Razed in 1995

3121

PARK AVENUE

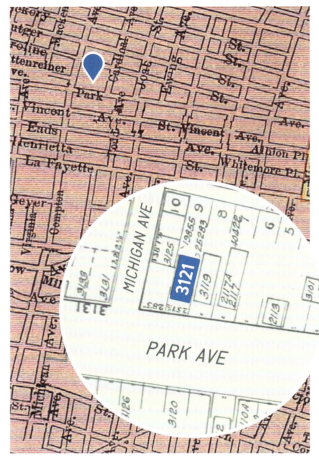

BUILDING PERMIT NO.
C-3073

APPEARED IN THE *DAILY RECORD*
09/06/1895

OWNER
A. A. Fischer

BUILDER
A. A. Fischer

DESCRIPTION
2-story brick dwelling; 22 feet × 30 feet

BROKEN FRIEZE
Unknown, but unlikely

PART OF A STREETSCAPE
Yes, 1 of 2 side by side (west to east: 3121, 3119)

NEIGHBORHOOD
● The Gate District

SIDE OF THE STREET
North

ABOVE
David Rumsey Map Collection, David Rumsey Map Center, Stanford Libraries at Stanford University.

CIRCLE
St. Louis Building Department Atlases, 1943–1946.
St. Louis Public Library.

6209

PERSHING AVENUE

ABOVE
Photo by Lori Berdak Miller, 2021

RIGHT
Photo by Nancy Moore Hamilton, 2000

DAILY RECORD NO.
3063

REALTY RECORD AND BUILDER NO.
6209

APPEARED IN THE REALTY RECORD AND BUILDER
Feb. 1910

OWNER
C. A. Garvey

ARCHITECT
A. A. Fischer Realty Company

BUILDER
A. A. Fischer Realty Company

DESCRIPTION
2.5-story dwelling; 32 feet × 33 feet

BROKEN FRIEZE
No

PART OF A STREETSCAPE
No

NEIGHBORHOOD
● Parkview subdivision of Skinker DeBaliviere

SIDE OF THE STREET
North

STATUS IN 2021
Restored

4620

PERSHING PLACE
This structure's original address was 4620 Berlin Avenue.

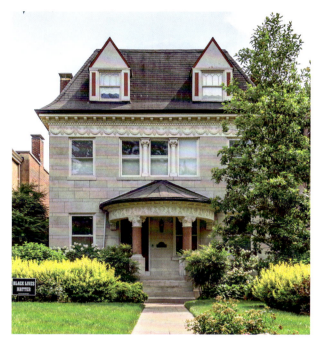

ABOVE Photos by Reed R. Radcliffe, 2022.

APPEARED IN THE *DAILY RECORD*
06/17/1899

HOUSE NUMBER SLIP
06/01/1899

OWNER
A. A. Fischer

BUILDER
A. A. Fischer

DESCRIPTION
2.5-story dwelling; 29 feet × 40 feet

BROKEN FRIEZE
No

PART OF A STREETSCAPE
Yes, 1 of 2 side by side (west to east: 4624, 4620)

NEIGHBORHOOD
● Central West End

SIDE OF THE STREET
South

STATUS IN 2021
Restored

4624

PERSHING PLACE
This structure's original address was 4624 Berlin Avenue.

ABOVE Photo by Reed R. Radcliffe, 2022.

APPEARED IN THE *DAILY RECORD*
06/17/1899

HOUSE NUMBER SLIP
06/01/1899

OWNER
A. A. Fischer

BUILDER
A. A. Fischer

DESCRIPTION
2.5-story dwelling; 29 feet × 40 feet

BROKEN FRIEZE
No

PART OF A STREETSCAPE
1 of 2 side by side (west to east: 4624, 4620)

NEIGHBORHOOD
● Central West End

SIDE OF THE STREET
South

STATUS IN 2021
Restored

3520-3522

PESTALOZZI STREET

This structure's original address was 3520 Pestalozzi Street.

APPEARED IN THE BUILDER
June 1905

OWNER
A. A. Fischer Architectural & Building Company

ARCHITECT
A. A. Fischer Architectural & Building Company

BUILDER
A. A. Fischer Architectural & Building Company

DESCRIPTION
2-story flats; 13 rooms; 28 feet × 60 feet

BROKEN FRIEZE
No

PART OF A STREETSCAPE
No

NEIGHBORHOOD
● Tower Grove East

SIDE OF THE STREET
South

STATUS IN 2021
Restored

TOP
Photo by Lori Berdak Miller, 2021.

LEFT
Photo by Nancy Moore Hamilton, 2001.

4233

WEST PINE BOULEVARD

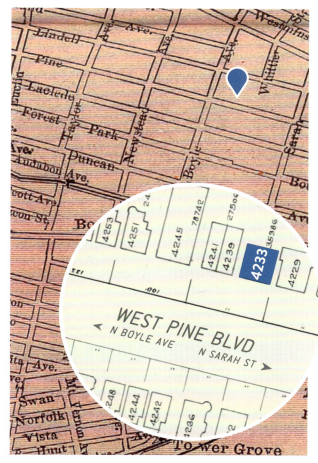

ABOVE
David Rumsey Map Collection, David Rumsey Map Center, Stanford Libraries at Stanford University.

CIRCLE
St. Louis Building Department Atlases, 1943–1946.
St. Louis Public Library.

BUILDING PERMIT NO.
E-3398

BUILDING PERMIT DATE
04/10/1905

DAILY RECORD NO.
3398

APPEARED IN THE DAILY RECORD
04/11/1905

OWNER
A. A. Fischer/A. A. Fischer Architectural & Building Company

ARCHITECT
A. A. Fischer/A. A. Fischer Architectural & Building Company

BUILDER
A. A. Fischer/A. A. Fischer Architectural & Building Company

DESCRIPTION
2-story brick residence; 33 feet × 33 feet; $6,000

BROKEN FRIEZE
Unknown

PART OF A STREETSCAPE
No

NEIGHBORHOOD
● Central West End

SIDE OF THE STREET
North

STATUS IN 2021
Razed

5184

PORTLAND PLACE
This structure is alternatively numbered 36 Portland Place.

ABOVE Photo by Reed R. Radcliffe, 2022.

BUILDING PERMIT NO.
E-9341

BUILDING PERMIT DATE
09/26/1906

DAILY RECORD NO.
4007

APPEARED IN THE DAILY RECORD
09/27/1906

OWNER
Herman C. G. Luyties

ARCHITECT
A. A. Fischer Realty Company

BUILDER
A. A. Fischer Realty Company

DESCRIPTION
3-story brick and stone residence; 50 feet × 50 feet; $40,000

BROKEN FRIEZE
No

PART OF A STREETSCAPE
No

NEIGHBORHOOD
● Central West End

SIDE OF THE STREET
North

STATUS IN 2021
Restored

5008
RAYMOND AVENUE

ABOVE
Photo by Reed R. Radcliffe, 2022.

RIGHT
Photo provided by Landmarks Association of St. Louis, 1980.

BUILDING PERMIT NO.
E-9519

BUILDING PERMIT DATE
10/12/1906

DAILY RECORD NO.
9519

APPEARED IN THE DAILY RECORD
10/13/1906

OWNER
Sigmund Hasgall

ARCHITECT
A. A. Fischer

BUILDER
A. A. Fischer Architectural & Building Company

DESCRIPTION
3-story brick residence; $9,500

BROKEN FRIEZE
No

PART OF A STREETSCAPE
No

NEIGHBORHOOD
● Academy

SIDE OF THE STREET
South

STATUS IN 2021
Occupied

5018
RAYMOND AVENUE

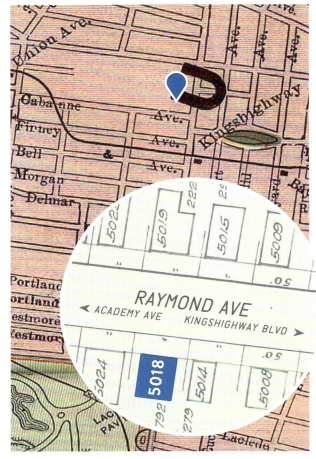

BUILDING PERMIT NO.
1657

BUILDING PERMIT DATE
09/15/1899

APPEARED IN THE DAILY RECORD
09/19/1899

OWNER
A. A. Fischer

DESCRIPTION
2.5-story dwelling; 38 feet × 32 feet; $4,000

BROKEN FRIEZE
Unknown

PART OF A STREETSCAPE
No

NEIGHBORHOOD
● Academy

SIDE OF THE STREET
South

STATUS IN 2021
Razed in 1995

ABOVE
David Rumsey Map Collection, David Rumsey Map Center, Stanford Libraries at Stanford University.

CIRCLE
St. Louis Building Department Atlases, 1943–1946.
St. Louis Public Library.

5031

RAYMOND AVENUE

BUILDING PERMIT NO.
E-1544

BUILDING PERMIT DATE
09/14/1904

DAILY RECORD NO.
1544

APPEARED IN THE DAILY RECORD
09/15/1904

APPEARED IN THE BUILDER
Oct. 1904

OWNER
A. A. Fischer Architectural & Building Company

ARCHITECT
A. A. Fischer Architectural & Building Company

BUILDER
A. A. Fischer Architectural & Building Company

BROKEN FRIEZE
No

DESCRIPTION
2-story dwelling; 36 feet × 33 feet; $6,000

PART OF A STREETSCAPE
Yes, 1 of 2 side by side (5035, 5031)

NEIGHBORHOOD
● Academy

SIDE OF THE STREET
North

STATUS IN 2021
Occupied

TOP AND CENTER
Photos by Reed R. Radcliffe, 2022.

BOTTOM
Photo provided by Landmarks Association of St. Louis, 1980.

5035

RAYMOND AVENUE

ABOVE
Photo by Reed R. Radcliffe, 2022.

RIGHT
Photo provided by Landmarks Association of St. Louis, 1980.

BUILDING PERMIT NO.
E-4912

BUILDING PERMIT DATE
08/23/1905

APPEARED IN THE *DAILY RECORD*
08/24/1905

APPEARED IN THE *BUILDER*
Sept. 1905

OWNER
Emma Cummings

ARCHITECT
A. A. Fischer Architectural & Building Company

BUILDER
A. A. Fischer Architectural & Building Company

DESCRIPTION
2-story brick mansard dwelling; 28 feet × 36 feet

BROKEN FRIEZE
Yes

PART OF A STREETSCAPE
Yes, 1 of 2 side by side (5035, 5031)

NEIGHBORHOOD
● Academy

SIDE OF THE STREET
North

STATUS IN 2021
Occupied

5060

RAYMOND AVENUE

ABOVE
Photo by Reed R. Radcliffe, 2022.

RIGHT
Photo provided by Landmarks Association of St. Louis, 1980.

BUILDING PERMIT NO.
E-8267

BUILDING PERMIT DATE
07/05/1906

REALTY RECORD AND BUILDER NO.
8267

APPEARED IN THE REALTY RECORD AND BUILDER
08/06/1906

OWNER
A. A. Fischer Architectural & Building Company

ARCHITECT
A. A. Fischer Architectural & Building Company

BUILDER
A. A. Fischer Architectural & Building Company

DESCRIPTION
2-story residence; 41 feet × 35 feet; $8,000

BROKEN FRIEZE
Yes

PART OF A STREETSCAPE
No

NEIGHBORHOOD
● Academy

SIDE OF THE STREET
South

STATUS IN 2021
Occupied

5075

RAYMOND AVENUE

ABOVE
Photo by Reed R. Radcliffe, 2022.

RIGHT
Photo provided by Landmarks Association of St. Louis, 1980.

BUILDING PERMIT NO.
E-3282

BUILDING PERMIT DATE
03/31/1905

DAILY RECORD NO.
3282

APPEARED IN THE DAILY RECORD
04/08/1905

OWNER
A. A. Fischer

ARCHITECT
A. A. Fischer

BUILDER
A. A. Fischer

DESCRIPTION
2-story dwelling; 39 feet × 35 feet

BROKEN FRIEZE
Yes

PART OF A STREETSCAPE
No

NEIGHBORHOOD
● Academy

SIDE OF THE STREET
North

STATUS IN 2021
Restored

5133

RAYMOND AVENUE

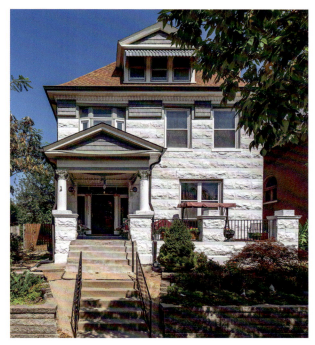

ABOVE
Photo by Reed R. Radcliffe, 2022.

RIGHT
Photo provided by Landmarks Association of St. Louis, 1980.

DAILY RECORD NO.
2402

APPEARED IN THE DAILY RECORD
01/06/1905

APPEARED IN THE BUILDER
Jan. 1905

OWNER
Sam Spiegel

ARCHITECT
A. A. Fischer Architectural & Building Company

BUILDER
A. A. Fischer Architectural & Building Company

DESCRIPTION
2-story dwelling; 31 feet × 51 feet

BROKEN FRIEZE
Yes

PART OF A STREETSCAPE
No

NEIGHBORHOOD
● Academy

SIDE OF THE STREET
North

STATUS IN 2021
Occupied

5167

RAYMOND AVENUE

ABOVE
Photo by Reed R. Radcliffe, 2022.

RIGHT
Photo by Lynn Josse for Landmarks Association of St. Louis, 2002.

DAILY RECORD NO.
31

APPEARED IN THE *DAILY RECORD*
11/05/1901

OWNER
A. A. Fischer

ARCHITECT
A. A. Fischer

BUILDER
A. A. Fischer

DESCRIPTION
Residence; 32.5 feet × 35 feet

BROKEN FRIEZE
Yes

PART OF A STREETSCAPE
No

NEIGHBORHOOD
● Academy

SIDE OF THE STREET
North

STATUS IN 2021
Occupied

5226
RAYMOND AVENUE

TOP Photo by Reed R. Radcliffe, 2022.
BOTTOM Photo by Lynn Josse for Landmarks Association of St. Louis, 2001.

DAILY RECORD NO.
8268

APPEARED IN THE DAILY RECORD
07/06/1906

REALTY RECORD NO.
8268

APPEARED IN THE REALTY RECORD
Aug. 1906

OWNER
A. A. Fischer Architectural & Building Company

ARCHITECT
A. A. Fischer Architectural & Building Company

BUILDER
A. A. Fischer Architectural & Building Company

DESCRIPTION
2-story residence; 41 feet × 35 feet; $8,000

BROKEN FRIEZE
Yes

PART OF A STREETSCAPE
No

NEIGHBORHOOD
● Academy

SIDE OF THE STREET
South

STATUS IN 2021
Occupied

5233

RAYMOND AVENUE

ABOVE
Photo by Reed R. Radcliffe, 2022.

RIGHT
Photo by Lynn Josse for Landmarks Association of St. Louis, 2002.

DAILY RECORD NO.
9520

APPEARED IN THE DAILY RECORD
10/13/1906

OWNER
Max Hasgall

ARCHITECT
A. A. Fischer

BUILDER
A. A. Fischer Architectural & Building Company

DESCRIPTION
2-story dwelling; 33 feet × 33 feet

BROKEN FRIEZE
No

PART OF A STREETSCAPE
Yes, 1 of 3 (west to east: 5243, 5237, 5233)

NEIGHBORHOOD
● Academy

SIDE OF THE STREET
North

STATUS IN 2021
Occupied

5237
RAYMOND AVENUE

TOP Photo by Reed R. Radcliffe, 2022.
BOTTOM Photo by Lynn Josse for Landmarks Association of St. Louis, 2002.

BUILDING PERMIT NO.
F-3419

BUILDING PERMIT DATE
09/19/1907

APPEARED IN THE *DAILY RECORD*
09/20/1907

***REALTY RECORD AND BUILDER* NO.**
3419

APPEARED IN THE *REALTY RECORD AND BUILDER*
10/07/1907

OWNER
A. A. Fischer Realty Company

ARCHITECT
A. A. Fischer Realty Company

BUILDER
A. A. Fischer Realty Company

DESCRIPTION
2-story dwelling; 36 feet × 30 feet; $5,000

BROKEN FRIEZE
Yes

PART OF A STREETSCAPE
Yes, 1 of 3 (west to east: 5243, 5237, 5233)

NEIGHBORHOOD
● Academy

SIDE OF THE STREET
North

STATUS IN 2021
Occupied

NOTE Described in a real estate listing in the September 13, 1908, *St. Louis Post-Dispatch* as "having wide front porch and Doric columns. The arrangement of the interior is new and attractive. The reception hall in the center is connected by a wide-columned opening to a large English living-room, 13 × 28, containing a large brick fireplace and heavy beamed ceiling. See this beautiful home."

5243

RAYMOND AVENUE

TOP Photo by Reed R. Radcliffe, 2022.
BOTTOM Photo by Lynn Josse for Landmarks Association of St. Louis, 2002.

BUILDING PERMIT NO.
F-3419

BUILDING PERMIT DATE
09/19/1907

APPEARED IN THE *DAILY RECORD*
09/20/1907

***REALTY RECORD AND BUILDER* NO.**
3419

APPEARED IN THE *REALTY RECORD AND BUILDER*
10/07/1907

OWNER
A. A. Fischer Realty Company

ARCHITECT
A. A. Fischer Realty Company

BUILDER
A. A. Fischer Realty Company

DESCRIPTION
2-story dwelling; 36 feet × 30 feet; $5,000

BROKEN FRIEZE
Yes

PART OF A STREETSCAPE
Yes, 1 of 3 (west to east: 5243, 5237, 5233)

NEIGHBORHOOD
● Academy

SIDE OF THE STREET
North

STATUS IN 2021
Occupied

5312

RIDGE AVENUE

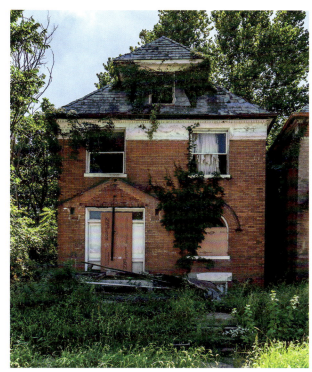

ABOVE Photo by Reed R. Radcliffe, 2022.

BUILDING PERMIT NO.
D-5368

BUILDING PERMIT DATE
01/15/1902

DAILY RECORD NO.
368

APPEARED IN THE DAILY RECORD
01/16/1902

OWNER
A. A. Fischer

ARCHITECT
A. A. Fischer

BUILDER
A. A. Fischer

DESCRIPTION
2-story residence; 25 feet × 34.5 feet; $3,000

BROKEN FRIEZE
Yes

PART OF A STREETSCAPE
Yes, 1 of 2 side by side (5312, 5314)

NEIGHBORHOOD
● Hamilton Heights

SIDE OF THE STREET
South

STATUS IN 2021
Condemned

5314

RIDGE AVENUE

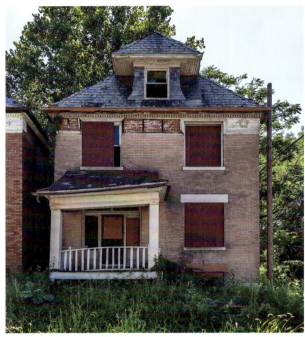

ABOVE Photo by Reed R. Radcliffe, 2022.

BUILDING PERMIT NO.
D-5368

BUILDING PERMIT DATE
01/15/1902

DAILY RECORD NO.
368

APPEARED IN THE DAILY RECORD
01/16/1902

OWNER
A. A. Fischer

ARCHITECT
A. A. Fischer

BUILDER
A. A. Fischer

DESCRIPTION
2-story residence; 25 feet × 34.5 feet; $3,000

BROKEN FRIEZE
Yes

PART OF A STREETSCAPE
Yes, 1 of 2 side by side (5312, 5314)

NEIGHBORHOOD
● Hamilton Heights

SIDE OF THE STREET
South

STATUS IN 2021
Condemned

5320

RIDGE AVENUE

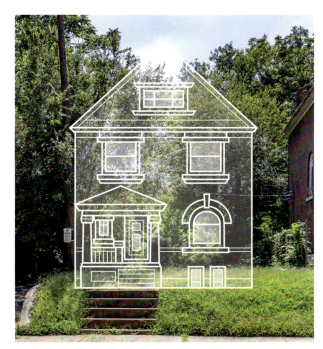

ABOVE Photo by Reed R. Radcliffe, 2022.

BUILDING PERMIT NO.
D-7160

BUILDING PERMIT DATE
10/15/1902

DAILY RECORD NO.
160

APPEARED IN THE DAILY RECORD
10/17/1902

OWNER
A. A. Fischer Architectural & Building Company

BUILDER
A. A. Fischer Architectural & Building Company

DESCRIPTION
2-story residence; 29.5 feet × 33 feet

BROKEN FRIEZE
Unknown

PART OF A STREETSCAPE
Yes, 1 of 2 side by side (5320, 5322)

NEIGHBORHOOD
● Hamilton Heights

SIDE OF THE STREET
South

STATUS IN 2021
Razed

5322

RIDGE AVENUE

ABOVE Photo by Reed R. Radcliffe, 2022.

BUILDING PERMIT NO.
D-7160

BUILDING PERMIT DATE
10/15/1902

DAILY RECORD NO.
160

APPEARED IN THE DAILY RECORD
10/17/1902

OWNER
A. A. Fischer Architectural
& Building Company

BUILDER
A. A. Fischer Architectural
& Building Company

DESCRIPTION
2-story residence; 29.5 feet × 33 feet

BROKEN FRIEZE
Yes

PART OF A STREETSCAPE
Yes, 1 of 2 side by side (5320, 5322)

NEIGHBORHOOD
● Hamilton Heights

SIDE OF THE STREET
South

STATUS IN 2021
Occupied

2326
RUSSELL BOULEVARD

ABOVE
Photo by Reed R. Radcliffe, 2022.

RIGHT
Photo by Cynthia Longwisch for Landmarks Association of St. Louis, 1984.

BUILDING PERMIT NO.
D-6211

BUILDING PERMIT DATE
05/29/1902

DAILY RECORD NO.
211

APPEARED IN THE DAILY RECORD
05/30/1902

OWNER
R. J. Henry

ARCHITECT
A. A. Fischer Architectural & Building Company

BUILDER
A. A. Fischer Architectural & Building Company

DESCRIPTION
3-story residence; 35 feet × 35 feet; $5,000

BROKEN FRIEZE
Yes

PART OF A STREETSCAPE
No

NEIGHBORHOOD
● McKinley Heights

SIDE OF THE STREET
South

STATUS IN 2021
Restored

3667

RUSSELL BOULEVARD

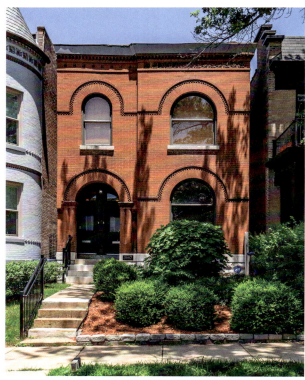

ABOVE
Photo by Reed R. Radcliffe, 2022.

RIGHT
Photo by Nancy Moore Hamilton, 2001.

APPEARED IN THE *DAILY RECORD*
10/25/1894

OWNER
A. A. Fischer

BUILDER
H. W. Mepham

DESCRIPTION
2-story brick dwelling; 22 feet × 50 feet

BROKEN FRIEZE
No

PART OF A STREETSCAPE
Yes, 1 of 2 side by side (west to east: 3669, 3667)

NEIGHBORHOOD
● Shaw

SIDE OF THE STREET
North

STATUS IN 2021
Restored

3669
RUSSELL BOULEVARD

ABOVE
Photo by Reed R. Radcliffe, 2022.

RIGHT
Photo by Nancy Moore Hamilton, 2001.

APPEARED IN THE *DAILY RECORD*
10/25/1894

OWNER
A. A. Fischer

BUILDER
H. W. Mepham

DESCRIPTION
2-story brick dwelling; 22 feet × 50 feet

BROKEN FRIEZE
No

PART OF A STREETSCAPE
Yes, 1 of 2 side by side (west to east: 3669, 3667)

NEIGHBORHOOD
● Shaw

SIDE OF THE STREET
North

STATUS IN 2021
Restored

3665
SHENANDOAH AVENUE

HOUSE NUMBER SLIP
10/15/1897

OWNER
John Hahn

ARCHITECT
A. A. Fischer

BUILDER
A. A. Fischer

DESCRIPTION
2-story flat; 25.3 feet × 45 feet; $3,000

BROKEN FRIEZE
No

PART OF A STREETSCAPE
No

NEIGHBORHOOD
● Shaw

SIDE OF THE STREET
North

STATUS IN 2021
Occupied

TOP
Photo by Reed R. Radcliffe, 2022.

LEFT
Photo by Nancy Moore Hamilton, 2001.

500

SKINKER BOULEVARD

This structure's original address was 6193 Westminster Place.

TOP AND BOTTOM Photos by Reed R. Radcliffe, 2022.

DAILY RECORD NO.
4812

APPEARED IN THE *DAILY RECORD*
06/15/1910

REALTY RECORD AND BUILDER NO.
4812

APPEARED IN THE *REALTY RECORD AND BUILDER*
July 1910

LANDMARKS
1910

OWNER
A. A. Fischer Realty Company

ARCHITECT
A. A. Fischer Realty Company

BUILDER
A. A. Fischer Realty Company

DESCRIPTION
2-story dwelling; 28 feet × 40 feet

BROKEN FRIEZE
No

PART OF A STREETSCAPE
Yes, 1 of 12 (west to east: 500 Skinker Boulevard, 6193, 6189, 6185, 6181, 6179, 6175, 6173, 6169, 6165, 6163, 6159, 6155 Westminster Place)

NEIGHBORHOOD
● Skinker DeBaliviere

SIDE OF THE STREET
North

STATUS IN 2021
Restored

NOTE This structure was originally built as a residence, but the City of St. Louis has rezoned it for commercial use.

520

SKINKER BOULEVARD
This structure's original address was 6194 Washington Terrace.

ABOVE Photos by Reed R. Radcliffe, 2022.

DAILY RECORD NO.
325

REALTY RECORD AND BUILDER NO.
325

APPEARED IN THE REALTY RECORD AND BUILDER
June 1909

LANDMARKS
1909

OWNER
A. A. Fischer Realty Company

ARCHITECT
A. A. Fischer Realty Company

BUILDER
A. A. Fischer Realty Company

DESCRIPTION
2.5-story dwelling; 28 feet × 39 feet

BROKEN FRIEZE
No

PART OF A STREETSCAPE
Yes, 1 of 6 (west to east: 520 Skinker Boulevard, 6190, 6186, 6182, 6178, 6174 Washington Boulevard)

NEIGHBORHOOD
● Skinker DeBaliviere

SIDE OF THE STREET
South

STATUS IN 2021
Restored

6

THORNBY PLACE
This structure's original address was 1014 Thornby Place.

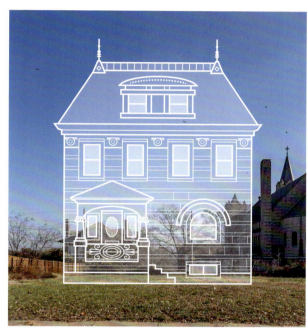

ABOVE Photo by Reed R. Radcliffe, 2022.

BUILDING PERMIT NO.
F-9696

BUILDING PERMIT DATE
04/15/1909

DAILY RECORD NO.
9696

REALTY RECORD AND BUILDER NO.
9696

APPEARED IN THE REALTY RECORD AND BUILDER
Apr. 1909

OWNER
William A. Lippman

ARCHITECT
A. A. Fischer Realty Company

BUILDER
A. A. Fischer Realty Company

DESCRIPTION
2-story and attic dwelling; 40 feet × 34 feet

BROKEN FRIEZE
No

PART OF A STREETSCAPE
No

NEIGHBORHOOD
● West End

SIDE OF THE STREET
East

STATUS IN 2021
Razed in 2019

1320-1322

UNION BOULEVARD
This structure's original address was 1322 Union Boulevard.

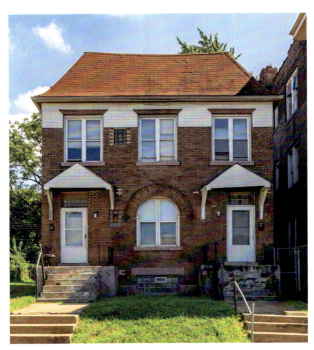

ABOVE Photo by Reed R. Radcliffe, 2022.

BUILDING PERMIT NO.
D-9499

BUILDING PERMIT DATE
11/10/1903

DAILY RECORD NO.
499

APPEARED IN THE DAILY RECORD
11/11/1903

OWNER
A. A. Fischer Architectural & Building Company

ARCHITECT
A. A. Fischer Architectural & Building Company

BUILDER
A. A. Fischer Architectural & Building Company

DESCRIPTION
2-story brick flats; 26.5 feet × 45 feet; $4,500

BROKEN FRIEZE
Yes

PART OF A STREETSCAPE
Yes, 1 of 3 (north to south: 1328-1330, 1324-1326, 1320-1322)

NEIGHBORHOOD
● Academy

SIDE OF THE STREET
East

STATUS IN 2021
Occupied

1324-1326

UNION BOULEVARD

This structure's original address was 1324 Union Boulevard.

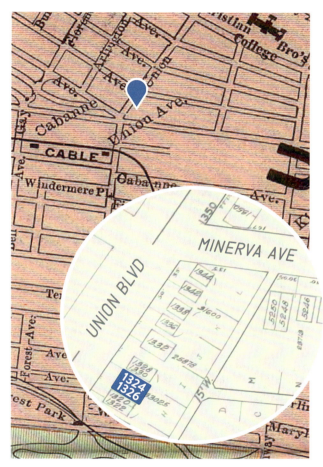

ABOVE
David Rumsey Map Collection, David Rumsey Map Center, Stanford Libraries at Stanford University.

CIRCLE
St. Louis Building Department Atlases, 1943–1946. St. Louis Public Library.

BUILDING PERMIT NO.
D-9499

BUILDING PERMIT DATE
11/10/1903

"USE" PER BUILDING PERMIT
2-story brick flats

DAILY RECORD NO.
499

APPEARED IN THE DAILY RECORD
11/11/1903

OWNER
A. A. Fischer Architectural & Building Company

ARCHITECT
A. A. Fischer Architectural & Building Company

BUILDER
A. A. Fischer Architectural & Building Company

DESCRIPTION
2-story brick flats; 26.5 feet × 45 feet; $4,500

BROKEN FRIEZE
Yes

PART OF A STREETSCAPE
Yes, 1 of 3 (north to south: 1328-1330, 1324-1326, 1320-1322)

NEIGHBORHOOD
● Academy

SIDE OF THE STREET
East

STATUS IN 2021
Razed in 2014

1328-1330

UNION BOULEVARD
This structure's original address was 1328 Union Boulevard.

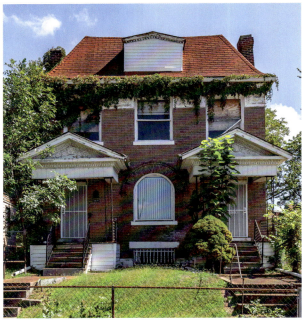

ABOVE Photo by Reed R. Radcliffe, 2022.

RIGHT Photo provided by City of St. Louis Address and Property Search, 2015.

BUILDING PERMIT NO.
D-9499

BUILDING PERMIT DATE
11/10/1903

DAILY RECORD NO.
499

APPEARED IN THE DAILY RECORD
11/11/1903

OWNER
A. A. Fischer Architectural & Building Company

ARCHITECT
A. A. Fischer Architectural & Building Company

BUILDER
A. A. Fischer Architectural & Building Company

DESCRIPTION
2-story brick flats; 26.5 feet × 45 feet; $4,500

BROKEN FRIEZE
Yes

PART OF A STREETSCAPE
Yes, 1 of 3 (north to south: 1328-1330, 1324-1326, 1320-1322)

NEIGHBORHOOD
● Academy

SIDE OF THE STREET
East

STATUS IN 2021
Condemned

1336

UNION BOULEVARD

ABOVE Photo by Reed R. Radcliffe, 2022.

BUILDING PERMIT NO.
D-6878

BUILDING PERMIT DATE
09/09/1902

DAILY RECORD NO.
878

APPEARED IN THE DAILY RECORD
09/10/1902

OWNER
A. A. Fischer

ARCHITECT
A. A. Fischer

BUILDER
A. A. Fischer

DESCRIPTION
2-story residence

BROKEN FRIEZE
Yes

PART OF A STREETSCAPE
Yes, 1 of 4 (north to south: 1344, 1342, 1338, 1336)

NEIGHBORHOOD
● Academy

SIDE OF THE STREET
East

STATUS IN 2021
Occupied

1338
UNION BOULEVARD

ABOVE Photo by Reed R. Radcliffe, 2022.

BUILDING PERMIT NO.
D-6878

BUILDING PERMIT DATE
09/09/1902

DAILY RECORD NO.
878

APPEARED IN THE DAILY RECORD
09/10/1902

OWNER
A. A. Fischer

ARCHITECT
A. A. Fischer

BUILDER
A. A. Fischer

BROKEN FRIEZE
Yes

PART OF A STREETSCAPE
Yes, 1 of 4 (north to south: 1344, 1342, 1338, 1336)

NEIGHBORHOOD
● Academy

SIDE OF THE STREET
East

STATUS IN 2021
Occupied

1342

UNION BOULEVARD

ABOVE Photo by Reed R. Radcliffe, 2022.

BUILDING PERMIT NO.
D-6878

BUILDING PERMIT DATE
09/09/1902

DAILY RECORD NO.
878

APPEARED IN THE DAILY RECORD
09/10/1902

OWNER
A. A. Fischer

ARCHITECT
A. A. Fischer

BUILDER
A. A. Fischer

BROKEN FRIEZE
Yes

PART OF A STREETSCAPE
Yes, 1 of 4 (north to south: 1344, 1342, 1338, 1336)

NEIGHBORHOOD
● Academy

SIDE OF THE STREET
East

STATUS IN 2021
Occupied

1344

UNION BOULEVARD

ABOVE Photo by Reed R. Radcliffe, 2022.

BUILDING PERMIT NO.
D-6878

BUILDING PERMIT DATE
09/09/1902

DAILY RECORD NO.
878

APPEARED IN THE DAILY RECORD
09/10/1902

OWNER
A. A. Fischer

ARCHITECT
A. A. Fischer

BUILDER
A. A. Fischer

DESCRIPTION
2-story residence

BROKEN FRIEZE
Yes

PART OF A STREETSCAPE
Yes, 1 of 4 (north to south: 1344, 1342, 1338, 1336)

NEIGHBORHOOD
● Academy

SIDE OF THE STREET
East

STATUS IN 2021
Restored

1384-1386

UNION BOULEVARD
This structure's original address was 1386 Union Boulevard.

ABOVE Photo by Reed R. Radcliffe, 2022.

BUILDING PERMIT NO.
E-4046

BUILDING PERMIT DATE
06/01/1905

DAILY RECORD NO.
4046

APPEARED IN THE DAILY RECORD
06/02/1905

OWNER
A. A. Fischer/A. A. Fischer Architectural & Building Company

ARCHITECT
A. A. Fischer/A. A. Fischer Architectural & Building Company

BUILDER
A. A. Fischer Architectural & Building Company

DESCRIPTION
2-story brick flat

BROKEN FRIEZE
Yes

PART OF A STREETSCAPE
Yes, 1 of 2 side by side (1384-1386, 1388-1390)

NEIGHBORHOOD
● Academy

SIDE OF THE STREET
East

STATUS IN 2021
Occupied

1387
UNION BOULEVARD

ABOVE Photo by Reed R. Radcliffe, 2022.

BUILDING PERMIT NO.
E-2354

BUILDING PERMIT DATE
12/23/1904

DAILY RECORD NO.
2354

APPEARED IN THE DAILY RECORD
12/24/1904

APPEARED IN THE BUILDER
Jan. 1905

OWNER
Mrs. Sarah M. Graves

ARCHITECT
A. A. Fischer

BUILDER
A. A. Fischer

DESCRIPTION
2-story brick dwelling; 26 feet × 36 feet; $6,000

BROKEN FRIEZE
Yes

PART OF A STREETSCAPE
No

NEIGHBORHOOD
● Hamilton Heights

SIDE OF THE STREET
West

STATUS IN 2021
Occupied

1388-1390

UNION BOULEVARD
This structure's original address was 1388 Union Boulevard.

ABOVE Photo by Reed R. Radcliffe, 2022.

BUILDING PERMIT NO.
E-3638

BUILDING PERMIT DATE
04/25/1906

DAILY RECORD NO.
3638

APPEARED IN THE DAILY RECORD
04/27/1905

OWNER
Cora N. Meers

ARCHITECT
A. A. Fischer/A. A. Fischer Architectural & Building Company

BUILDER
A. A. Fischer Architectural & Building Company

DESCRIPTION
2-story brick flats; 28 feet × 55 feet

BROKEN FRIEZE
Yes

PART OF A STREETSCAPE
Yes, 1 of 2 side by side (1384-1386, 1388-1390)

NEIGHBORHOOD
● Academy

SIDE OF THE STREET
East

STATUS IN 2021
Occupied

1391

UNION BOULEVARD

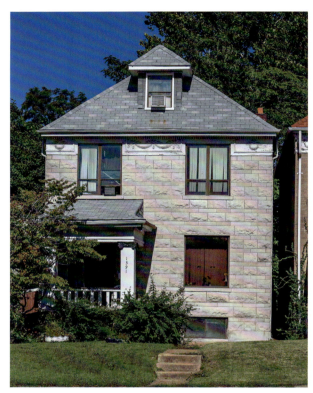

ABOVE Photo by Reed R. Radcliffe, 2022.

BUILDING PERMIT NO.
D-4960

BUILDING PERMIT DATE
10/24/1901

DAILY RECORD NO.
960

APPEARED IN THE DAILY RECORD
10/28/1901

OWNER
A. A. Fischer/A. A. Fischer Architectural & Building Company

ARCHITECT
A. A. Fischer/A. A. Fischer Architectural & Building Company

BUILDER
A. A. Fischer Architectural & Building Company

DESCRIPTION
2-story brick dwelling; 25 feet × 34.5 feet; $3,000

BROKEN FRIEZE
Yes

PART OF A STREETSCAPE
Yes, 1 of 4 (north to south: 1399, 1397, 1395, 1391)

NEIGHBORHOOD
● Hamilton Heights

SIDE OF THE STREET
West

STATUS IN 2021
Occupied

1395

UNION BOULEVARD

ABOVE Photo by Reed R. Radcliffe, 2022.

BUILDING PERMIT NO.
D-4960

BUILDING PERMIT DATE
10/24/1901

DAILY RECORD NO.
960

APPEARED IN THE DAILY RECORD
10/28/1901

OWNER
A. A. Fischer/A. A. Fischer Architectural & Building Company

ARCHITECT
A. A. Fischer/A. A. Fischer Architectural & Building Company

BUILDER
A. A. Fischer Architectural & Building Company

DESCRIPTION
2-story brick dwelling; 25 feet × 34.5 feet; $3,000

BROKEN FRIEZE
Yes

PART OF A STREETSCAPE
Yes, 1 of 4 (north to south: 1399, 1397, 1395, 1391)

NEIGHBORHOOD
● Hamilton Heights

SIDE OF THE STREET
West

STATUS IN 2021
Occupied

1397
UNION BOULEVARD

ABOVE Photo by Reed R. Radcliffe, 2022.

BUILDING PERMIT NO.
D-4960

BUILDING PERMIT DATE
10/24/1901

DAILY RECORD NO.
960

APPEARED IN THE DAILY RECORD
10/28/1901

OWNER
A. A. Fischer/A. A. Fischer Architectural & Building Company

ARCHITECT
A. A. Fischer/A. A. Fischer Architectural & Building Company

BUILDER
A. A. Fischer Architectural & Building Company

DESCRIPTION
2-story brick dwelling; 25 feet × 34.5 feet; $3,000

BROKEN FRIEZE
Unknown

PART OF A STREETSCAPE
Yes, 1 of 4 (north to south: 1399, 1397, 1395, 1391)

NEIGHBORHOOD
● Hamilton Heights

SIDE OF THE STREET
West

STATUS IN 2021
Razed

1399

UNION BOULEVARD

ABOVE Photo by Reed R. Radcliffe, 2022.

BUILDING PERMIT NO.
D-4960

BUILDING PERMIT DATE
10/24/1901

DAILY RECORD NO.
960

APPEARED IN THE DAILY RECORD
10/28/1901

OWNER
A. A. Fischer/A. A. Fischer Architectural & Building Company

ARCHITECT
A. A. Fischer/A. A. Fischer Architectural & Building Company

BUILDER
A. A. Fischer Architectural & Building Company

DESCRIPTION
2-story brick dwelling; 25 feet × 34.5 feet; $3,000

BROKEN FRIEZE
Yes

PART OF A STREETSCAPE
Yes, 1 of 4 (north to south: 1399, 1397, 1395, 1391)

NEIGHBORHOOD
● Hamilton Heights

SIDE OF THE STREET
West

STATUS IN 2021
Occupied

3627
UTAH PLACE

ABOVE
Photo by Reed R. Radcliffe, 2022.

BUILDING PERMIT NO.
E-3634

BUILDING PERMIT DATE
04/26/1905

DAILY RECORD NO.
3634

APPEARED IN THE DAILY RECORD
04/27/1905

OWNER
Joseph M. and Jessie Griffin

ARCHITECT
A. A. Fischer/A. A. Fischer Architectural & Building Company

BUILDER
A. A. Fischer Architectural & Building Company

BROKEN FRIEZE
Yes

DESCRIPTION
2-story brick dwelling; 35 feet × 38 feet; $7,000

PART OF A STREETSCAPE
No

NEIGHBORHOOD
● Tower Grove South

SIDE OF THE STREET
North

STATUS IN 2021
Occupied

5039

VERNON AVENUE

ABOVE
Photo by Reed R. Radcliffe, 2022.

RIGHT
Photo provided by Landmarks Association of St. Louis, 1980.

BUILDING PERMIT NO.
9005

APPEARED IN THE *DAILY RECORD*
03/09/1898

HOUSE NUMBER SLIP
03/10/1898

OWNER
A. A. Fischer

ARCHITECT
A. A. Fischer

BUILDER
A. A. Fischer

DESCRIPTION
2.5-story dwelling; 27.5 feet × 36 feet

BROKEN FRIEZE
No

PART OF A STREETSCAPE
Yes, 1 of 3 (west to east: 5045, 5043, 5039)

NEIGHBORHOOD
● Academy

SIDE OF THE STREET
North

STATUS IN 2021
Occupied

5043

VERNON AVENUE

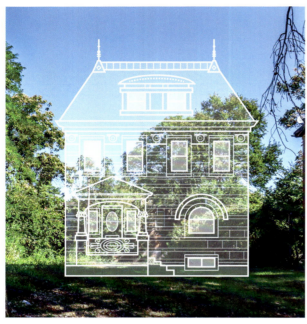

ABOVE
Photo by Reed R. Radcliffe, 2022

RIGHT
Photo provided by Landmarks Association of St. Louis, 1980.

BUILDING PERMIT NO.
9005

APPEARED IN THE *DAILY RECORD*
03/09/1898

OWNER
A. A. Fischer

ARCHITECT
A. A. Fischer

BUILDER
A. A. Fischer

DESCRIPTION
2.5-story dwelling; 27.6 feet × 36 feet

BROKEN FRIEZE
No

PART OF A STREETSCAPE
Yes, 1 of 3 (west to east: 5045, 5043, 5039)

NEIGHBORHOOD
● Academy

SIDE OF THE STREET
North

STATUS IN 2021
Razed in 2018

5045

VERNON AVENUE

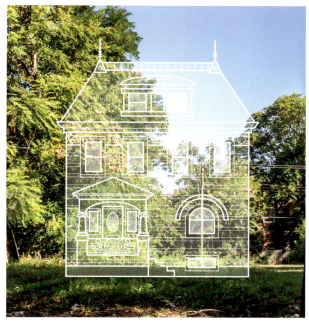

ABOVE
Photo by Reed R. Radcliffe, 2022.

RIGHT
Photo provided by Landmarks Association of St. Louis, 1980.

BUILDING PERMIT NO.
9005

APPEARED IN THE *DAILY RECORD*
03/09/1898

OWNER
A. A. Fischer

ARCHITECT
A. A. Fischer

BUILDER
A. A. Fischer

DESCRIPTION
2.5-story dwelling; 27.6 feet × 36 feet

BROKEN FRIEZE
No

PART OF A STREETSCAPE
Yes, 1 of 3 (west to east: 5045, 5043, 5039)

NEIGHBORHOOD
● Academy

SIDE OF THE STREET
North

STATUS IN 2021
Razed in 2018

5169

VERNON AVENUE

ABOVE
Photo by Reed R. Radcliffe, 2022.

RIGHT
Photo provided by Landmarks Association of St. Louis, 1980.

BUILDING PERMIT NO.
1658

BUILDING PERMIT DATE
09/15/1899

APPEARED IN THE *DAILY RECORD*
09/19/1899

OWNER
A. A. Fischer

BROKEN FRIEZE
No

DESCRIPTION
2.5-story dwelling; 38 feet × 32 feet; $4,000

PART OF A STREETSCAPE
No

NEIGHBORHOOD
● Academy

SIDE OF THE STREET
North

STATUS IN 2021
Occupied

5195
VERNON AVENUE

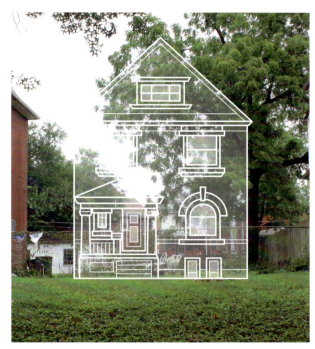

ABOVE
Photo by Lori Berdak Miller, 2021.

RIGHT
Photo provided by Landmarks Association of St. Louis, 1980.

BUILDING PERMIT NO.
D-5588

BUILDING PERMIT DATE
03/04/1902

DAILY RECORD NO.
588

APPEARED IN THE DAILY RECORD
03/05/1902

OWNER
A. A. Fischer

ARCHITECT
A. A. Fischer

BUILDER
A. A. Fischer

DESCRIPTION
2-story brick dwelling; 31.5 feet × 35 feet; $4,000

BROKEN FRIEZE
Unknown

PART OF A STREETSCAPE
No

NEIGHBORHOOD
North

NEIGHBORHOOD
● Academy

STATUS IN 2021
Razed in 2000

5227

VERNON AVENUE

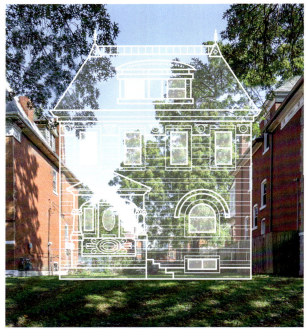

ABOVE Photo by Reed R. Radcliffe, 2022.

BUILDING PERMIT NO.
6650

BUILDING PERMIT DATE
03/26/1897

APPEARED IN THE *DAILY RECORD*
03/27/1897

OWNER
A. A. Fischer

BUILDER
A. A. Fischer

DESCRIPTION
2.5-story brick dwelling; $4,000

BROKEN FRIEZE
Unknown

PART OF A STREETSCAPE
Yes, originally 1 of 11 (west to east: 5263, 5259, 5255, 5253, 5249, 5147, 5243, 5237, 5233, 5231, 5227)

NEIGHBORHOOD
● Academy

SIDE OF THE STREET
North

STATUS IN 2021
Razed

NOTE The 2002 Mount Cabanne–Raymond Place Historic District nomination apparently confused this home, 5227 Vernon, with 5223 Vernon. The latter house had been demolished and attributed to Fischer, but in fact 5233 was built in 1903 by F. E. A. Darr. Fischer built 5227 Vernon.

5231

VERNON AVENUE

ABOVE
Photo by Reed R. Radcliffe, 2022.

RIGHT
Photo provided by Landmarks Association of St. Louis, 1980.

BUILDING PERMIT NO.
6651

BUILDING PERMIT DATE
03/26/1897

APPEARED IN THE *DAILY RECORD*
03/27/1897

OWNER
A. A. Fischer

BUILDER
A. A. Fischer

DESCRIPTION
2.5-story brick dwelling; $4,000

BROKEN FRIEZE
No

PART OF A STREETSCAPE
Yes, originally 1 of 11 (west to east: 5263, 5259, 5255, 5253, 5249, 5147, 5243, 5237, 5233, 5231, 5227)

NEIGHBORHOOD
● Academy

SIDE OF THE STREET
North

STATUS IN 2021
Occupied

NOTE The 2002 Mount Cabanne–Raymond Place Historic District nomination describes 5231 as representing late 19th and 20th century revival styles. The nomination further states, "This building has a hipped roof of asphalt shingle. The brown Roman brick façade is two stories high. The four-bay façade has an entrance in the second bay. Frieze has swags. Twin steep gable dormers. Similar to 5233-5237 Vernon. The building appears to be in good condition with no character-impairing alterations."

5233

VERNON AVENUE

ABOVE
Photo by Reed R. Radcliffe, 2022.

RIGHT
Photo provided by Landmarks Association of St. Louis, 1980.

BUILDING PERMIT NO.
6652

BUILDING PERMIT DATE
03/26/1897

APPEARED IN THE *DAILY RECORD*
03/27/1897

OWNER
A. A. Fischer

BUILDER
A. A. Fischer

DESCRIPTION
2.5-story brick dwelling; $4,000

BROKEN FRIEZE
No

PART OF A STREETSCAPE
Yes, originally 1 of 11 (west to east: 5263, 5259, 5255, 5253, 5249, 5147, 5243, 5237, 5233, 5231, 5227)

NEIGHBORHOOD
● Academy

SIDE OF THE STREET
North

STATUS IN 2021
Occupied

NOTE The 2002 Mount Cabanne–Raymond Place Historic District nomination describes 5233 Vernon as representing late 19th and 20th century revival styles. The nomination further states, "The building has a hipped slate roof. The Roman brick (brown at the foundation level and buff above) façade is 2 stories high and 4 bays wide. Rinceau relief at frieze. Twin steep gable dormers. Round-arched openings at the first floor, including the arch to the recessed entrance in the second bay. Similar to 5231, 5237 Vernon. The building appears to be in fair condition and has the following alterations: The front porch has been removed."

5237

VERNON AVENUE

ABOVE Photo by Reed R. Radcliffe, 2022.

HOUSE NUMBER CERTIFICATE
10/15/1897

OWNER
Allen T. Latta

BUILDER
A. A. Fischer

DESCRIPTION
1 house; 28 feet wide

BROKEN FRIEZE
No

PART OF A STREETSCAPE
Yes, originally 1 of 11 (west to east: 5263, 5259, 5255, 5253, 5249, 5147, 5243, 5237, 5233, 5231, 5227)

NEIGHBORHOOD
● Academy

SIDE OF THE STREET
North

STATUS IN 2021
Restored

NOTE The 2002 Mount Cabanne–Raymond Place Historic District nomination describes 5237 Vernon Avenue as representing late 19th and 20th century revival styles. The nomination further states, "This building has a hipped slate roof. The Roman brick (brown at the foundation level and red above) façade is 2 stories high and 4 bays wide. Twin steep gable dormers. Recessed entrance in the second bay. Round-arched windows at the second story except for the small rectangular window above the entrance. Similar to 5231, 5233 Vernon. The building appears to be in fair condition and has the following alterations: original porch missing."

5243

VERNON AVENUE

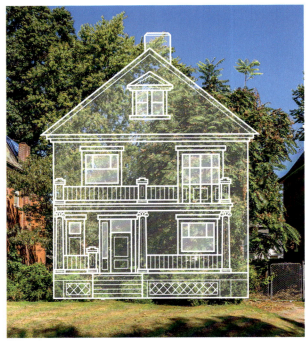

ABOVE Photo by Reed R. Radcliffe, 2022.

BUILDING PERMIT NO.
8124

BUILDING PERMIT DATE
09/28/1897

APPEARED IN THE *DAILY RECORD*
09/29/1897

OWNER
A. A. Fischer

ARCHITECT
A. A. Fischer

BUILDER
A. A. Fischer

DESCRIPTION
2-story dwelling; 28 feet × 40 feet; $4,000

BROKEN FRIEZE
Unknown

PART OF A STREETSCAPE
Yes, originally 1 of 11 (west to east: 5263, 5259, 5255, 5253, 5249, 5147, 5243, 5237, 5233, 5231, 5227)

NEIGHBORHOOD
● Academy

SIDE OF THE STREET
North

STATUS IN 2021
Razed

5247

VERNON AVENUE

This structure's original address was 5245 Vernon Avenue.

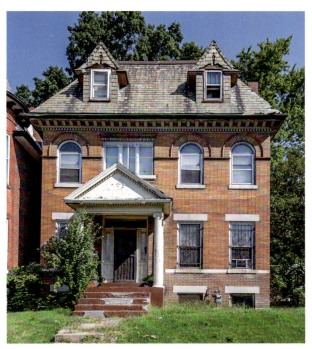

ABOVE Photo by Reed R. Radcliffe, 2022.

YEAR BUILT
1897

BROKEN FRIEZE
No

PART OF A STREETSCAPE
Yes, originally 1 of 11 (west to east: 5263, 5259, 5255, 5253, 5249, 5147, 5243, 5237, 5233, 5231, 5227)

NEIGHBORHOOD
● Academy

SIDE OF THE STREET
North

STATUS IN 2021
Occupied

NOTE The 2002 Mount Cabanne–Raymond Place Historic District nomination describes 5247 Vernon Avenue as representing late 19th and 20th century revival styles. The nomination further states, "This building has a hipped slate front roof. The Roman brick (brown at the foundation level and orangish above) façade is 2 stories high and 4 bays wide. Twin steep gable dormers. Gable front porch (original & intact) at the second bay. Round-arched windows at the second story except for a small rectangular triple window above the entrance. Similar to 5231, 5233, 5237 Vernon. The building appears to be in fair condition."

5248

VERNON AVENUE

ABOVE Photo by Lori Berdak Miller, 2021.

BUILDING PERMIT NO.
D-5689

DAILY RECORD NO.
689

APPEARED IN THE DAILY RECORD
03/21/1902

OWNER
A. A. Fischer/A. A. Fischer Architectural & Building Company

ARCHITECT
A. A. Fischer Architectural & Building Company

BUILDER
A. A. Fischer/A. A. Fischer Architectural & Building Company

DESCRIPTION
2-story brick dwelling; 34 feet × 34 feet; $4,000

BROKEN FRIEZE
Unknown

PART OF A STREETSCAPE
Yes, 1 of 3 (5248, 5252, 5256)

NEIGHBORHOOD
● Academy

SIDE OF THE STREET
South

STATUS IN 2021
Razed

5249

VERNON AVENUE

ABOVE
Photo by Reed R. Radcliffe, 2022.

RIGHT
Photo provided by Landmarks Association of St. Louis, 1980.

BUILDING PERMIT NO.
C-5531

BUILDING PERMIT DATE
09/05/1896

APPEARED IN THE *DAILY RECORD*
09/07/1896

OWNER
A. A. Fischer

BUILDER
A. A. Fischer

DESCRIPTION
2.5-story brick dwelling; 28 feet × 43 feet; $5,000

BROKEN FRIEZE
No

PART OF A STREETSCAPE
Yes, originally 1 of 11 (west to east: 5263, 5259, 5255, 5253, 5249, 5147, 5243, 5237, 5233, 5231, 5227)

NEIGHBORHOOD
● Academy

SIDE OF THE STREET
North

STATUS IN 2021
Occupied

NOTE The 2002 Mount Cabanne–Raymond Place Historic District nomination describes 5249 Vernon as representing Queen Anne and Romanesque Revival styles. The nomination further states, "This building has a complex roof of asphalt shingle. The red brick façade is 2 stories high and 3 bays wide. This house is a more intact mirror image of the house just west at 5253 Vernon. Rounded left bay has steep conical roof. Right bay projects slightly. Stone sill course under first floor sills. The building appears to be in fair condition and has the following alterations: Front door recess filled in; added hood. Lower center window opening altered."

5252

VERNON AVENUE

TOP Photo by Reed R. Radcliffe, 2022.
BOTTOM Photo by Lynn Josse for Landmarks Association of St. Louis, 2002.

BUILDING PERMIT NO.
D-5689

BUILDING PERMIT DATE
03/19/1902

DAILY RECORD NO.
689

APPEARED IN THE DAILY RECORD
03/21/1902

OWNER
A. A. Fischer/A. A. Fischer Architectural & Building Company

ARCHITECT
A. A. Fischer Architectural & Building Company

BUILDER
A. A. Fischer/A. A. Fischer Architectural & Building Company

DESCRIPTION
2-story brick dwelling; 34 feet × 34 feet; $4,000

BROKEN FRIEZE
Yes

PART OF A STREETSCAPE
Yes, 1 of 3 (5248, 5252, 5256)

NEIGHBORHOOD
● Academy

SIDE OF THE STREET
South

STATUS IN 2021
Occupied

5253

VERNON AVENUE

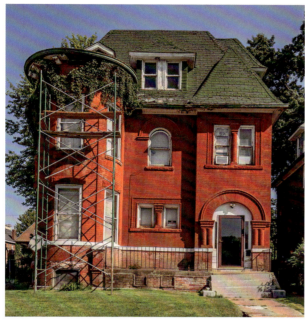

ABOVE
Photo by Reed R. Radcliffe, 2022.

RIGHT
Photo provided by Landmarks Association of St. Louis, 1980.

BUILDING PERMIT NO.
C-5532

BUILDING PERMIT DATE
09/05/1896

APPEARED IN THE *DAILY RECORD*
09/07/1896

OWNER
A. A. Fischer

BUILDER
A. A. Fischer

DESCRIPTION
2.5-story brick dwelling; 28 feet × 43 feet; $5,000

BROKEN FRIEZE
No

PART OF A STREETSCAPE
Yes, originally 1 of 11 (west to east: 5263, 5259, 5255, 5253, 5249, 5147, 5243, 5237, 5233, 5231, 5227)

NEIGHBORHOOD
● Academy

SIDE OF THE STREET
North

STATUS IN 2021
Occupied, under renovation

NOTE The 2002 Mount Cabanne–Raymond Place Historic District nomination describes 5253 Vernon Avenue as representing Queen Anne and Romanesque Revival styles. The nomination further states, "This building has a complex roof of asphalt shingle. The brick (painted red) façade is 2 stones high and 3 bays wide. Very similar to the house just east at 5249 Vernon, this house has a rounded left bay missing the conical roof and some brackets. Right bay projects slightly. Stone sill course under first floor sills, the building appears to be in fair condition and has the following alterations: Filled-in front door recess."

5255
VERNON AVENUE

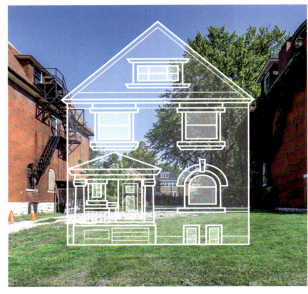

ABOVE Photo by Reed R. Radcliffe, 2022.

BUILDING PERMIT DATE
10/13/1898

APPEARED IN THE *DAILY RECORD*
10/13/1898

HOUSE NUMBER CERTIFICATE
09/12/1898

OWNER
A. A. Fischer

BUILDER
A. A. Fischer

DESCRIPTION
2.5-story bake shop; 28 feet × 39 feet; $4,200

BROKEN FRIEZE
Unknown

PART OF A STREETSCAPE
Yes, originally 1 of 11 (west to east: 5263, 5259, 5255, 5253, 5249, 5147, 5243, 5237, 5233, 5231, 5227)

NEIGHBORHOOD
● Academy

SIDE OF THE STREET
North

STATUS IN 2021
Razed

5256

VERNON AVENUE

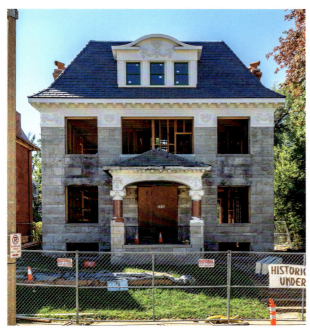

ABOVE Photo by Reed R. Radcliffe, 2022.

BUILDING PERMIT NO.
D-5126

BUILDING PERMIT DATE
11/21/1901

DAILY RECORD NO.
126

APPEARED IN THE DAILY RECORD
11/22/1901

OWNER
A. A. Fischer

ARCHITECT
A. A. Fischer

BUILDER
A. A. Fischer

DESCRIPTION
2-story brick residence; 38 feet × 31.3 feet; $4,000

BROKEN FRIEZE
Yes

PART OF A STREETSCAPE
Yes, 1 of 3 (5248, 5252, 5256)

NEIGHBORHOOD
● Academy

SIDE OF THE STREET
South

STATUS IN 2021
Under renovation

NOTE A. A. Fischer built this home for himself and his family. According to the City of St. Louis's online Address and Property Search portal, in 2021 its owners invested more than $450,000 in construction costs toward this home's restoration.

5259

VERNON AVENUE

ABOVE
Photo by Reed R. Radcliffe, 2022.

RIGHT
Photo by Lynn Josse for Landmarks Association of St. Louis, 2002.

APPEARED IN THE *DAILY RECORD*
03/23/1899

HOUSE NUMBER CERTIFICATE
03/24/1899

OWNER
A. A. Fischer

ARCHITECT
A. A. Fischer

BUILDER
A. A. Fischer

DESCRIPTION
2-story stone dwelling; 29 feet × 40 feet; $4,000

BROKEN FRIEZE
No

PART OF A STREETSCAPE
Yes, originally 1 of 11 (west to east: 5263, 5259, 5255, 5253, 5249, 5147, 5243, 5237, 5233, 5231, 5227)

NEIGHBORHOOD
● Academy

SIDE OF THE STREET
North

STATUS IN 2021
Occupied

NOTE It is possible this building originally had a broken frieze. The 2002 Mount Cabanne–Raymond Place Historic District nomination describes 5259 Vernon Avenue as representing late 19th and 20th century revival styles. The nomination further states, "This building has a mansard roof of asphalt shingle. The façade is 2 stories high and 3 bays wide. Shallow porch hood at center two bays is not original. At the second story, smooth limestone courses alternate wide and narrow width. The building appears to be in good condition and has the following alterations: First story of façade covered with imitation stone veneer. Massing, fenestration, and second story are intact, tipping the scales toward contributing status."

5263

VERNON AVENUE

ABOVE
Photo by Reed R. Radcliffe, 2022.

RIGHT
Photo by Lynn Josse for Landmarks Association of St. Louis, 2002.

BUILDING PERMIT NO.
9870

BUILDING PERMIT DATE
08/10/1898

APPEARED IN THE *DAILY RECORD*
08/12/1898

OWNER
A. A. Fischer

BUILDER
A. A. Fischer

DESCRIPTION
2.5-story brick dwelling; $4,000

BROKEN FRIEZE
No

PART OF A STREETSCAPE
Yes, originally 1 of 11 (west to east: 5263, 5259, 5255, 5253, 5249, 5147, 5243, 5237, 5233, 5231, 5227)

NEIGHBORHOOD
● Academy

SIDE OF THE STREET
North

STATUS IN 2021
Occupied

NOTE The 2002 Mount Cabanne–Raymond Place Historic District nomination describes 5263 Vernon Avenue as representing a French Renaissance style. The nomination further states, "This building has a complex roof of asphalt shingle. The brown brick façade is 2 stories high and 3 bays wide. Outer bays of this three-bay façade project forward, round, with conical roofs. At the center bay, a steep roof with a hipped dormer connects the two cone shapes. Porch at the center bay has red granite columns; palmetto frieze. The building appears to be in good condition and has the following alterations: Awnings added."

5359

VERNON AVENUE

ABOVE Photo by Reed R. Radcliffe, 2022.

***REALTY RECORD AND BUILDER* NO.**
2246

APPEARED IN THE *REALTY RECORD AND BUILDER*
07/07/1907

OWNER
A. A. Fischer Realty Company

ARCHITECT
A. A. Fischer Realty Company

BUILDER
A. A. Fischer Realty Company

DESCRIPTION
2-story dwelling; 23 feet × 33 feet; $4,500

BROKEN FRIEZE
Yes

PART OF A STREETSCAPE
No

NEIGHBORHOOD
● Visitation Park

SIDE OF THE STREET
North

STATUS IN 2021
Condemned

5363

VERNON AVENUE

ABOVE Photo by Reed R. Radcliffe, 2022.

DAILY RECORD NO.
1933

APPEARED IN THE DAILY RECORD
05/18/1907

REALTY RECORD AND BUILDER NO.
1933

APPEARED IN THE REALTY RECORD AND BUILDER
06/07/1907

OWNER
A. A. Fischer Realty Company

ARCHITECT
A. A. Fischer Realty Company

BUILDER
A. A. Fischer Realty Company

DESCRIPTION
2-story dwelling; 23 feet × 33 feet; $4,500

BROKEN FRIEZE
Yes

PART OF A STREETSCAPE
No

NEIGHBORHOOD
● Visitation Park

SIDE OF THE STREET
North

STATUS IN 2021
Occupied

5616-5618

VERNON AVENUE

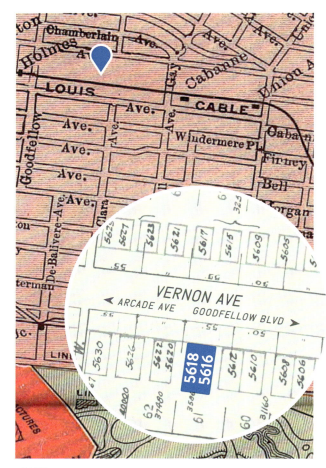

ABOVE
David Rumsey Map Collection, David Rumsey Map Center, Stanford Libraries at Stanford University.

CIRCLE
St. Louis Building Department Atlases, 1943–1946. St. Louis Public Library.

DAILY RECORD NO.
4134

APPEARED IN THE *BUILDER*
June 1905

APPEARED IN THE *REALTY RECORD*
June 1905

HOUSE NUMBER CERTIFICATE
06/08/1905

OWNER
A. A. Fischer/A. A. Fischer Architectural & Building Company

ARCHITECT
A. A. Fischer/A. A. Fischer Architectural & Building Company

BUILDER
A. A. Fischer/A. A. Fischer Architectural & Building Company

DESCRIPTION
28.1-foot-wide house

BROKEN FRIEZE
Unknown

PART OF A STREETSCAPE
Yes, 1 of 2 side by side (west to east: 5620-5622, 5616-5618)

NEIGHBORHOOD
● West End

SIDE OF THE STREET
South

STATUS IN 2021
Razed in 1991

5620-5622
VERNON AVENUE

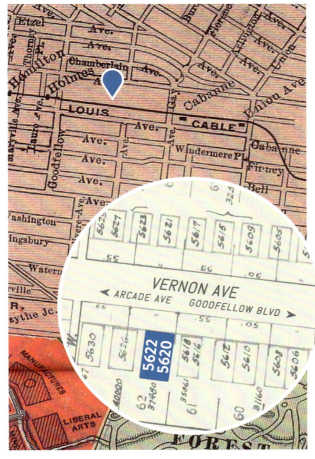

ABOVE
David Rumsey Map Collection, David Rumsey Map Center, Stanford Libraries at Stanford University.

CIRCLE
St. Louis Building Department Atlases, 1943–1946.
St. Louis Public Library.

DAILY RECORD NO.
6514

APPEARED IN THE DAILY RECORD
02/10/1906

HOUSE NUMBER CERTIFICATE
02/09/1906

OWNER
A. A. Fischer Architectural & Building Company

ARCHITECT
A. A. Fischer Architectural & Building Company

BUILDER
A. A. Fischer Architectural & Building Company

DESCRIPTION
2-story flats; 28 feet × 47 feet

BROKEN FRIEZE
Unknown

PART OF A STREETSCAPE
Yes, 1 of 2 side by side (west to east: 5620-5622, 5616-5618)

NEIGHBORHOOD
● West End

SIDE OF THE STREET
South

STATUS IN 2021
Razed

6224
WASHINGTON AVENUE

ABOVE Photo by Reed R. Radcliffe, 2022.

***REALTY RECORD AND BUILDER* NO.**
7426

APPEARED IN THE *REALTY RECORD AND BUILDER*
Oct. 1908

OWNER
Nathaniel S. Brown

ARCHITECT
A. A. Fischer Realty Company/L. F. Gardner

BUILDER
A. A. Fischer Realty Company

DESCRIPTION
2-story dwelling; 34 feet × 46 feet; $7,000

BROKEN FRIEZE
No

PART OF A STREETSCAPE
No

NEIGHBORHOOD
● Parkview subdivision of Skinker DeBaliviere

SIDE OF THE STREET
South

STATUS IN 2021
Restored

NOTE The owner of this Washington Avenue home, Nathaniel S. Brown, was living in a recently constructed Fischer home at 915 Clarendon when this building permit was filed.

6309
WASHINGTON AVENUE

ABOVE Photo by Reed R. Radcliffe, 2022.

RIGHT Photo by Nancy Moore Hamilton, 2001.

DAILY RECORD NO.
3986

APPEARED IN THE DAILY RECORD
11/27/1909

OWNER
Mrs. Jennie S. Garvey

BUILDER
A. A. Fischer Realty Company

DESCRIPTION
Brick Craftsman-style residence; $6,000

BROKEN FRIEZE
No

PART OF A STREETSCAPE
Yes, 1 of 2 side by side (6311, 6309)

NEIGHBORHOOD
● Parkview subdivision of University City

SIDE OF THE STREET
North

STATUS IN 2021
Restored

6311

WASHINGTON AVENUE

ABOVE
Photo by Lori Berdak Miller, 2021.

RIGHT
Photo by Nancy Moore Hamilton, 2001.

DAILY RECORD NO.
2755

APPEARED IN THE DAILY RECORD
03/23/1909

OWNER
Mrs. Jennie S. Garvey

BUILDER
A. A. Fischer Realty Company

DESCRIPTION
Brick Craftsman-style residence; $5,000

BROKEN FRIEZE
No

PART OF A STREETSCAPE
Yes, 1 of 2 side by side (6311, 6309)

NEIGHBORHOOD
● Parkview subdivision of University City

SIDE OF THE STREET
North

STATUS IN 2021
Restored

6317
WASHINGTON AVENUE

ABOVE Photo by Reed R. Radcliffe, 2022.

DAILY RECORD NO.
1594

APPEARED IN THE DAILY RECORD
06/25/1908

OWNER
Mrs. Jennie S. Garvey

ARCHITECT
Chris Garvey

BUILDER
A. A. Fischer

DESCRIPTION
Brick Colonial Revival residence; $5,000

BROKEN FRIEZE
No

PART OF A STREETSCAPE
No

NEIGHBORHOOD
● Parkview subdivision of University City

SIDE OF THE STREET
North

STATUS IN 2021
Occupied

6353
WASHINGTON AVENUE

ABOVE Photo by Lori Berdak Miller, 2021.

DAILY RECORD NO.
1812

APPEARED IN THE DAILY RECORD
08/12/1908

OWNER
L. H. Winter

ARCHITECT
A. A. Fischer

BUILDER
A. A. Fischer/A. A. Fischer Architectural & Building Company

DESCRIPTION
Brick residence; $5,000

BROKEN FRIEZE
No

PART OF A STREETSCAPE
No

NEIGHBORHOOD
● Parkview subdivision of University City

SIDE OF THE STREET
North

STATUS IN 2021
Restored

5916-18
WASHINGTON BOULEVARD

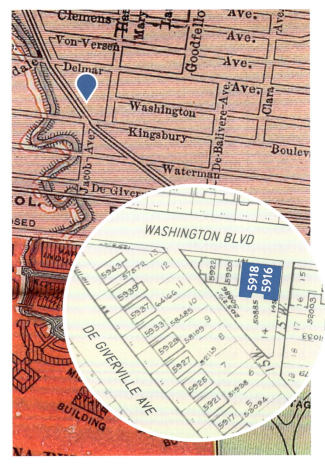

ABOVE
David Rumsey Map Collection, David Rumsey Map Center, Stanford Libraries at Stanford University.

CIRCLE
St. Louis Building Department Atlases, 1943–1946.
St. Louis Public Library.

APPEARED IN THE *DAILY RECORD*
11/12/1910

***REALTY RECORD AND BUILDER* NO.**
6438

APPEARED IN THE *REALTY RECORD AND BUILDER*
Nov. 1910

OWNER
A. A. Fischer Realty Company

ARCHITECT
A. A. Fischer Realty Company

BUILDER
A. A. Fischer Realty Company

DESCRIPTION
3-story tenement; 52 feet × 42 feet

BROKEN FRIEZE
Unknown

PART OF A STREETSCAPE
No

NEIGHBORHOOD
● Skinker DeBaliviere

SIDE OF THE STREET
South

STATUS IN 2021
Razed (current site of Lucier Park)

DIRECTORY OF A. A. FISCHER BUILDS | 371

6101

WASHINGTON BOULEVARD

This structure is also known as 541-543 Rosedale Avenue. Its original address was 6101-6103 Washington Boulevard.

ABOVE Photo by Reed R. Radcliffe, 2022.

DAILY RECORD NO.
3768

APPEARED IN THE DAILY RECORD
03/29/1910

REALTY RECORD AND BUILDER NO.
3768

APPEARED IN THE REALTY RECORD AND BUILDER
Apr. 1910

LANDMARKS
1910

OWNER
A. A. Fischer Realty Company

ARCHITECT
A. A. Fischer Realty Company

BUILDER
A. A. Fischer Realty Company

DESCRIPTION
3-story tenement; 55 feet × 95 feet

BROKEN FRIEZE
Yes

PART OF A STREETSCAPE
Yes, 1 of 3 apartment buildings (west to east: 6115-17, 6109-11, 6101-03)

NEIGHBORHOOD
● Skinker DeBaliviere

SIDE OF THE STREET
North

STATUS IN 2021
Occupied

6102-6104
WASHINGTON BOULEVARD
This structure is also known as 519-521 Rosedale Avenue.

TOP Photo by Reed R. Radcliffe, 2022.
BOTTOM Photo by Nancy Moore Hamilton, 2001.

DAILY RECORD NO.
3563

APPEARED IN THE DAILY RECORD
03/16/1910

REALTY RECORD AND BUILDER NO.
3563

APPEARED IN THE REALTY RECORD AND BUILDER
Apr. 1910

LANDMARKS
1910

OWNER
A. A. Fischer Realty Company

ARCHITECT
A. A. Fischer Realty Company

BUILDER
A. A. Fischer Realty Company

DESCRIPTION
3-story tenement; 55 feet × 95 feet

BROKEN FRIEZE
Yes

PART OF A STREETSCAPE
Yes, 1 of 7 (west to east: 6134, 6130, 6126-6128, 6120-6122, 6114-6116, 6108-6110, 6102-6104)

NEIGHBORHOOD
● Skinker DeBaliviere

SIDE OF THE STREET
South

STATUS IN 2021
Occupied

6108-6110
WASHINGTON BOULEVARD

ABOVE Photo by Reed R. Radcliffe, 2022.

DAILY RECORD NO.
3171

REALTY RECORD AND BUILDER NO.
3171

APPEARED IN THE REALTY RECORD AND BUILDER
Mar. 1910

LANDMARKS
1910

OWNER
A. A. Fischer Realty Company

ARCHITECT
A. A. Fischer Realty Company

BUILDER
A. A. Fischer Realty Company

DESCRIPTION
3-story apartments; 51 feet × 33 feet

BROKEN FRIEZE
Yes

PART OF A STREETSCAPE
Yes, 1 of 7 (west to east: 6134, 6130, 6126-6128, 6120-6122, 6114-6116, 6108-6110, 6102-6104)

NEIGHBORHOOD
● Skinker DeBaliviere

SIDE OF THE STREET
South

STATUS IN 2021
Restored

6109-6111

WASHINGTON BOULEVARD

ABOVE Photo by Reed R. Radcliffe, 2022.

DAILY RECORD NO.
3923

APPEARED IN THE DAILY RECORD
04/08/1910

LANDMARKS
1910

OWNER
A. A. Fischer Realty Company

ARCHITECT
A. A. Fischer Realty Company

BUILDER
A. A. Fischer Realty Company

DESCRIPTION
3-story tenement; 33 feet × 53 feet

BROKEN FRIEZE
This home features a variation on Fischer's traditional broken frieze — an example of which can be seen next door at 6101 Washington Boulevard. On this apartment building Fischer installed corbels that protrude downward from the frieze to the space in between the windows. This building is one of four structures on the 6100 block of Washington Boulevard that has this variation on the broken frieze. The others are 6115-6117, 6114-6116, and 6173.

PART OF A STREETSCAPE
Yes, 1 of 3 apartment buildings (west to east: 6115-17, 6109-11, 6101-03)

NEIGHBORHOOD
● Skinker DeBaliviere

SIDE OF THE STREET
North

STATUS IN 2021
Occupied

6114-6116

WASHINGTON BOULEVARD

TOP Photo by Reed R. Radcliffe, 2022.
BOTTOM Photo by Nancy Moore Hamilton, 2001.

LANDMARKS
1910

APPEARED IN THE *REALTY RECORD AND BUILDER*
Mar. 1910

OWNER
A. A. Fischer Realty Company

ARCHITECT
A. A. Fischer Realty Company

BUILDER
A. A. Fischer Realty Company

DESCRIPTION
3-story apartments; 51 feet × 33 feet

BROKEN FRIEZE
This home features a variation on Fischer's traditional broken frieze. On this apartment building Fischer installed corbels that protrude downward from the frieze to the space in between the windows. This building is one of four structures on the 6100 block of Washington Boulevard that has this variation on the broken frieze. The others are 6109-6111, 6115-6117, and 6173.

PART OF A STREETSCAPE
Yes, 1 of 7 (west to east: 6134, 6130, 6126-6128, 6120-6122, 6114-6116, 6108-6110, 6102-6104)

NEIGHBORHOOD
● Skinker DeBaliviere

SIDE OF THE STREET
South

STATUS IN 2021
Occupied

6115-6117

WASHINGTON BOULEVARD

ABOVE Photo by Reed R. Radcliffe, 2022.

DAILY RECORD NO.
4039

APPEARED IN THE DAILY RECORD
04/15/1910

REALTY RECORD AND BUILDER NO.
4039

APPEARED IN THE REALTY RECORD AND BUILDER
May 1910

LANDMARKS
1910

OWNER
A. A. Fischer Realty Company

ARCHITECT
A. A. Fischer Realty Company

BUILDER
A. A. Fischer Realty Company

DESCRIPTION
3-story tenement; 55 feet × 44 feet

BROKEN FRIEZE
On this apartment building, Fischer installed corbels that protrude downward from the frieze to the space in between the windows. This building is one of four structures on the 6100 block of Washington Boulevard that has this variation on the broken frieze. The others are 6109-6111, 6114-6116, and 6173.

PART OF A STREETSCAPE
Yes, 1 of 3 apartment buildings (west to east: 6115-17, 6109-11, 6101-03)

NEIGHBORHOOD
● Skinker DeBaliviere

SIDE OF THE STREET
North

STATUS IN 2021
Restored

6120-6122
WASHINGTON BOULEVARD

ABOVE Photo by Reed R. Radcliffe, 2022.

REALTY RECORD AND BUILDER NO.
2949

APPEARED IN THE REALTY RECORD AND BUILDER
Jan. 1910

LANDMARKS
1910

OWNER
A. A. Fischer Realty Company

ARCHITECT
A. A. Fischer Realty Company

BUILDER
A. A. Fischer Realty Company

DESCRIPTION
3-story apartments; 51 feet × 33 feet

BROKEN FRIEZE
Yes

PART OF A STREETSCAPE
Yes, 1 of 7 (west to east: 6134, 6130, 6126-6128, 6120-6122, 6114-6116, 6108-6110, 6102-6104)

NEIGHBORHOOD
● Skinker DeBaliviere

SIDE OF THE STREET
South

STATUS IN 2021
Restored

6126-6128
WASHINGTON BOULEVARD

ABOVE Photo by Reed R. Radcliffe, 2022.

REALTY RECORD AND BUILDER NO.
2949

APPEARED IN THE *REALTY RECORD AND BUILDER*
Feb. 1910

LANDMARKS
1910

OWNER
A. A. Fischer Realty Company

ARCHITECT
A. A. Fischer Realty Company

BUILDER
A. A. Fischer Realty Company

DESCRIPTION
3-story apartment building; 51 feet × 33 feet

BROKEN FRIEZE
Yes

PART OF A STREETSCAPE
Yes, 1 of 7 (west to east: 6134, 6130, 6126-6128, 6120-6122, 6114-6116, 6108-6110, 6102-6104)

NEIGHBORHOOD
● Skinker DeBaliviere

SIDE OF THE STREET
South

STATUS IN 2021
Restored

6130
WASHINGTON BOULEVARD

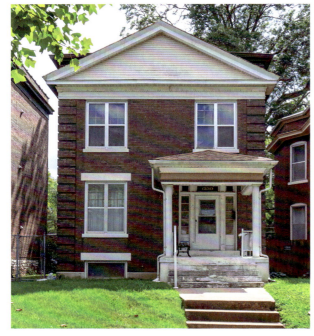

ABOVE Photo by Reed R. Radcliffe, 2022.

REALTY RECORD AND BUILDER NO.
2441

APPEARED IN THE REALTY RECORD AND BUILDER
Nov. 1909

LANDMARKS
1909

OWNER
A. A. Fischer Realty Company

ARCHITECT
A. A. Fischer Realty Company

BUILDER
A. A. Fischer Realty Company

DESCRIPTION
2-story dwelling; 24 feet × 33 feet; $4,500

BROKEN FRIEZE
No

PART OF A STREETSCAPE
Yes, 1 of 7 (west to east: 6134, 6130, 6126-6128, 6120-6122, 6114-6116, 6108-6110, 6102-6104)

NEIGHBORHOOD
● Skinker DeBaliviere

SIDE OF THE STREET
South

STATUS IN 2021
Occupied

6134

WASHINGTON BOULEVARD

ABOVE Photo by Reed R. Radcliffe, 2022.

REALTY RECORD AND BUILDER NO.
2441

APPEARED IN THE REALTY RECORD AND BUILDER
Nov. 1909

LANDMARKS
1909

OWNER
A. A. Fischer Realty Company

ARCHITECT
A. A. Fischer Realty Company

BUILDER
A. A. Fischer Realty Company

DESCRIPTION
2-story dwelling; 24 feet × 33 feet; $4,500

BROKEN FRIEZE
No

PART OF A STREETSCAPE
Yes, 1 of 7 (west to east: 6134, 6130, 6126-6128, 6120-6122, 6114-6116, 6108-6110, 6102-6104)

NEIGHBORHOOD
● Skinker DeBaliviere

SIDE OF THE STREET
South

STATUS IN 2021
Occupied

6144

WASHINGTON BOULEVARD

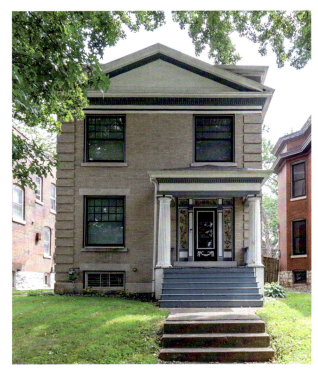

ABOVE Photo by Reed R. Radcliffe, 2022.

***REALTY RECORD AND BUILDER* NO.**
6895

APPEARED IN THE *REALTY RECORD AND BUILDER*
Aug. 1908

LANDMARKS
1908

OWNER
A. A. Fischer Realty Company

ARCHITECT
A. A. Fischer Realty Company

BUILDER
A. A. Fischer Realty Company

DESCRIPTION
2-story residence; 24 feet × 33 feet

BROKEN FRIEZE
No

PART OF A STREETSCAPE
Yes, 1 of 7 (west to east: 6164, 6160, 6158, 6154, 6152, 6148, 6144)

NEIGHBORHOOD
● Skinker DeBaliviere

SIDE OF THE STREET
South

STATUS IN 2021
Occupied

6145

WASHINGTON BOULEVARD

ABOVE Photo by Reed R. Radcliffe, 2022.

REALTY RECORD AND BUILDER NO.
9477

APPEARED IN THE REALTY RECORD AND BUILDER
Mar. 1909

LANDMARKS
1909

OWNER
A. A. Fischer Realty Company

ARCHITECT
A. A. Fischer Realty Company

BUILDER
A. A. Fischer Realty Company

DESCRIPTION
2-story dwelling; 30 feet × 32 feet; $5,000

BROKEN FRIEZE
No

PART OF A STREETSCAPE
Yes, 1 of 10 (west to east: 6177, 6173, 6169, 6167, 6163, 6159, 6155, 6151, 6149, 6145)

NEIGHBORHOOD
● Skinker DeBaliviere

SIDE OF THE STREET
North

STATUS IN 2021
Restored

6148

WASHINGTON BOULEVARD

ABOVE Photos by Reed R. Radcliffe, 2022.

BUILDING PERMIT DATE
08/15/1908

REALTY RECORD AND BUILDER NO.
6895

APPEARED IN THE REALTY RECORD AND BUILDER
Aug. 1908

LANDMARKS
1908

OWNER
A. A. Fischer Realty Company

ARCHITECT
A. A. Fischer Realty Company

BUILDER
A. A. Fischer Realty Company

DESCRIPTION
2-story residence; 24 feet × 33 feet

BROKEN FRIEZE
Yes

PART OF A STREETSCAPE
Yes, 1 of 7 (west to east: 6164, 6160, 6158, 6154, 6152, 6148, 6144)

NEIGHBORHOOD
● Skinker DeBaliviere

SIDE OF THE STREET
South

STATUS IN 2021
Occupied

6149
WASHINGTON BOULEVARD

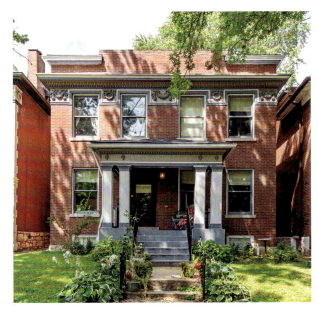

ABOVE Photo by Reed R. Radcliffe, 2022.

REALTY RECORD AND BUILDER NO.
9477

APPEARED IN THE REALTY RECORD AND BUILDER
Mar. 1909

LANDMARKS
1909

OWNER
A. A. Fischer Realty Company

ARCHITECT
A. A. Fischer Realty Company

BUILDER
A. A. Fischer Realty Company

DESCRIPTION
2-story dwelling; 30 feet × 32 feet; $5,000

BROKEN FRIEZE
Yes

PART OF A STREETSCAPE
Yes, 1 of 10 (west to east: 6177, 6173, 6169, 6167, 6163, 6159, 6155, 6151, 6149, 6145)

NEIGHBORHOOD
● Skinker DeBaliviere

SIDE OF THE STREET
North

STATUS IN 2021
Occupied

6151
WASHINGTON BOULEVARD

ABOVE Photo by Reed R. Radcliffe, 2022.

REALTY RECORD AND BUILDER NO.
9477

APPEARED IN THE *REALTY RECORD AND BUILDER*
Mar. 1909

LANDMARKS
1909

OWNER
A. A. Fischer Realty Company

ARCHITECT
A. A. Fischer Realty Company

BUILDER
A. A. Fischer Realty Company

DESCRIPTION
2-story dwelling; 30 feet × 32 feet; $5,000

BROKEN FRIEZE
Yes

PART OF A STREETSCAPE
Yes, 1 of 10 (west to east: 6177, 6173, 6169, 6167, 6163, 6159, 6155, 6151, 6149, 6145)

NEIGHBORHOOD
● Skinker DeBaliviere

SIDE OF THE STREET
North

STATUS IN 2021
Occupied

6152
WASHINGTON BOULEVARD

ABOVE Photo by Reed R. Radcliffe, 2022.

BUILDING PERMIT DATE
08/15/1908

REALTY RECORD AND BUILDER NO.
6895

APPEARED IN THE REALTY RECORD AND BUILDER
Aug. 1908

LANDMARKS
1908

OWNER
A. A. Fischer Realty Company

ARCHITECT
A. A. Fischer Realty Company

BUILDER
A. A. Fischer Realty Company

DESCRIPTION
2-story residence; 24 feet × 33 feet

BROKEN FRIEZE
No

PART OF A STREETSCAPE
Yes, 1 of 7 (west to east: 6164, 6160, 6158, 6154, 6152, 6148, 6144)

NEIGHBORHOOD
● Skinker DeBaliviere

SIDE OF THE STREET
South

STATUS IN 2021
Occupied

6154

WASHINGTON BOULEVARD

ABOVE Photo by Reed R. Radcliffe, 2022.

BUILDING PERMIT DATE
08/01/1908

REALTY RECORD AND BUILDER NO.
6700

APPEARED IN THE REALTY RECORD AND BUILDER
Aug. 1908

LANDMARKS
1908

OWNER
A. A. Fischer Realty Company

ARCHITECT
A. A. Fischer Realty Company

BUILDER
A. A. Fischer Realty Company

DESCRIPTION
2-story dwelling; 24 feet × 33 feet; $4,000

BROKEN FRIEZE
No

PART OF A STREETSCAPE
Yes, 1 of 7 (west to east: 6164, 6160, 6158, 6154, 6152, 6148, 6144)

NEIGHBORHOOD
● Skinker DeBaliviere

SIDE OF THE STREET
South

STATUS IN 2021
Occupied

6155

WASHINGTON BOULEVARD

ABOVE
Photo by Reed R. Radcliffe, 2022.

RIGHT
Photo by Nancy Moore Hamilton, 2001.

DAILY RECORD NO.
5096

APPEARED IN THE DAILY RECORD
03/27/1908

REALTY RECORD AND BUILDER NO.
5096

APPEARED IN THE REALTY RECORD AND BUILDER
May 1908

LANDMARKS
1908

OWNER
A. A. Fischer Realty Company

ARCHITECT
A. A. Fischer Realty Company

BUILDER
A. A. Fischer Realty Company

DESCRIPTION
1 dwelling; 24 feet × 33 feet; $4,000

BROKEN FRIEZE
Yes

PART OF A STREETSCAPE
Yes, 1 of 10 (west to east: 6177, 6173, 6169, 6167, 6163, 6159, 6155, 6151, 6149, 6145)

NEIGHBORHOOD
● Skinker DeBaliviere

SIDE OF THE STREET
North

STATUS IN 2021
Occupied

6158
WASHINGTON BOULEVARD

ABOVE Photos by Reed R. Radcliffe, 2022.

BUILDING PERMIT DATE
08/01/1908

REALTY RECORD AND BUILDER NO.
6700

APPEARED IN THE REALTY RECORD AND BUILDER
Aug. 1908

LANDMARKS
1908

OWNER
A. A. Fischer Realty Company

ARCHITECT
A. A. Fischer Realty Company

BUILDER
A. A. Fischer Realty Company

DESCRIPTION
2-story dwelling; 24 feet × 33 feet; $4,000

BROKEN FRIEZE
No

PART OF A STREETSCAPE
Yes, 1 of 7 (west to east: 6164, 6160, 6158, 6154, 6152, 6148, 6144)

NEIGHBORHOOD
● Skinker DeBaliviere

SIDE OF THE STREET
South

STATUS IN 2021
Occupied

6159

WASHINGTON BOULEVARD

ABOVE Photo by Reed R. Radcliffe, 2022.

DAILY RECORD NO.
5096

APPEARED IN THE DAILY RECORD
03/27/1908

REALTY RECORD AND BUILDER NO.
5096

APPEARED IN THE REALTY RECORD AND BUILDER
May 1908

LANDMARKS
1908

OWNER
A. A. Fischer Realty Company

ARCHITECT
A. A. Fischer Realty Company

BUILDER
A. A. Fischer Realty Company

DESCRIPTION
1 dwelling; 24 feet × 33 feet; $4,000

BROKEN FRIEZE
Yes

PART OF A STREETSCAPE
Yes, 1 of 10 (west to east: 6177, 6173, 6169, 6167, 6163, 6159, 6155, 6151, 6149, 6145)

NEIGHBORHOOD
● Skinker DeBaliviere

SIDE OF THE STREET
North

STATUS IN 2021
Occupied

6160

WASHINGTON BOULEVARD

ABOVE Photo by Reed R. Radcliffe, 2022.

BUILDING PERMIT DATE
07/13/1908

REALTY RECORD AND BUILDER NO.
6472

APPEARED IN THE REALTY RECORD AND BUILDER
Aug. 1908

LANDMARKS
1908

OWNER
A. A. Fischer Realty Company

ARCHITECT
A. A. Fischer Realty Company

BUILDER
A. A. Fischer Realty Company

DESCRIPTION
2-story dwelling; 30 feet × 32 feet; $5,000

BROKEN FRIEZE
Yes

PART OF A STREETSCAPE
Yes, 1 of 7 (west to east: 6164, 6160, 6158, 6154, 6152, 6148, 6144)

NEIGHBORHOOD
● Skinker DeBaliviere

SIDE OF THE STREET
South

STATUS IN 2021
Restored

6163

WASHINGTON BOULEVARD

ABOVE Photo by Reed R. Radcliffe, 2022.

DAILY RECORD NO.
5095

APPEARED IN THE DAILY RECORD
03/27/1908

REALTY RECORD AND BUILDER NO.
5095

APPEARED IN THE REALTY RECORD AND BUILDER
May 1908

LANDMARKS
1908

OWNER
A. A. Fischer Realty Company

ARCHITECT
A. A. Fischer Realty Company

BUILDER
A. A. Fischer Realty Company

DESCRIPTION
2-story dwelling; 31 feet × 32 feet

BROKEN FRIEZE
Yes

PART OF A STREETSCAPE
Yes, 1 of 10 (west to east: 6177, 6173, 6169, 6167, 6163, 6159, 6155, 6151, 6149, 6145)

NEIGHBORHOOD
● Skinker DeBaliviere

SIDE OF THE STREET
North

STATUS IN 2021
Occupied

6164
WASHINGTON BOULEVARD

ABOVE Photo by Reed R. Radcliffe, 2022.

REALTY RECORD AND BUILDER NO.
6472

APPEARED IN THE REALTY RECORD AND BUILDER
Aug. 1908

LANDMARKS
1908

OWNER
A. A. Fischer Realty Company

ARCHITECT
A. A. Fischer Realty Company

BUILDER
A. A. Fischer Realty Company

DESCRIPTION
2-story dwelling; 30 feet × 32 feet; $5,000

BROKEN FRIEZE
Yes

PART OF A STREETSCAPE
Yes, 1 of 7 (west to east: 6164, 6160, 6158, 6154, 6152, 6148, 6144)

NEIGHBORHOOD
● Skinker DeBaliviere

SIDE OF THE STREET
South

STATUS IN 2021
Occupied

6167

WASHINGTON BOULEVARD

ABOVE Photo by Reed R. Radcliffe, 2022.

LANDMARKS
1909

BUILDER
A. A. Fischer

BROKEN FRIEZE
Yes

PART OF A STREETSCAPE
Yes, 1 of 10 (west to east: 6177, 6173, 6169, 6167, 6163, 6159, 6155, 6151, 6149, 6145)

NEIGHBORHOOD
● Skinker DeBaliviere

SIDE OF THE STREET
North

STATUS IN 2021
Occupied

6169
WASHINGTON BOULEVARD

ABOVE Photo by Reed R. Radcliffe, 2022.

LANDMARKS
1909

BUILDER
A. A. Fischer

BROKEN FRIEZE
No

PART OF A STREETSCAPE
Yes, 1 of 10 (west to east: 6177, 6173, 6169, 6167, 6163, 6159, 6155, 6151, 6149, 6145)

NEIGHBORHOOD
● Skinker DeBaliviere

SIDE OF THE STREET
North

STATUS IN 2021
Restored

6173

WASHINGTON BOULEVARD

ABOVE Photo by Lori Berdak Miller, 2022.

LANDMARKS
1909

BUILDER
A. A. Fischer

BROKEN FRIEZE
On this home Fischer installed corbels that protrude downward from the frieze to the space in between the windows. This building is one of three structures on the 6100 block of Washington Boulevard that has this variation on the broken frieze. The others are 6109-6111 and 6115-6117 on the north side and 6114-6116 on the south side.

PART OF A STREETSCAPE
Yes, 1 of 10 (west to east: 6177, 6173, 6169, 6167, 6163, 6159, 6155, 6151, 6149, 6145)

NEIGHBORHOOD
● Skinker DeBaliviere

SIDE OF THE STREET
North

STATUS IN 2021
Occupied

6174

WASHINGTON BOULEVARD

This structure's original address was 6176 Washington Boulevard.

ABOVE Photo by Reed R. Radcliffe, 2022.

DAILY RECORD NO.
5513

LANDMARKS
1908

OWNER
A. A. Fischer Realty Company

ARCHITECT
A. A. Fischer Realty Company

BUILDER
A. A. Fischer Realty Company

DESCRIPTION
2-story dwelling; 30 feet × 32 feet

BROKEN FRIEZE
Yes

PART OF A STREETSCAPE
Yes, 1 of 6 (west to east: 520 Skinker Boulevard, 6190, 6186, 6182, 6178, 6174 Washington Boulevard)

NEIGHBORHOOD
● Skinker DeBaliviere

SIDE OF THE STREET
South

STATUS IN 2021
Occupied

6177
WASHINGTON BOULEVARD

ABOVE Photo by Reed R. Radcliffe, 2022.

LANDMARKS
1909

BUILDER
A. A. Fischer

BROKEN FRIEZE
Yes

PART OF A STREETSCAPE
Yes, 1 of 10 (west to east: 6177, 6173, 6169, 6167, 6163, 6159, 6155, 6151, 6149, 6145)

NEIGHBORHOOD
● Skinker DeBaliviere

SIDE OF THE STREET
North

STATUS IN 2021
Restored

6178

WASHINGTON BOULEVARD

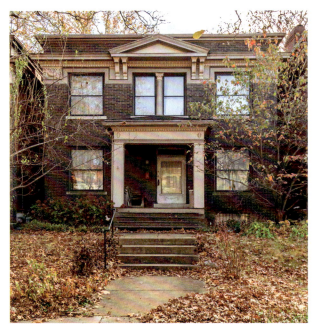

ABOVE Photos by Reed R. Radcliffe, 2022.

DAILY RECORD NO.
5513

LANDMARKS
1908

BUILDER
A. A. Fischer

DESCRIPTION
2-story dwelling; 30 feet × 32 feet

BROKEN FRIEZE
Yes

PART OF A STREETSCAPE
Yes, 1 of 6 (west to east: 520 Skinker Boulevard, 6190, 6186, 6182, 6178, 6174 Washington Boulevard)

NEIGHBORHOOD
● Skinker DeBaliviere

SIDE OF THE STREET
South

STATUS IN 2021
Occupied

6182

WASHINGTON BOULEVARD

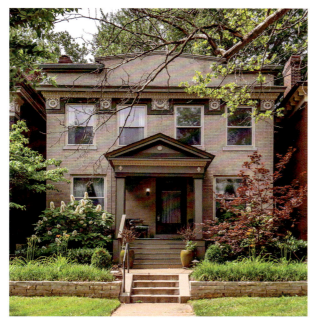

ABOVE Photo by Reed R. Radcliffe, 2022.

DAILY RECORD NO.
5513

LANDMARKS
1908

BUILDER
A. A. Fischer

DESCRIPTION
2-story dwelling; 30 feet × 32 feet

BROKEN FRIEZE
Yes

PART OF A STREETSCAPE
Yes, 1 of 6 (west to east: 520 Skinker Boulevard, 6190, 6186, 6182, 6178, 6174 Washington Boulevard)

NEIGHBORHOOD
● Skinker DeBaliviere

SIDE OF THE STREET
South

STATUS IN 2021
Restored

6186

WASHINGTON BOULEVARD

ABOVE Photo by Reed R. Radcliffe, 2022.

DAILY RECORD NO.
5513

LANDMARKS
1908

OWNER
A. A. Fischer Realty Company

ARCHITECT
A. A. Fischer Realty Company

BUILDER
A. A. Fischer Realty Company

DESCRIPTION
2-story dwelling; 30 feet × 32 feet

BROKEN FRIEZE
No

PART OF A STREETSCAPE
Yes, 1 of 6 (west to east: 520 Skinker Boulevard, 6190, 6186, 6182, 6178, 6174 Washington Boulevard)

NEIGHBORHOOD
● Skinker DeBaliviere

SIDE OF THE STREET
South

STATUS IN 2021
Occupied

6190

WASHINGTON BOULEVARD

ABOVE Photo by Reed R. Radcliffe, 2022.

REALTY RECORD AND BUILDER NO.
8839

APPEARED IN THE REALTY RECORD AND BUILDER
Feb. 1909

HOUSE NUMBER CERTIFICATE
02/09/1909

LANDMARKS
1909

OWNER
Ralph H. Orthwein

ARCHITECT
A. A. Fischer Realty Company

BUILDER
A. A. Fischer Realty Company

DESCRIPTION
2-story dwelling; 35 feet × 30 feet; $5,000

BROKEN FRIEZE
No

PART OF A STREETSCAPE
Yes, 1 of 6 (west to east: 520 Skinker Boulevard, 6190, 6186, 6182, 6178, 6174 Washington Boulevard))

NEIGHBORHOOD
● Skinker DeBaliviere

SIDE OF THE STREET
South

STATUS IN 2021
Restored

5088
WASHINGTON PLACE

ABOVE Photos by Reed R. Radcliffe, 2022.

DAILY RECORD NO.
956

APPEARED IN THE DAILY RECORD
03/18/1903

OWNER
W. E. Ingalls

BUILDER
A. A. Fischer/A. A. Fischer Architectural & Building Company

DESCRIPTION
3-story residence; 35 feet × 35 feet

BROKEN FRIEZE
Yes

PART OF A STREETSCAPE
Yes, 1 of 2 side by side (5090, 5088)

NEIGHBORHOOD
● Central West End

SIDE OF THE STREET
South

STATUS IN 2021
Restored

5090

WASHINGTON PLACE

ABOVE Photo by Reed R. Radcliffe, 2022.

DAILY RECORD NO.
6515

APPEARED IN THE DAILY RECORD
02/10/1906

OWNER
A. A. Fischer Architectural & Building Company

ARCHITECT
A. A. Fischer Architectural & Building Company

BUILDER
A. A. Fischer Architectural & Building Company

DESCRIPTION
2-story mansard dwelling; 39 feet × 33 feet

BROKEN FRIEZE
No

PART OF A STREETSCAPE
Yes, 1 of 2 side by side (5090, 5088)

NEIGHBORHOOD
● Central West End

SIDE OF THE STREET
South

STATUS IN 2021
Occupied

5129

WASHINGTON PLACE

ABOVE Photo by Reed R. Radcliffe, 2022.

DAILY RECORD NO.
152

APPEARED IN THE DAILY RECORD
11/02/1900

HOUSE NUMBER SLIP
11/01/1900

OWNER
McKinley Realty Company

ARCHITECT
McKinley Realty Company

BUILDER
McKinley Realty Company/A. A. Fischer

DESCRIPTION
Dwelling; 43 feet × 35 feet; $5,000

BROKEN FRIEZE
No

PART OF A STREETSCAPE
Yes, 1 of 3 (west to east: 5137, 5133, 5129)

NEIGHBORHOOD
● Central West End

SIDE OF THE STREET
North

STATUS IN 2021
Occupied

5133

WASHINGTON PLACE

ABOVE Photo by Reed R. Radcliffe, 2022.

LANDMARKS
1899

BUILDER
A. A. Fischer

BROKEN FRIEZE
No

PART OF A STREETSCAPE
Yes, 1 of 3 (west to east: 5137, 5133, 5129)

NEIGHBORHOOD
● Central West End

SIDE OF THE STREET
North

STATUS IN 2021
Restored

5137

WASHINGTON PLACE

ABOVE Photo by Reed R. Radcliffe, 2022.

HOUSE NUMBER CERTIFICATE
11/22/1899

BUILDER
A. A. Fischer

DESCRIPTION
1 house; 30 feet wide

BROKEN FRIEZE
No

PART OF A STREETSCAPE
Yes, 1 of 3 (west to east: 5137, 5133, 5129)

NEIGHBORHOOD
● Central West End

SIDE OF THE STREET
North

STATUS IN 2021
Restored

6217
WATERMAN AVENUE
This structure's original address was 6231 Waterman Avenue.

ABOVE Photo by Reed R. Radcliffe, 2022.

APPEARED IN THE *REALTY RECORD AND BUILDER*
Jan. 1907

***REALTY RECORD* NO.**
219

OWNER
Lulu L. Smith

ARCHITECT
A. A. Fischer Architectural & Building Company

BUILDER
A. A. Fischer Architectural & Building Company

DESCRIPTION
2.5-story dwelling; 40 feet × 37 feet; $12,000

BROKEN FRIEZE
No

PART OF A STREETSCAPE
No

NEIGHBORHOOD
● Parkview subdivision of Skinker DeBaliviere

SIDE OF THE STREET
North

STATUS IN 2021
Relocated

NOTE In 1923, this home was moved from its original location at 6231 Waterman Avenue to its current-day location at 6217 Waterman Avenue.

6307
WATERMAN AVENUE

DAILY RECORD NO.
4026

OWNER
Mrs. Jennie S. Garvey

BUILDER
A. A. Fischer

DESCRIPTION
Craftsman-style residence

BROKEN FRIEZE
No

PART OF A STREETSCAPE
No

NEIGHBORHOOD
● Parkview subdivision of University City

SIDE OF THE STREET
North

STATUS IN 2021
Restored

ABOVE
Photo by Reed R. Radcliffe, 2022.

RIGHT
Photo by Nancy Moore Hamilton, 2000.

5073
WATERMAN BOULEVARD
This structure's original address was 5073 McPherson Boulevard.

ABOVE
Photo by Reed R. Radcliffe, 2022.

RIGHT
Photo by Nancy Moore Hamilton, 2001.

DAILY RECORD NO.
30

APPEARED IN THE DAILY RECORD
11/05/1901

OWNER
Chris Garvey

BUILDER
A. A. Fischer Architectural & Building Company

DESCRIPTION
2-story residence; 32.5 feet × 35 feet; $6,000

BROKEN FRIEZE
Yes

PART OF A STREETSCAPE
No

NEIGHBORHOOD
● Central West End

SIDE OF THE STREET
North

STATUS IN 2021
Occupied

NOTE Chris Garvey — the owner of this property and its likely architect — frequently collaborated with Fischer. He lived here in 1903.

5212

WATERMAN BOULEVARD

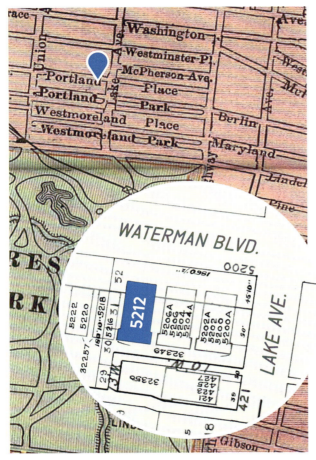

ABOVE
David Rumsey Map Collection, David Rumsey Map Center, Stanford Libraries at Stanford University.

CIRCLE
St. Louis Building Department Atlases, 1943–1946.
St. Louis Public Library.

REALTY RECORD AND BUILDER NO.
8658

APPEARED IN THE REALTY RECORD AND BUILDER
Sept. 1906

OWNER
Harry H. Linnemann

ARCHITECT
A. A. Fischer Realty Company

BUILDER
A. A. Fischer Realty Company

DESCRIPTION
2-story mansard dwelling; 33 feet × 29 feet; $9,000

BROKEN FRIEZE
Unknown

PART OF A STREETSCAPE
No

NEIGHBORHOOD
● Central West End

SIDE OF THE STREET
South

STATUS IN 2021
Razed

5227
WATERMAN BOULEVARD
This structure's original address was 5227 McPherson Avenue.

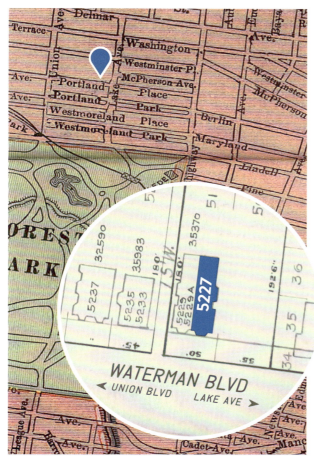

ABOVE
David Rumsey Map Collection, David Rumsey Map Center, Stanford Libraries at Stanford University.

CIRCLE
St. Louis Building Department Atlases, 1943–1946. St. Louis Public Library.

DAILY RECORD NO.
3381

APPEARED IN THE DAILY RECORD
04/10/1905

THE BUILDER NO.
3381

APPEARED IN THE BUILDER
May 1905

OWNER
Daniel Abramsky

ARCHITECT
A. A. Fischer

BUILDER
J. D. Quillin

DESCRIPTION
3-story dwelling; 45 feet × 81 feet

BROKEN FRIEZE
Unknown

PART OF A STREETSCAPE
Yes, 1 of 2 side by side (5227, 5229)

NEIGHBORHOOD
● Central West End

SIDE OF THE STREET
North

STATUS IN 2021
Razed

5229

WATERMAN BOULEVARD

This structure's original address was 5229 McPherson Avenue.

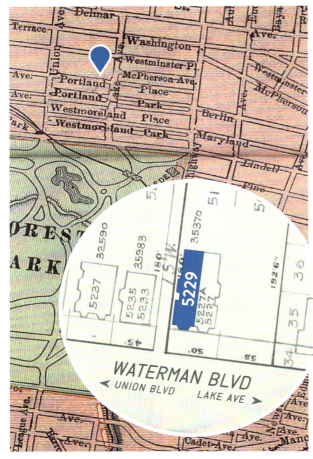

ABOVE
David Rumsey Map Collection, David Rumsey Map Center, Stanford Libraries at Stanford University.

CIRCLE
St. Louis Building Department Atlases, 1943–1946.
St. Louis Public Library.

DAILY RECORD NO.
3381

APPEARED IN THE DAILY RECORD
04/10/1905

THE BUILDER NO.
3381

APPEARED IN THE BUILDER
May 1905

OWNER
Daniel Abramsky

ARCHITECT
A. A. Fischer

BUILDER
J. D. Quillin

DESCRIPTION
3-story dwelling; 45 feet × 81 feet

BROKEN FRIEZE
Unknown

PART OF A STREETSCAPE
Yes, 1 of 2 side by side (5227, 5229)

NEIGHBORHOOD
● Central West End

SIDE OF THE STREET
North

STATUS IN 2021
Razed

5241-5243

WATERMAN BOULEVARD

This structure's original address was 5241 McPherson Avenue.

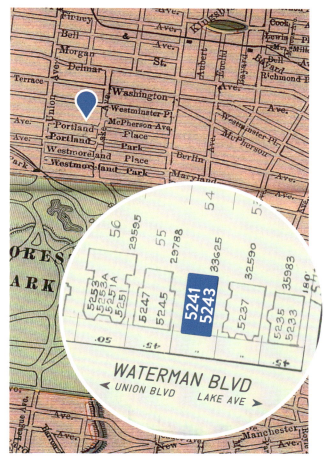

ABOVE
David Rumsey Map Collection, David Rumsey Map Center, Stanford Libraries at Stanford University.

CIRCLE
St. Louis Building Department Atlases, 1943–1946.
St. Louis Public Library.

DAILY RECORD NO.
682

APPEARED IN THE *DAILY RECORD*
05/27/1904

OWNER
Jennie F. Garvey

ARCHITECT
A. A. Fischer Architectural & Building Company

BUILDER
A. A. Fischer Architectural & Building Company

DESCRIPTION
2-story dwelling; 30 feet × 60 feet

BROKEN FRIEZE
Unknown

PART OF A STREETSCAPE
No

NEIGHBORHOOD
● Central West End

SIDE OF THE STREET
North

STATUS IN 2021
Razed

5740
WATERMAN BOULEVARD

ABOVE
Photo by Reed R. Radcliffe, 2022.

RIGHT
Photo by Nancy Moore Hamilton, 2000.

DAILY RECORD NO.
8088

APPEARED IN THE DAILY RECORD
04/21/1911

LANDMARKS
1911

OWNER
A. A. Fischer Realty Company

ARCHITECT
A. A. Fischer Realty Company

BUILDER
A. A. Fischer Realty Company

DESCRIPTION
2-story dwelling; 28 feet × 33 feet

BROKEN FRIEZE
No

PART OF A STREETSCAPE
No

NEIGHBORHOOD
● Skinker DeBaliviere

SIDE OF THE STREET
South

STATUS IN 2021
Occupied

5334
WELLS AVENUE

ABOVE Photo by Reed R. Radcliffe, 2022.

BUILDING PERMIT NO.
E-3933

BUILDING PERMIT DATE
05/22/1905

DAILY RECORD NO.
3933

APPEARED IN THE DAILY RECORD
05/23/1905

APPEARED IN THE BUILDER
June 1905

OWNER
John F. Werman (or "Worman")

ARCHITECT
A. A. Fischer

BUILDER
A. A. Fischer

DESCRIPTION
2-story flat; 26 feet × 44 feet

BROKEN FRIEZE
Yes

PART OF A STREETSCAPE
No

NEIGHBORHOOD
● Hamilton Heights

SIDE OF THE STREET
South

STATUS IN 2021
Occupied

4614

WESTMINSTER PLACE

ABOVE Photo by Lori Berdak Miller, 2022.

DAILY RECORD NO.
2835

APPEARED IN THE DAILY RECORD
03/07/1905

HOUSE NUMBER CERTIFICATE
03/04/1905

OWNER
A. A. Fischer Architectural & Building Company

ARCHITECT
A. A. Fischer Architectural & Building Company

BUILDER
A. A. Fischer Architectural & Building Company

DESCRIPTION
2-story dwelling; 33 feet × 33 feet

BROKEN FRIEZE
Yes

PART OF A STREETSCAPE
Yes, 1 of 3 (west to east: 4620-4622, 4618-4616, 4614)

NEIGHBORHOOD
● Central West End

SIDE OF THE STREET
South

4616

WESTMINSTER PLACE

This structure's original address was 4618 Westminster Place.

ABOVE Photo by Reed R. Radcliffe, 2022.

DAILY RECORD NO.
2836

APPEARED IN THE DAILY RECORD
03/07/1905

HOUSE NUMBER CERTIFICATE
03/04/1905

OWNER
A. A. Fischer Architectural & Building Company

ARCHITECT
A. A. Fischer Architectural & Building Company

BUILDER
A. A. Fischer Architectural & Building Company

DESCRIPTION
2-story dwelling; 28 feet × 38 feet

BROKEN FRIEZE
Yes

PART OF A STREETSCAPE
Yes, 1 of 3 (west to east: 4620-4622, 4618-4616, 4614)

NEIGHBORHOOD
● Central West End

SIDE OF THE STREET
South

STATUS IN 2021
Occupied

4622
WESTMINSTER PLACE
This structure's original address was 4620 Westminster Place.

ABOVE
Photo by Reed R. Radcliffe, 2022.

RIGHT
Photo by Nancy Moore Hamilton, 2001.

DAILY RECORD NO.
2835

APPEARED IN THE DAILY RECORD
03/07/1905

HOUSE NUMBER CERTIFICATE
03/04/1905

OWNER
A. A. Fischer Architectural & Building Company

ARCHITECT
A. A. Fischer Architectural & Building Company

BUILDER
A. A. Fischer Architectural & Building Company

DESCRIPTION
2-story dwelling; 33 feet × 33 feet

BROKEN FRIEZE
No

PART OF A STREETSCAPE
Yes, 1 of 3 (west to east: 4620-4622, 4618-4616, 4614)

NEIGHBORHOOD
● Central West End

SIDE OF THE STREET
South

STATUS IN 2021
Occupied

4721

WESTMINSTER PLACE

ABOVE Photo by Reed R. Radcliffe, 2022.

DAILY RECORD NO.
11

APPEARED IN THE *DAILY RECORD*
11/28/1906

REALTY RECORD AND BUILDER NO.
11

APPEARED IN THE *REALTY RECORD AND BUILDER*
12/06/1906

OWNER
Chas. F. Levy, care of Hub Furniture Company

ARCHITECT
A. A. Fischer

BUILDER
A. A. Fischer

DESCRIPTION
2.5-story dwelling; 39 feet × 34 feet; $12,000

BROKEN FRIEZE
Yes

PART OF A STREETSCAPE
No

NEIGHBORHOOD
● Central West End

SIDE OF THE STREET
North

STATUS IN 2021
Restored

4749

WESTMINSTER PLACE

ABOVE
Photo by Reed R. Radcliffe, 2022.

RIGHT
Photo by Nancy Moore Hamilton, 2001.

BUILDING PERMIT NO.
5515

DAILY RECORD NO.
5515

APPEARED IN THE DAILY RECORD
10/19/1905

OWNER
Alby Mason

ARCHITECT
A. A. Fischer Architectural & Building Company

BUILDER
A. A. Fischer/A. A. Fischer Architectural & Building Company

DESCRIPTION
2-story dwelling; 34 feet × 33 feet

BROKEN FRIEZE
Yes

PART OF A STREETSCAPE
No

NEIGHBORHOOD
● Central West End

SIDE OF THE STREET
North

STATUS IN 2021
Occupied

5250
WESTMINSTER PLACE

ABOVE Photos by Reed R. Radcliffe, 2022.

BUILDING PERMIT NO.
830

DAILY RECORD NO.
830

APPEARED IN THE DAILY RECORD
08/08/1903

BUILDER NO.
830

APPEARED IN THE BUILDER
08/17/1903

OWNER
F. H. Ingalls

BUILDER
A. A. Fischer Architectural & Building Company

DESCRIPTION
2-story residence; 41.16 feet × 55.16 feet

BROKEN FRIEZE
No

PART OF A STREETSCAPE
No

NEIGHBORHOOD
● Central West End

SIDE OF THE STREET
South

STATUS IN 2021
Restored

6121
WESTMINSTER PLACE

ABOVE Photo by Reed R. Radcliffe, 2022.

DAILY RECORD NO.
3463

APPEARED IN THE DAILY RECORD
03/09/1910

REALTY RECORD AND BUILDER NO.
3463

APPEARED IN THE REALTY RECORD AND BUILDER
Apr. 1910

LANDMARKS
1910

OWNER
A. A. Fischer Realty Company

ARCHITECT
A. A. Fischer Realty Company

BUILDER
A. A. Fischer Realty Company

DESCRIPTION
2-story dwelling; 30 feet × 32 feet

BROKEN FRIEZE
No

PART OF A STREETSCAPE
Yes, 1 of 3 (west to east: 6127, 6123, 6121)

NEIGHBORHOOD
● Skinker DeBaliviere

SIDE OF THE STREET
North

STATUS IN 2021
Occupied

6123

WESTMINSTER PLACE

ABOVE Photo by Reed R. Radcliffe, 2022.

DAILY RECORD NO.
3463

APPEARED IN THE DAILY RECORD
03/09/1910

REALTY RECORD AND BUILDER NO.
3463

APPEARED IN THE REALTY RECORD AND BUILDER
Apr. 1910

LANDMARKS
1910

OWNER
A. A. Fischer Realty Company

ARCHITECT
A. A. Fischer Realty Company

BUILDER
A. A. Fischer Realty Company

DESCRIPTION
2-story dwelling; 30 feet × 32 feet

BROKEN FRIEZE
No

PART OF A STREETSCAPE
1 of 3 (west to east: 6127, 6123, 6121)

NEIGHBORHOOD
● Skinker DeBaliviere

SIDE OF THE STREET
North

STATUS IN 2021
Restored

6124

WESTMINSTER PLACE

ABOVE Photo by Lori Berdak Miller, 2021.

DAILY RECORD NO.
6460

APPEARED IN THE DAILY RECORD
11/16/1910

REALTY RECORD AND BUILDER NO.
6460

APPEARED IN THE REALTY RECORD AND BUILDER
Nov. 1910

OWNER
A. A. Fischer Realty Company

ARCHITECT
A. A. Fischer Realty Company

BUILDER
A. A. Fischer Realty Company

DESCRIPTION
2-story dwelling; 30 feet × 32 feet

BROKEN FRIEZE
No

PART OF A STREETSCAPE
Yes, originally 1 of 20 (west to east: 6192, 6188, 6186, 6182, 6178, 6174, 6172, 6168, 6164, 6160, 6158, 6154, 6150, 6146, 6142, 6140, 6136, 6132, 6128, 6124)

NEIGHBORHOOD
● Skinker DeBaliviere

SIDE OF THE STREET
South

STATUS IN 2021
Restored

6127

WESTMINSTER PLACE

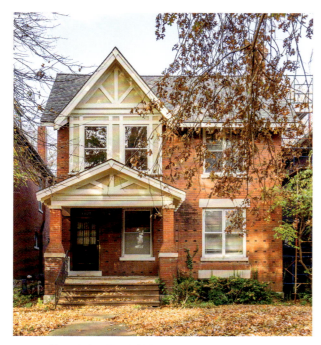

ABOVE Photo by Lori Berdak Miller, 2022.

DAILY RECORD NO.
3107

REALTY RECORD AND BUILDER NO.
3107

APPEARED IN THE REALTY RECORD AND BUILDER
Feb. 1910

LANDMARKS
1910

OWNER
A. A. Fischer Realty Company

ARCHITECT
A. A. Fischer Realty Company

BUILDER
A. A. Fischer Realty Company

DESCRIPTION
2-story dwelling; 30 feet × 32 feet

BROKEN FRIEZE
No

PART OF A STREETSCAPE
1 of 3 (west to east: 6127, 6123, 6121)

NEIGHBORHOOD
● Skinker DeBaliviere

SIDE OF THE STREET
North

STATUS IN 2021
Restored

6128

WESTMINSTER PLACE

ABOVE Photo by Reed R. Radcliffe, 2022.

DAILY RECORD NO.
6460

APPEARED IN THE DAILY RECORD
11/16/1910

REALTY RECORD AND BUILDER NO.
6460

APPEARED IN THE REALTY RECORD AND BUILDER
Nov. 1910

OWNER
A. A. Fischer Realty Company

ARCHITECT
A. A. Fischer Realty Company

BUILDER
A. A. Fischer Realty Company

DESCRIPTION
2-story dwelling; 30 feet × 32 feet

BROKEN FRIEZE
No

PART OF A STREETSCAPE
Yes, originally 1 of 20 (west to east: 6192, 6188, 6186, 6182, 6178, 6174, 6172, 6168, 6164, 6160, 6158, 6154, 6150, 6146, 6142, 6140, 6136, 6132, 6128, 6124)

NEIGHBORHOOD
● Skinker DeBaliviere

SIDE OF THE STREET
South

STATUS IN 2021
Restored

6132

WESTMINSTER PLACE

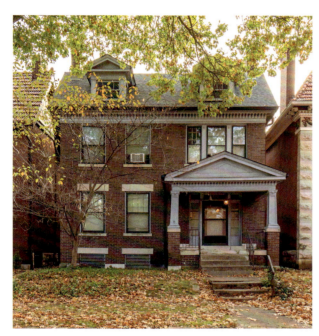

TOP Photo by Reed R. Radcliffe, 2022.
BOTTOM Photo by Lori Berdak Miller, 2022.

DAILY RECORD NO.
6460

APPEARED IN THE DAILY RECORD
11/16/1910

REALTY RECORD AND BUILDER NO.
6460

APPEARED IN THE REALTY RECORD AND BUILDER
Nov. 1910

OWNER
A. A. Fischer Realty Company

ARCHITECT
A. A. Fischer Realty Company

BUILDER
A. A. Fischer Realty Company

DESCRIPTION
2-story dwelling; 30 feet × 32 feet

BROKEN FRIEZE
No

PART OF A STREETSCAPE
Yes, originally 1 of 20 (west to east: 6192, 6188, 6186, 6182, 6178, 6174, 6172, 6168, 6164, 6160, 6158, 6154, 6150, 6146, 6142, 6140, 6136, 6132, 6128, 6124)

NEIGHBORHOOD
● Skinker DeBaliviere

SIDE OF THE STREET
South

STATUS IN 2021
Occupied

6136

WESTMINSTER PLACE

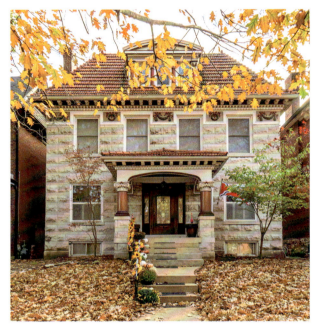

TOP Photo by Reed R. Radcliffe, 2022.
BOTTOM Photo by Nancy Moore Hamilton, 1995.

REALTY RECORD AND BUILDER NO.
6044

APPEARED IN THE REALTY RECORD AND BUILDER
Oct. 1910

OWNER
A. A. Fischer Realty Company

ARCHITECT
A. A. Fischer Realty Company

BUILDER
A. A. Fischer Realty Company

DESCRIPTION
2.5-story dwelling; 35 feet × 33 feet

BROKEN FRIEZE
Yes

PART OF A STREETSCAPE
Yes, originally 1 of 20 (west to east: 6192, 6188, 6186, 6182, 6178, 6174, 6172, 6168, 6164, 6160, 6158, 6154, 6150, 6146, 6142, 6140, 6136, 6132, 6128, 6124)

NEIGHBORHOOD
● Skinker DeBaliviere

SIDE OF THE STREET
South

STATUS IN 2021
Restored

6140

WESTMINSTER PLACE

ABOVE Photo by Reed R. Radcliffe, 2022.

REALTY RECORD AND BUILDER NO.
5008

APPEARED IN THE REALTY RECORD AND BUILDER
Aug. 1910

OWNER
A. A. Fischer Realty Company

ARCHITECT
A. A. Fischer Realty Company

BUILDER
A. A. Fischer Realty Company

DESCRIPTION
2-story dwelling; 30 feet × 32 feet

BROKEN FRIEZE
Yes

PART OF A STREETSCAPE
Yes, originally 1 of 20 (west to east: 6192, 6188, 6186, 6182, 6178, 6174, 6172, 6168, 6164, 6160, 6158, 6154, 6150, 6146, 6142, 6140, 6136, 6132, 6128, 6124)

NEIGHBORHOOD
● Skinker DeBaliviere

SIDE OF THE STREET
South

STATUS IN 2021
Occupied

6142

WESTMINSTER PLACE

ABOVE Photos by Reed R. Radcliffe, 2022.

DAILY RECORD NO.
4536

APPEARED IN THE DAILY RECORD
05/21/1910

OWNER
A. A. Fischer Realty Company

ARCHITECT
A. A. Fischer Realty Company

BUILDER
A. A. Fischer Realty Company

DESCRIPTION
2.5-story dwelling; 28 feet × 41 feet

BROKEN FRIEZE
No

PART OF A STREETSCAPE
Yes, originally 1 of 20 (west to east: 6192, 6188, 6186, 6182, 6178, 6174, 6172, 6168, 6164, 6160, 6158, 6154, 6150, 6146, 6142, 6140, 6136, 6132, 6128, 6124)

NEIGHBORHOOD
● Skinker DeBaliviere

SIDE OF THE STREET
South

STATUS IN 2021
Restored

6146

WESTMINSTER PLACE

TOP Photo by Lori Berdak Miller, 2021.
BOTTOM Photo by Joan Young, 2006.

DAILY RECORD NO.
324

REALTY RECORD AND BUILDER NO.
324

APPEARED IN THE REALTY RECORD AND BUILDER
June 1909

OWNER
A. A. Fischer Realty Company

ARCHITECT
A. A. Fischer Realty Company

BUILDER
A. A. Fischer Realty Company

DESCRIPTION
2-story dwelling; 30 feet × 32 feet

BROKEN FRIEZE
No

PART OF A STREETSCAPE
Yes, originally 1 of 20 (west to east: 6192, 6188, 6186, 6182, 6178, 6174, 6172, 6168, 6164, 6160, 6158, 6154, 6150, 6146, 6142, 6140, 6136, 6132, 6128, 6124)

NEIGHBORHOOD
● Skinker DeBaliviere

SIDE OF THE STREET
South

STATUS IN 2021
Restored

6150
WESTMINSTER PLACE

ABOVE Photo by Reed R. Radcliffe, 2022.

DAILY RECORD NO.
324

REALTY RECORD AND BUILDER NO.
324

APPEARED IN THE REALTY RECORD AND BUILDER
June 1909

OWNER
A. A. Fischer Realty Company

ARCHITECT
A. A. Fischer Realty Company

BUILDER
A. A. Fischer Realty Company

DESCRIPTION
2-story dwelling; 30 feet × 32 feet

BROKEN FRIEZE
No

PART OF A STREETSCAPE
Yes, originally 1 of 20 (west to east: 6192, 6188, 6186, 6182, 6178, 6174, 6172, 6168, 6164, 6160, 6158, 6154, 6150, 6146, 6142, 6140, 6136, 6132, 6128, 6124)

NEIGHBORHOOD
● Skinker DeBaliviere

SIDE OF THE STREET
South

STATUS IN 2021
Occupied

6154
WESTMINSTER PLACE

TOP Photo by Reed R. Radcliffe, 2022.
BOTTOM Photo by Joan Young, 2006.

DAILY RECORD NO.
324

REALTY RECORD AND BUILDER NO.
324

APPEARED IN THE REALTY RECORD AND BUILDER
June 1909

OWNER
A. A. Fischer Realty Company

ARCHITECT
A. A. Fischer Realty Company

BUILDER
A. A. Fischer Realty Company

DESCRIPTION
2-story dwelling; 30 feet × 32 feet

BROKEN FRIEZE
No

PART OF A STREETSCAPE
Yes, originally 1 of 20 (west to east: 6192, 6188, 6186, 6182, 6178, 6174, 6172, 6168, 6164, 6160, 6158, 6154, 6150, 6146, 6142, 6140, 6136, 6132, 6128, 6124)

NEIGHBORHOOD
● Skinker DeBaliviere

SIDE OF THE STREET
South

STATUS IN 2021
Restored

6155

WESTMINSTER PLACE

ABOVE Photo by Reed R. Radcliffe, 2022.

DAILY RECORD NO.
3971

REALTY RECORD AND BUILDER NO.
3971

APPEARED IN THE REALTY RECORD AND BUILDER
12/07/1907

LANDMARKS
1907

OWNER
A. A. Fischer Realty Company

ARCHITECT
A. A. Fischer Realty Company

BUILDER
A. A. Fischer Realty Company

DESCRIPTION
2-story dwelling; 24 feet × 3 feet; $5,000

BROKEN FRIEZE
Yes

PART OF A STREETSCAPE
Yes, 1 of 12 (west to east: 500 Skinker Boulevard, 6189, 6185, 6181, 6179, 6175, 6173, 6169, 6165, 6163, 6159, 6155 Westminster Place)

NEIGHBORHOOD
● Skinker DeBaliviere

SIDE OF THE STREET
North

STATUS IN 2021
Occupied

6158

WESTMINSTER PLACE

ABOVE Photo by Reed R. Radcliffe, 2022.

DAILY RECORD NO.
4898

APPEARED IN THE DAILY RECORD
03/17/1908

REALTY RECORD AND BUILDER NO.
4898

APPEARED IN THE REALTY RECORD AND BUILDER
Mar. 1908

OWNER
A. A. Fischer Realty Company

ARCHITECT
A. A. Fischer Realty Company

BUILDER
A. A. Fischer Realty Company

DESCRIPTION
2-story dwelling; 24 feet × 33 feet

BROKEN FRIEZE
Yes

PART OF A STREETSCAPE
Yes, originally 1 of 20 (west to east: 6192, 6188, 6186, 6182, 6178, 6174, 6172, 6168, 6164, 6160, 6158, 6154, 6150, 6146, 6142, 6140, 6136, 6132, 6128, 6124)

NEIGHBORHOOD
● Skinker DeBaliviere

SIDE OF THE STREET
South

STATUS IN 2021
Occupied

6159

WESTMINSTER PLACE

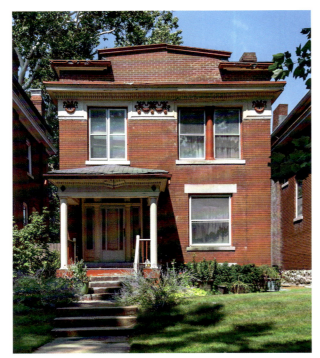

ABOVE Photo by Reed R. Radcliffe, 2022.

DAILY RECORD NO.
3971

REALTY RECORD AND BUILDER NO.
3971

APPEARED IN THE REALTY RECORD AND BUILDER
12/07/1907

LANDMARKS
1907

OWNER
A. A. Fischer Realty Company

ARCHITECT
A. A. Fischer Realty Company

BUILDER
A. A. Fischer Realty Company

DESCRIPTION
2-story dwelling; 24 feet × 33 feet; $5,000

BROKEN FRIEZE
Yes

PART OF A STREETSCAPE
Yes, 1 of 12 (west to east: 500 Skinker Boulevard, 6189, 6185, 6181, 6179, 6175, 6173, 6169, 6165, 6163, 6159, 6155 Westminster Place)

NEIGHBORHOOD
● Skinker DeBaliviere

SIDE OF THE STREET
North

STATUS IN 2021
Occupied

6160

WESTMINSTER PLACE

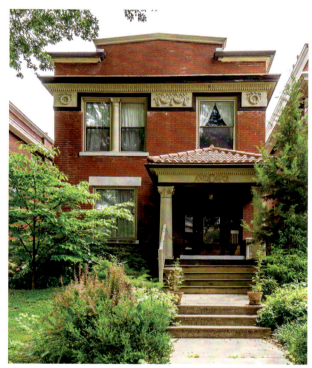

ABOVE Photo by Reed R. Radcliffe, 2022.

DAILY RECORD NO.
4898

APPEARED IN THE DAILY RECORD
03/17/1908

REALTY RECORD AND BUILDER NO.
4898

APPEARED IN THE REALTY RECORD AND BUILDER
Mar. 1908

OWNER
A. A. Fischer Realty Company

ARCHITECT
A. A. Fischer Realty Company

BUILDER
A. A. Fischer Realty Company

DESCRIPTION
2-story dwelling; 24 feet × 33 feet

BROKEN FRIEZE
Yes

PART OF A STREETSCAPE
Yes, originally 1 of 20 (west to east: 6192, 6188, 6186, 6182, 6178, 6174, 6172, 6168, 6164, 6160, 6158, 6154, 6150, 6146, 6142, 6140, 6136, 6132, 6128, 6124)

NEIGHBORHOOD
● Skinker DeBaliviere

SIDE OF THE STREET
South

STATUS IN 2021
Occupied

6163

WESTMINSTER PLACE

ABOVE Photo by Reed R. Radcliffe, 2022.

REALTY RECORD AND BUILDER NO.
4006

APPEARED IN THE REALTY RECORD AND BUILDER
12/07/1907

LANDMARKS
1907

OWNER
A. A. Fischer Realty Company

ARCHITECT
A. A. Fischer Realty Company

BUILDER
A. A. Fischer Realty Company

DESCRIPTION
2-story dwelling; 35 feet × 30 feet; $6,000

BROKEN FRIEZE
Yes

PART OF A STREETSCAPE
Yes, 1 of 12 (west to east: 500 Skinker Boulevard, 6189, 6185, 6181, 6179, 6175, 6173, 6169, 6165, 6163, 6159, 6155 Westminster Place)

NEIGHBORHOOD
● Skinker DeBaliviere

SIDE OF THE STREET
North

STATUS IN 2021
Restored

6164

WESTMINSTER PLACE

ABOVE Photo by Reed R. Radcliffe, 2022.

DAILY RECORD NO.
4897

APPEARED IN THE DAILY RECORD
03/17/1908

REALTY RECORD AND BUILDER NO.
4897

APPEARED IN THE REALTY RECORD AND BUILDER
Mar. 1908

OWNER
A. A. Fischer Realty Company

ARCHITECT
A. A. Fischer Realty Company

BUILDER
A. A. Fischer Realty Company

DESCRIPTION
2-story dwelling; 30 feet × 32 feet; $5,000

BROKEN FRIEZE
Yes

PART OF A STREETSCAPE
Yes, originally 1 of 20 (west to east: 6192, 6188, 6186, 6182, 6178, 6174, 6172, 6168, 6164, 6160, 6158, 6154, 6150, 6146, 6142, 6140, 6136, 6132, 6128, 6124)

NEIGHBORHOOD
● Skinker DeBaliviere

SIDE OF THE STREET
South

STATUS IN 2021
Restored

6165

WESTMINSTER PLACE

ABOVE Photo by Reed R. Radcliffe, 2022.

REALTY RECORD AND BUILDER NO.
3971

APPEARED IN THE REALTY RECORD AND BUILDER
12/07/1907

LANDMARKS
1907

OWNER
A. A. Fischer Realty Company

ARCHITECT
A. A. Fischer Realty Company

BUILDER
A. A. Fischer Realty Company

DESCRIPTION
2-story dwelling; 24 feet × 33 feet

BROKEN FRIEZE
Yes

PART OF A STREETSCAPE
Yes, 1 of 12 (west to east: 500 Skinker Boulevard, 6189, 6185, 6181, 6179, 6175, 6173, 6169, 6165, 6163, 6159, 6155 Westminster Place)

NEIGHBORHOOD
● Skinker DeBaliviere

SIDE OF THE STREET
North

STATUS IN 2021
Occupied

6168

WESTMINSTER PLACE

ABOVE Photo by Reed R. Radcliffe, 2022.

DAILY RECORD NO.
4897

APPEARED IN THE DAILY RECORD
03/17/1908

REALTY RECORD AND BUILDER NO.
4897

APPEARED IN THE REALTY RECORD AND BUILDER
Mar. 1908

OWNER
A. A. Fischer Realty Company

ARCHITECT
A. A. Fischer Realty Company

BUILDER
A. A. Fischer Realty Company

DESCRIPTION
2-story dwelling; 30 feet × 32 feet

BROKEN FRIEZE
Yes

PART OF A STREETSCAPE
Yes, originally 1 of 20 (west to east: 6192, 6188, 6186, 6182, 6178, 6174, 6172, 6168, 6164, 6160, 6158, 6154, 6150, 6146, 6142, 6140, 6136, 6132, 6128, 6124)

NEIGHBORHOOD
● Skinker DeBaliviere

SIDE OF THE STREET
South

STATUS IN 2021
Restored

6169

WESTMINSTER PLACE

ABOVE Photo by Reed R. Radcliffe, 2022.

REALTY RECORD AND BUILDER **NO.**
3971

APPEARED IN THE *REALTY RECORD AND BUILDER*
12/07/1907

LANDMARKS
1907

OWNER
A. A. Fischer Realty Company

ARCHITECT
A. A. Fischer Realty Company

BUILDER
A. A. Fischer Realty Company

DESCRIPTION
2-story dwelling; 24 feet × 33 feet

BROKEN FRIEZE
Yes

PART OF A STREETSCAPE
Yes, 1 of 12 (west to east: 500 Skinker Boulevard, 6189, 6185, 6181, 6179, 6175, 6173, 6169, 6165, 6163, 6159, 6155 Westminster Place)

NEIGHBORHOOD
● Skinker DeBaliviere

SIDE OF THE STREET
North

STATUS IN 2021
Occupied

6172
WESTMINSTER PLACE

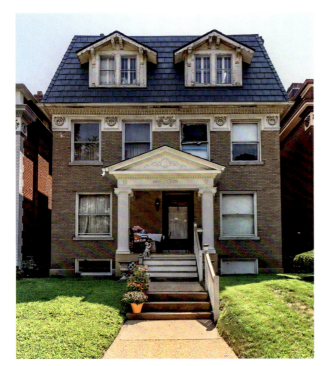

ABOVE Photo by Reed R. Radcliffe, 2022.

DAILY RECORD NO.
4897

APPEARED IN THE DAILY RECORD
03/17/1908

REALTY RECORD AND BUILDER NO.
4897

APPEARED IN THE REALTY RECORD AND BUILDER
Mar. 1908

OWNER
A. A. Fischer Realty Company

ARCHITECT
A. A. Fischer Realty Company

BUILDER
A. A. Fischer Realty Company

DESCRIPTION
2-story dwelling; 30 feet × 32 feet; $5,000

BROKEN FRIEZE
Yes

PART OF A STREETSCAPE
Yes, originally 1 of 20 (west to east: 6192, 6188, 6186, 6182, 6178, 6174, 6172, 6168, 6164, 6160, 6158, 6154, 6150, 6146, 6142, 6140, 6136, 6132, 6128, 6124)

NEIGHBORHOOD
● Skinker DeBaliviere

SIDE OF THE STREET
South

STATUS IN 2021
Occupied

6173

WESTMINSTER PLACE

TOP Photo by Reed R. Radcliffe, 2022.
BOTTOM Photo by Joan Young, 2006.

REALTY RECORD AND BUILDER NO.
3971

APPEARED IN THE REALTY RECORD AND BUILDER
12/07/1907

LANDMARKS
1907

OWNER
A. A. Fischer Realty Company

ARCHITECT
A. A. Fischer Realty Company

BUILDER
A. A. Fischer Realty Company

DESCRIPTION
2-story dwelling; 24 feet × 33 feet; $5,000

BROKEN FRIEZE
Yes

PART OF A STREETSCAPE
Yes, 1 of 12 (west to east: 500 Skinker Boulevard, 6189, 6185, 6181, 6179, 6175, 6173, 6169, 6165, 6163, 6159, 6155 Westminster Place)

NEIGHBORHOOD
● Skinker DeBaliviere

SIDE OF THE STREET
North

STATUS IN 2021
Occupied

6174

WESTMINSTER PLACE

ABOVE Photo by Reed R. Radcliffe, 2022.

DAILY RECORD NO.
4814

APPEARED IN THE DAILY RECORD
03/10/1908

OWNER
A. A. Fischer Realty Company

ARCHITECT
A. A. Fischer Realty Company

BUILDER
A. A. Fischer Realty Company

DESCRIPTION
2-story dwelling; 30 feet × 32 feet

BROKEN FRIEZE
Yes

PART OF A STREETSCAPE
Yes, originally 1 of 20 (west to east: 6192, 6188, 6186, 6182, 6178, 6174, 6172, 6168, 6164, 6160, 6158, 6154, 6150, 6146, 6142, 6140, 6136, 6132, 6128, 6124)

NEIGHBORHOOD
● Skinker DeBaliviere

SIDE OF THE STREET
South

STATUS IN 2021
Occupied

6175

WESTMINSTER PLACE

ABOVE Photo by Reed R. Radcliffe, 2022.

DAILY RECORD NO.
1558

APPEARED IN THE DAILY RECORD
04/20/1907

REALTY RECORD AND BUILDER NO.
1558

APPEARED IN THE REALTY RECORD AND BUILDER
05/07/1907

LANDMARKS
1907

OWNER
A. A. Fischer Realty Company

ARCHITECT
A. A. Fischer Realty Company

BUILDER
A. A. Fischer Realty Company

DESCRIPTION
2-story dwelling; 27 feet × 37 feet

BROKEN FRIEZE
Yes

PART OF A STREETSCAPE
Yes, 1 of 12 (west to east: 500 Skinker Boulevard, 6189, 6185, 6181, 6179, 6175, 6173, 6169, 6165, 6163, 6159, 6155 Westminster Place)

NEIGHBORHOOD
● Skinker DeBaliviere

SIDE OF THE STREET
North

STATUS IN 2021
Restored

6178

WESTMINSTER PLACE

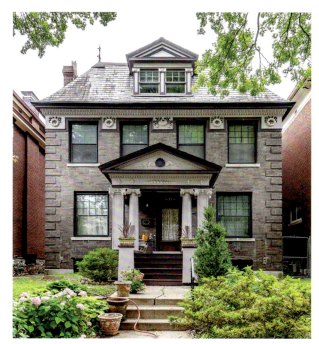

ABOVE Photo by Reed R. Radcliffe, 2022.

DAILY RECORD NO.
4815

APPEARED IN THE DAILY RECORD
03/10/1908

OWNER
A. A. Fischer Realty Company

ARCHITECT
A. A. Fischer Realty Company

BUILDER
A. A. Fischer Realty Company

DESCRIPTION
2-story dwelling; 33 feet × 31 feet

BROKEN FRIEZE
Yes

PART OF A STREETSCAPE
Yes, originally 1 of 20 (west to east: 6192, 6188, 6186, 6182, 6178, 6174, 6172, 6168, 6164, 6160, 6158, 6154, 6150, 6146, 6142, 6140, 6136, 6132, 6128, 6124)

NEIGHBORHOOD
● Skinker DeBaliviere

SIDE OF THE STREET
South

STATUS IN 2021
Occupied

6179

WESTMINSTER PLACE

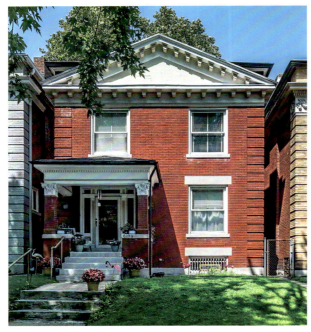

ABOVE Photo by Reed R. Radcliffe, 2022.

REALTY RECORD AND BUILDER NO.
4667

APPEARED IN THE REALTY RECORD AND BUILDER
Mar. 1908

LANDMARKS
1908

OWNER
Frances C. Wines

ARCHITECT
A. A. Fischer Realty Company

BUILDER
A. A. Fischer Realty Company

DESCRIPTION
2-story dwelling; 26 feet × 34 feet; $4,500

BROKEN FRIEZE
No

PART OF A STREETSCAPE
Yes, 1 of 12 (west to east: 500 Skinker Boulevard, 6189, 6185, 6181, 6179, 6175, 6173, 6169, 6165, 6163, 6159, 6155 Westminster Place)

NEIGHBORHOOD
● Skinker DeBaliviere

SIDE OF THE STREET
North

STATUS IN 2021
Occupied

6181

WESTMINSTER PLACE

ABOVE Photo by Reed R. Radcliffe, 2022.

DAILY RECORD NO.
1558

APPEARED IN THE DAILY RECORD
04/20/1907

REALTY RECORD AND BUILDER NO.
1558

APPEARED IN THE REALTY RECORD AND BUILDER
05/07/1907

LANDMARKS
1907

OWNER
A. A. Fischer Realty Company

ARCHITECT
A. A. Fischer Realty Company

BUILDER
A. A. Fischer Realty Company

DESCRIPTION
2-story dwelling; 27 feet × 37 feet

BROKEN FRIEZE
No

PART OF A STREETSCAPE
Yes, 1 of 12 (west to east: 500 Skinker Boulevard, 6189, 6185, 6181, 6179, 6175, 6173, 6169, 6165, 6163, 6159, 6155 Westminster Place)

NEIGHBORHOOD
● Skinker DeBaliviere

SIDE OF THE STREET
North

STATUS IN 2021
Occupied

6182

WESTMINSTER PLACE

ABOVE Photo by Reed R. Radcliffe, 2022.

DAILY RECORD NO.
1557

APPEARED IN THE DAILY RECORD
04/20/1907

REALTY RECORD AND BUILDER NO.
1557

APPEARED IN THE REALTY RECORD AND BUILDER
05/07/1907

OWNER
A. A. Fischer Realty Company

ARCHITECT
A. A. Fischer Realty Company

BUILDER
A. A. Fischer Realty Company

DESCRIPTION
2-story dwelling; 27 feet × 37 feet

BROKEN FRIEZE
Yes

PART OF A STREETSCAPE
Yes, originally 1 of 20 (west to east: 6192, 6188, 6186, 6182, 6178, 6174, 6172, 6168, 6164, 6160, 6158, 6154, 6150, 6146, 6142, 6140, 6136, 6132, 6128, 6124)

NEIGHBORHOOD
● Skinker DeBaliviere

SIDE OF THE STREET
South

STATUS IN 2021
Occupied

6185

WESTMINSTER PLACE

ABOVE
Photo by Reed R. Radcliffe, 2022.

RIGHT
Photo by Lori Berdak Miller, 2022.

***REALTY RECORD AND BUILDER* NO.**
4669

APPEARED IN THE *REALTY RECORD AND BUILDER*
Mar. 1908

LANDMARKS
1908

OWNER
A. A. Fischer Realty Company

ARCHITECT
A. A. Fischer Realty Company

BUILDER
A. A. Fischer Realty Company

DESCRIPTION
2.5-story dwelling; 26 feet × 35 feet; $5,000

BROKEN FRIEZE
No

PART OF A STREETSCAPE
Yes, 1 of 12 (west to east: 500 Skinker Boulevard, 6189, 6185, 6181, 6179, 6175, 6173, 6169, 6165, 6163, 6159, 6155 Westminster Place)

NEIGHBORHOOD
● Skinker DeBaliviere

SIDE OF THE STREET
North

STATUS IN 2021
Restored

6186

WESTMINSTER PLACE

ABOVE
Photo by Reed R. Radcliffe, 2022.

RIGHT
Photo by Nancy Moore Hamilton, 1995.

DAILY RECORD NO.
4816

APPEARED IN THE DAILY RECORD
03/10/1908

OWNER
A. A. Fischer Realty Company

ARCHITECT
A. A. Fischer Realty Company

BUILDER
A. A. Fischer Realty Company

DESCRIPTION
2.5-story dwelling; 26 feet × 35 feet

BROKEN FRIEZE
Yes

PART OF A STREETSCAPE
Yes, originally 1 of 20 (west to east: 6192, 6188, 6186, 6182, 6178, 6174, 6172, 6168, 6164, 6160, 6158, 6154, 6150, 6146, 6142, 6140, 6136, 6132, 6128, 6124)

NEIGHBORHOOD
● Skinker DeBaliviere

SIDE OF THE STREET
South

STATUS IN 2021
Occupied

6188

WESTMINSTER PLACE

ABOVE Photo by Reed R. Radcliffe, 2022.

REALTY RECORD AND BUILDER **NO.**
1555

APPEARED IN THE *REALTY RECORD AND BUILDER*
05/07/1907

OWNER
A. A. Fischer Realty Company

ARCHITECT
A. A. Fischer Realty Company

BUILDER
A. A. Fischer Realty Company

DESCRIPTION
2.5-story dwelling; 33 feet × 33 feet; $8,000

BROKEN FRIEZE
Yes

PART OF A STREETSCAPE
Yes, originally 1 of 20 (west to east: 6192, 6188, 6186, 6182, 6178, 6174, 6172, 6168, 6164, 6160, 6158, 6154, 6150, 6146, 6142, 6140, 6136, 6132, 6128, 6124)

NEIGHBORHOOD
● Skinker DeBaliviere

SIDE OF THE STREET
South

STATUS IN 2021
Restored

6189

WESTMINSTER PLACE

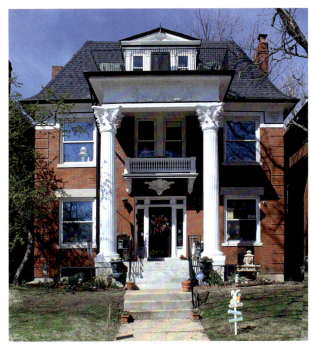

ABOVE Photo by Lori Berdak Miller, 2022.

DAILY RECORD NO.
1556

APPEARED IN THE *DAILY RECORD*
04/20/1907

REALTY RECORD AND BUILDER NO.
1556

APPEARED IN THE *REALTY RECORD AND BUILDER*
05/07/1907

LANDMARKS
1907

OWNER
A. A. Fischer Realty Company

ARCHITECT
A. A. Fischer Realty Company

BUILDER
A. A. Fischer Realty Company

DESCRIPTION
2.5-story dwelling; 33 feet × 33 feet

BROKEN FRIEZE
Yes

PART OF A STREETSCAPE
Yes, 1 of 12 (west to east: 500 Skinker Boulevard, 6189, 6185, 6181, 6179, 6175, 6173, 6169, 6165, 6163, 6159, 6155 Westminster Place)

NEIGHBORHOOD
● Skinker DeBaliviere

SIDE OF THE STREET
North

STATUS IN 2021
Restored

6192

WESTMINSTER PLACE

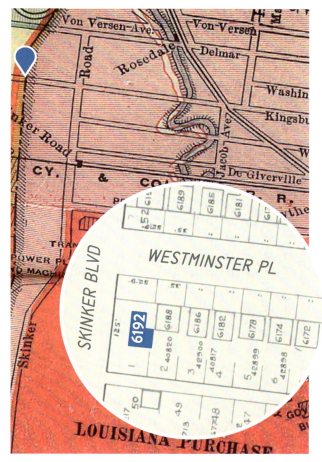

ABOVE
David Rumsey Map Collection, David Rumsey Map Center, Stanford Libraries at Stanford University.

CIRCLE
St. Louis Building Department Atlases, 1943–1946.
St. Louis Public Library.

DAILY RECORD NO.
3010

REALTY RECORD AND BUILDER NO.
3010

APPEARED IN THE REALTY RECORD AND BUILDER
Jan. 1910

OWNER
A. A. Fischer Realty Company

ARCHITECT
A. A. Fischer Realty Company

BUILDER
A. A. Fischer Realty Company

DESCRIPTION
2-story dwelling; 28 feet × 39 feet

BROKEN FRIEZE
Unknown

PART OF A STREETSCAPE
Yes, originally 1 of 20 (west to east: 6192, 6188, 6186, 6182, 6178, 6174, 6172, 6168, 6164, 6160, 6158, 6154, 6150, 6146, 6142, 6140, 6136, 6132, 6128, 6124)

NEIGHBORHOOD
● Skinker DeBaliviere

SIDE OF THE STREET
South

STATUS IN 2021
Razed

7327
WESTMORELAND DRIVE

TOP Photo by Reed R. Radcliffe, 2022.
BOTTOM Photo by Lori Berdak Miller, 2022.

BUILDING PERMIT NO.
3142

BUILDING PERMIT DATE
11/03/1925

BUILDING PERMIT FILED BY
A. A. Fischer

DAILY RECORD NO.
3142

APPEARED IN THE DAILY RECORD
11/10/1925

OWNER
Adolph Boldt

ARCHITECT
William W. Sabin

BUILDER
A. A. Fischer

DESCRIPTION
2-story brick, tile, and stucco Spanish Revival house; 66 feet × 25 feet × 32 feet; $15,000

BROKEN FRIEZE
No

PART OF A STREETSCAPE
No

NEIGHBORHOOD
● University City

SIDE OF THE STREET
North

STATUS IN 2021
Restored

52

WESTMORELAND PLACE
This structure's original address was 5284 Westmoreland Place.

TOP Photo by Reed R. Radcliffe, 2022.
BOTTOM Photo by S. J. Raiche for Landmarks Association of St. Louis, 1972.

DAILY RECORD NO.
4550

APPEARED IN THE
DAILY RECORD
07/21/1905

APPEARED IN THE
BUILDER
Aug. 1905

HOUSE NUMBER
CERTIFICATE
07/20/1905

OWNER
A. A. Fischer

ARCHITECT
A. A. Fischer

BUILDER
A. A. Fischer

DESCRIPTION
3-story dwelling;
52 feet × 37 feet

BROKEN FRIEZE
No

PART OF A
STREETSCAPE
No

NEIGHBORHOOD
● Central West End

SIDE OF THE STREET
South

STATUS IN 2021
Restored

NOTES

1. Ralph Gregory, *A History of Washington, Missouri* (Washington: Missourian Printing Co., 1991), 18.
2. "Germany, Select Births and Baptisms, 1558–1898," Ancestry.com.
3. Ira Glazier and P. Filby, *Germans to America* 1 (Lanham, MD: Scarecrow Press, 1988).
4. Herrmann Heinrich Ferdinand Fischer, birth certificate, Ancestry.com.
5. Herrmann Heinrich Ferdinand Fischer and Henriette Marie Johanne Karoline Fischer, baptismal certificates, Ancestry.com.
6. Herrmann Heinrich Ferdinand Fischer birth certificate, Ancestry.com.
7. "New York, Passenger and Crew Lists (including Castle Garden and Ellis Island), 1820–1957," Ancestry.com.
8. Ira Glazier and P. Filby, *Germans to America* 6 (Lanham, MD: Scarecrow Press, 1989), 296; "Selected Passenger and Crew Lists and Manifests" (National Archives, Washington, DC).
9. Ira Glazier and P. Filby, *Germans to America* 21 (Lanham, MD: Scarecrow Press, 1989), 17.
10. 1860 United States Federal Census, population schedule, Franklin County, Missouri.
11. Gregory, *A History of Washington, Missouri*, 55.
12. Ibid.
13. William L. Shea and Earl J. Hess, "Marching Through Arkansas." *From Pea Ridge: Civil War Campaign in the West* (Chapel Hill: Chapel Hill University Press, 1992), 284–306.
14. Ibid.
15. Missouri marriage records for August Fischer and Maria Heining, Jefferson City, Missouri State Archives microfilm.
16. 1860 United States Federal Census, population schedule, Franklin County, Missouri.
17. "Missouri, U.S., Compiled Marriage Index, 1766–1983," Ancestry.com.
18. 1910 United States Federal Census.
19. Missouri death records, 1910–1971.
20. 1870 United States Federal Census.
21. *History of Benton, Washington, Carroll, Madison, Crawford, Franklin, and Sebastian Counties, Arkansas* (reprinted for the Franklin County Historical Association, 1889), 660.
22. Missouri marriage records, Jefferson City, Missouri State Archives microfilm.
23. *Arkansas Democrat*, March 25, 1898, 4.
24. 1910 United States Federal Census.
25. Albert Nelson Marquis, *The Book of St. Louisans* (St. Louis: St. Louis Republic Publishers, 1912), 364.
26. Ibid.
27. Ibid.
28. Ibid.
29. Marquis, *The Book of St. Louisans*, 364.
30. "Missouri, U.S., Marriage Records, 1805–2002," Ancestry.com.
31. Ibid.
32. Ibid.
33. *Die Washingtoner Post*, August 30, 1889. Washington Historical Society, Washington, MO.
34. Marquis, *The Book of St. Louisans*, 197.
35. Missouri marriage records, Jefferson City, Missouri State Archives microfilm.
36. *Franklin County Observer*, February 21, 1890, Washington Historical Society, Washington, MO.
37. Polk-Gould Directory Company, *St. Louis City and County Directory*, 1889 (https://dl.mospace.umsystem.edu/umsl/islandora/object/umsl%3A40412#page/402/mode/2up).
38. Polk-Gould Directory Company, *St. Louis City and County Directory*, 1889. https://dl.mospace.umsystem.edu/umsl/islandora/object/umsl%3A40412#page/402/mode/2up
39. Missouri birth records, Jefferson City, Missouri State Archives microfilm.
40. Missouri marriage records, Jefferson City, Missouri State Archives microfilm.
41. Marquis, *The Book of St. Louisans*, 251.
42. Charles C. Savage, *Architecture of the Private Streets of St. Louis* (Columbia: University of Missouri Press, 1987).
43. Ibid.
44. Ibid.
45. "Alabama Deaths and Burials, 1881–1952," Ancestry.com.
46. George McCue and Frank Peters, *A Guide to the Architecture of St. Louis* (Columbia: University of Missouri Press, 1989), 168.
47. Marquis, *The Book of St. Louisans*, 197.
48. "Articles of Incorporation of Cleveland Realty & Building Co.," Archives, St. Louis City Hall (December 13, 1902).
49. *The Builder* (United States: n.p., 1905).
50. *Corporation Report of Secretary of State: Charter Issued to and Other Proceedings Concerning Corporations* (United States: Tribune Printing Company, 1907), 481–482.
51. Gregory, *A History of Washington, Missouri*, 56.
52. Dianna Graveman and Don Graveman, *Washington* (Mt. Pleasant, SC: Arcadia Publishing, 2010).
53. Marquis, *The Book of St. Louisans*.
54. Polk-Gould Directory Company, *St. Louis City and County Directories*, 1916–1922.
55. U.S. Selective Service System, *World War I Selective Service System Draft Registration Cards, 1917–1918*, accessed January 2022.
56. Polk-Gould Directory Company, *St. Louis City and County Directories*, 1924–1943.
57. "Rowland A. Fisher death certificate"; "Obituary [Rowland A. Fischer]," *St. Louis Post-Dispatch*, 1936; "[Rowland A. Fischer] Obituary," Nieburg-Vitt Funeral Home, 1948.
58. "Rowland A. Fischer Funeral Tomorrow," *St. Louis-Globe Democrat*, 1948.

OPPOSITE
6170 McPherson Avenue.
Photo by Reed R. Radcliffe, 2022.

NEXT
Vernon Avenue streetscape with 5247 Vernon in the foreground followed by 5249, 5253, and 5259.
Photo by Reed R. Radcliffe, 2022.

ACKNOWLEDGMENTS

The research for this book was completed over the course of many years and with the help of local historians, librarians, archivists, city clerks, Fischer family members, and others. For each person named here, I know and regret in advance that there is another (or two others) whom I am failing to name.

I'd like to begin by thanking the entire staff—generations of staff, in fact—at the Missouri Historical Society's Library & Research Center, the public libraries in St. Louis and University City, the Landmarks Association of St. Louis, the Washington (Missouri) Historical Society, and the City of St. Louis Records Service Center. I have a long, old list of individuals who, in some instances, helped facilitate my research more than 20 years ago. Because I unfortunately do not know where most of these talented professionals are currently employed, I will not attempt to link them to former or current institutions unless that is my only hope of identifying them. Thank you to Esley Hamilton, Sue Rehkopf, Anne Prichard, Barbara Moorman, Cyndi Longwisch, Nola Rhodes, Noel at the St. Louis Public Library, Ed Machowski, Jeannie Head, Angie Polito, Gloria Carreathers, Marc Houseman, Nick Ballta, Bob Schneider, Emily Troxell Jaycox, Ethelyn Gonsoulin, and Murella Powell. You helped me gather all of the bread crumbs I needed to tell the story of A. A. Fischer and his impact on St. Louis's built environment, and I am forever appreciative of each and every detail you checked for me and/or made possible for me to check myself.

PREVIOUS

Westminster Place streetscape with 6160 Westminster in the foreground followed by 6164, 6168, 6172, 6174, 6178, and 6182.

Photo by Reed R. Radcliffe, 2022.

In the introduction to this book, I go into some detail regarding the profound impact that former executive director of the Landmarks Association of St. Louis, historian, and author Carolyn Hewes Toft had on me. I will forever be indebted to Carolyn for piquing my interest in A. A. Fischer and for giving me the opportunity to hone my research skills while working on my Union Sarah West report in the 1990s.

I would also like to thank the current executive director of Landmarks, Andrew Weil, for his many years of encouraging my research. Andrew generously granted me use of the photographs originally commissioned by Landmarks for use in Historic District nominations, which allowed me to show the rise and fall of houses, blocks, and neighborhoods, particularly in the directory, simply by juxtaposing Landmarks' historical photographs with contemporary images. Historical photographs of the Mount Cabanne–Raymond Place Historic District were taken by former Landmarks staff member Lynn Josse, and I thank Lynn for the time she spent on the streets capturing these priceless images and for her enthusiastic permission to reproduce them in this book.

When researcher Lori Berdak Miller began retracing my steps in 2020, she worked with all of the same institutions that had originally supported my research, and many, but not all, of the cultural stewards with whom Lori connected were new to their institutions since my last in-person visit. Of particularly great help were Kathleen Gallagher and Kara Krekeler of the University City Public Library, Adele Heagney of the St. Louis (Local History) Room at the central branch of the St. Louis Public Library, and Rickey R. Jones and Joseph Sims of the City of the St. Louis Public Records Center. At the Missouri Historical Society's Library & Research Center, Lori's mission was aided immeasurably by Molly Kodner, Jason Stratman, and Dennis Northcott. Given the ongoing pandemic, Lori's research was, by and large, completed remotely, enabled by the creativity and resourcefulness of the individuals named above, as well as by Victoria Ashley Miller, who provided invaluable data retrieval skills. I would also like to thank Kalamazoo College history major Fiona Holmes for her early work on this project, sifting through my original research files, and helping to identify and think through gaps in the narrative.

I am also indebted to David Rumsey and the David Rumsey Map Collection at Stanford University for use of two stunning historical maps. The first, an 1854 map of Germany, appears in Chapter 1, and the second appears in Chapter 5, which details in striking color the city of St. Louis in 1903. This latter map was absolutely vital to my research and in visualizing the spread of Fischer's builds.

Thank you to graphic designer Mary Haskin of Mary Haskin Designs LLC for the thoughtful design of this book and for all of the special care and attention she dedicated to the photographs of Fischer's homes. Mary directed the cover photography and much of the photography used throughout the book, and she is also responsible for designing the foldout map. Mary was supported in her work by the talented and dedicated graphic designer Carolyn Fink. Carolyn was essential in drawing the Fischer house outlines featured in conjunction with photos of empty lots and fine-tuning myriad other details in Chapter 5: Directory of A. A. Fischer Builds as well as helping with the development of the inset maps for the foldout map.

For photographs, I owe great thanks to two native St. Louisans whom I met and worked with separately: Lori Berdak Miller of Redbird Research LLC and Reed R. Radcliffe of TripleRPhotography LLC. Lori spent many long days taking the first and second rounds of reference photographs for all of the confirmed Fischer homes in St. Louis and University City. She was curious and good-natured throughout this endeavor, even when I sent her back out to photograph empty lots where Fischer houses had once stood in an effort to give me a better sense of what was missing. Many of Lori's photos are used in the directory. During my research, I learned that the condition of houses on any given block (probably in any given city) can change rapidly, so Lori's photographs—taken in 2021 and early 2022—gave me a good idea of the present condition of Fischer's individual structures and of entire streetscapes. This in turn allowed me to direct professional photographer Reed R. Radcliffe in his work shooting the cover photo and the majority of the photos you see on the inside pages. Reed's love for St. Louis comes through in his photography. Lori and Reed both made important contributions to the work of documenting Fischer's structures, and I thank them for their dedication to this undertaking and for the friendships we've formed over Fischer and his career. I would also like to thank Marty D. Spikener, a friend of Reed's, for accompanying him on several days of shooting, and Stephen Weiss, the Photo Pros/Creve Coeur Camera, for the skills with which he armed Lori before sending her into the city with a camera.

For historical photos of the Fischer family and for much of the genealogy research, I offer my deep and sincere thanks to the great-granddaughter of A. A. Fischer, Diane Barrett, and to her late mother, Lorraine Fischer Cruise. Both Diane and her mother before her are passionate keepers of their family history, and in cooperation with cousins, they generously provided the family photographs and numerous official business documents featured in the book. I also had the great pleasure of meeting and corresponding with several other Fischer family members, including Lorraine's brother Norman Fischer and his wife, Dorothy, and Richard K. Fischer, the son of Lorraine's other brother, Kenneth, as well as Richard's wife, Christine. Thank you to the Fischer family for opening up your homes and hearts to me and for embracing me and my research.

I am grateful for the opportunity to thank my dearest friends and family for their many years of support as I researched, wrote about, and talked about A. A. Fischer with near single-minded attention. In particular, I owe thanks to my late husband, Ramon "Ray" Hamilton, who encouraged me to pursue my interest in A. A. Fischer; accompanied me on research trips to Missouri and Arkansas; and supported me at every turn, in every way he could, including as research assistant, early reader, and sounding board. Thank you to my dear friend Joan Young, who accompanied me on a research trip to St. Louis and believed in me, my research, and this book from the very beginning; Joan is also responsible for a number of the archival photographs featured in the book. I'd also like to thank my daughter and son-in-law, Debby and Chris Radcliffe, for sticking with me and my research, and for their special commitment to facilitating the publication of this book. I thank my son, Doug Hamilton, for his many years of encouragement and support. Thank you also to two very special women from my inner circle, Sydney Parfet and Geralyn Pasi, for the parts they played in getting this book to print. I am especially grateful to my daughter Debby and friend Geralyn for all of the time they spent reading drafts, thinking deeply about them, and weighing in—I couldn't have done this without you. I thank two longtime friends and advisors, Jim Thompson and Pauline Blanton, for their enduring interest in my research and their encouragement to publish. I would also like to thank Mary Brigid Becktell (née Corcoran) for managing this project and guiding it to publication.

And last but not least, I would like to thank Lauren Mitchell, the Missouri Historical Society's director of publications, for giving this book a chance. Her kindness and expertise in guiding me and my team throughout a lengthy publication process, all of which was completed remotely and during a pandemic, was invaluable. I also owe considerable thanks to Kristie Lein, the Missouri Historical Society's editor, for her meticulous attention to detail and great efforts to prepare the manuscript for publication.